MEDICAL CRISIS COUNSELING

SHORT-TERM THERAPY
FOR
LONG-TERM ILLNESS

Irene Pollin, M.S.W.
with Susan Baird Kanaan

W. W. NORTON & COMPANY • New York • London

A NORTON PROFESSIONAL BOOK

Also by Irene Pollin

Taking Charge: Overcoming the Challenges of Long-Term Illness
(with Susan K. Golant)

Printed in the United States of America

First Edition

Composition by Bytheway Typesetting Services, Inc.
Manufacturing by Haddon Craftsmen, Inc.

Library of Congress Cataloging-in-Publication Data

Pollin, Irene, 1924–
    Medical crisis counseling : short-term therapy for long-term
illness / Irene Pollin with Susan Baird Kanaan.
      p.   cm.
    "A Norton professional book."
    ISBN 0-393-70195-6
    1. Chronically ill – Counseling of. 2. Crisis intervention
(Psychiatry) I. Kanaan, Susan Baird. II. Title.
RC108.P648   1995
362.1'04256 – dc20   95-3391 CIP

W. W. Norton & Company, Inc., 500 Fifth Avenue, New York, NY 10110
W. W. Norton & Company, Ltd., 10 Coptic Street, London WC1A 1PU

1 2 3 4 5 6 7 8 9 0

Contents

Foreword

Traditional models of psychotherapy training have not prepared clinicians to meet the needs of people caught up in the maelstrom of a medical crisis. The usual training of psychotherapists involves a heavy component of human psychopathology taught from a framework that is inevitably reductionistic in focus. The student-therapist is taught to conduct an assessment, identify the problem behaviors, and break them into component parts. In many ways the source of the problem is viewed as though it were the heart of an artichoke or onion, buried beneath layers to be slowly peeled back and stripped away in quest of some inner kernel of emotional conflict to be interpreted or altered.

Such strategies are of little help to patients newly diagnosed with a chronic illness. What the patient really needs is acknowledgment that life has been stood on its head. The world will never be back to where it was, but that does not mean all control is lost. There are ways to cope. There are strategies that can help. There are ways to find a new balance and move ahead with joy, zest, and satisfaction in life. To facilitate this process of adaptation, the therapist must have an orientation that recognizes normal behavior in the abnormal psychosocial ecology of a medical crisis. Helping to impart that orientation is a primary goal of *Medical Crisis Counseling: Short-Term Therapy for Long-Term Illness*.

Primary care providers in both adult and pediatric medicine are well aware that many patient visits and telephone calls ostensibly about medical problems are actually driven by emotional concerns. They know about overutilization, noncompliance, and simple distress that are generated by feelings linked to stresses of adapting to chronic illness. Too often such primary care providers have little time, limited training, and no temperament for dealing with such patient needs. Most would welcome the services of a skilled mental health professional who could step in to address these issues and foster improved coping responses in their patients.

The template for intervention and the ways of thinking about the stresses of serious medical illness that are detailed in the pages of this book provide a valuable guide to the psychotherapist. Irene Pollin has drawn on her rich experiences as a social worker, clinic administrator, medical team member, and mother of seriously ill children to map out an active intervention plan that can easily be generalized across illnesses and treatment sites. Together with Susan Kanaan she has detailed diagnostic cues, management strategies, and problem-solving techniques that map the way toward highly effective focal interventions in times of urgent need.

Gerald P. Koocher, Ph.D.
January, 1995

Acknowledgments

As with any long and difficult project, there are a number of people who helped me complete the formulation of medical crisis counseling and the writing of this book—those who believed in it and provided the kind of support that allowed me to continue. I am forever grateful to each of them.

Reflecting on the catalyst that helped me envision what would be an important mission for the rest of my life, I see a small moment in time with a person—a nun—whose name I never knew. We shared our burning hot coffee in soggy paper cups during a coffee break in a night class at Catholic University. In casual conversation, this woman asked me if I had decided on a subject for my master's thesis. I replied that I hadn't, even though time was running out. I had enjoyed my training but had not yet focused on what I would do with it.

Based on what she had just heard me discuss in our Ethics class, she offered a suggestion. "Irene," she said, "why don't you write about what you just told us?" As I considered her idea, she added, "You have so much to offer. You have had a unique experience and could teach us so much."

At that moment, without realizing it, she touched on what I had sought for the last eleven years—a purpose in my life. The title of my thesis: "The Dying Adolescent, Effects on the Family."

With this now clearly defined direction, I carefully planned the steps I would have to take to achieve my goal of helping patients, families, and professionals understand the problems of coping with chronic illness. Where could I gain more experience? I had spent a year as a career counselor for the Peace Corps and now used all of my skills and experience to guide myself.

Since I wanted to work with children and their families, I applied to

Children's Hospital in Washington, D.C. for my first job. And Dr. William Stark, a child psychiatrist on the staff, was the first to help me. I taught family dynamics to medical residents in the Department of Psychiatry, and was fortunate in having the support of a wonderful woman, Dot Scallon, the chief social worker. Sadly, Dot has since died and cannot read this, but I owe her much for her constant understanding of what I wished to accomplish. She helped me become a part of a newly formed Consultation/Liaison unit where I learned so very much about families and staff support. It was also at Children's Hospital that I met Dr. Reginald Lourie, a world-reknowned child psychiatrist who was to become my mentor.

As I became increasingly convinced that my goals had merit, I decided to open a private practice specializing in chronically ill patients and their families. With that in mind, I contacted a number of physicians, including oncologists, neurologists, and nephrologists, to inform them of my plans and encourage referrals. There was no rush of patients, but there was a phone call from Dr. Marvin Korengold, the senior physician at The Neurology Center, a large group practice. In our first meeting we became aware that our interests meshed neatly and we agreed to work together. Although initially I wanted him to refer clients to my nearby office, he presented good arguments to keep me on the premises. And so I began working three days a week to build a service that would fit with an already comprehensive array of other services offered by the Center.

This was a wonderful opportunity for me to achieve what I had wished to accomplish: I provided a new type of counseling and confirmed my nascent theories about medical crisis counseling. I had the benefit of three outstanding, dedicated, and caring physicians who supervised my work: Dr. Korengold, Dr. Richard Edelson, and Dr. Lourie. Margaret Patton had worked with Dr. Korengold for some years and was my first important staff contact and support. In fact, I owe her a debt of gratitude for helping me start my first clinic at the Center. For within three months, I was working full time and had to hire another full-time social worker.

Indeed, I was so successful I now wished to spread my wings even further. I wanted to treat patients who suffered from other diseases and encounter different situations in order to confirm my developing theory. And so, with the wonderful support from the greater community—the public sector, business, academia, and medicine—I opened a private, non-profit, community-based clinic. Here I had the opportunity to develop clinical and administrative staff.

The new clinic also thrived, but after a while I discovered that I was trying to do too much at once. Fundraising and the development of a clinical model each tugged me in different directions—I began to fear burnout. I made an extremely difficult decision to put my energies into developing the model. That was always where my heart was—where professionally and personally I knew the need existed.

I continued with my private practice for some time, but always sought other settings to deliver services on a larger scale. This occurred as the result of my work with the Humanizing Task Force at the Washington Hospital Center in the District of Columbia. I began to wonder if this institution was interested in an outpatient clinic to treat the same individuals I wished to serve. When I approached John McDaniel, the CEO of the parent corporation, he was as eager and supportive as Dr. Korengold had been, and again I received another wonderful opportunity.

At Washington Hospital Center, I was also fortunate to be working with Dr. James Sayers, then the Chief of Social Work. He was my guide and partner in every way. He compensated for my weaknesses and supported my strengths. We were a great team, and together carefully developed a new clinic with a single purpose—medical crisis counseling. Having this kind of institutional support allowed me to develop my ideas even more fully. Dr. Jimmy Light, a nephrologist, was the first to give me the green light to develop a group program.

While I was working with outstanding professionals at Washington Hospital Center, as I had in my own clinic, I realized that none of these individuals had had any specialized training. They were relying on their traditional backgrounds which limited their ability to focus, as I had trained myself to do, solely on the issues related to chronic illness. These experienced professionals needed another way to envision the struggles of those coping with long-term medical conditions. Case conferences simply weren't adequate. I decided that I had delayed disseminating my views and theories long enough; I would write a book, perhaps even two—one for the general public and one for professionals. I would have to work at this full-time. I had been fiddling around with these ideas long enough.

But I also recognized that professionals working in medical settings with this population had few places to obtain training, even if they wanted it. I decided that in my daughter's memory, my husband and I would create a foundation specifically dedicated to training professionals in medical crisis counseling. I chose several of the most outstanding institutions in the country as well as their equally excellent personnel to serve as medical crisis counseling mentors: Dr. Jimmie Holland, Dr. James Strain, Dr. Fawzy Fawzy, Dr. Margaret Lederberg, Dr. Michael Jellinek, Dr. Ruth McCorkle, and Dr. David Spiegel. The Linda Pollin Foundation held several NIMH-supported conferences, all directed at the further development of medical crisis counseling.

I learned much from every one of these professionals but wanted to take one more step. In my own model, I favored a short-term method, focused and structured. Again, I was fortunate to have discovered another outstanding professional, Dr. Gerald Koocher, a psychologist on the staff of the Harvard Medical School who also worked at the Dana-Farber Institute and Boston Children's Hospital. During his tenure on the board of the Linda Pollin Foundation, I learned that he shared my interst in short-term therapy for long-term illness. Here is where we have trained more outstanding fellows and where the Linda Pollin Institute is newly housed. Dr. Koocher has been a vital support to me professionally and personally and we have many plans for the future.

My mentor, Dr. Lourie, had been very approving of my methods many years ago, yet when he prodded me to tell him exactly what it was that I was doing, I had great difficulty. Abstracting and articulating clinical process is not easy. And so I also wish to thank Susan Kanaan for helping me bring to fruition this long-planned book. Since she is not a clinician, she has forced me to explain my theory and therapeutic process during medical crisis counseling. Her help over the years has been most valuable.

I am also fortunate to have two others in my life: my husband, Abe, and my dear friend, Cherry Adler. Both have stayed with me throughout the long and difficult process, always interested, always supportive. I cannot state my appreciation to them in mere words.

And finally, thanks to my many patients and their families for teaching me what they learned about coping. It is through them that I was able to define and refine, and most importantly, to confirm my theories. I hope that this will in some way be valuable to you as well.

Irene S. Pollin, M.S.W.
Chevy Chase, Maryland

Working with Irene Pollin on this important project has been both educational and inspiring, and I thank her for giving me the opportunity. I have learned much about the profound challenges people face as they live with chronic illness. But more importantly, I have learned from her instruction and example that they can draw on many resources, both personal and external, to meet those challenges.

Many people have contributed to this book. First, my thanks to those who shared their time and insights in lengthy interviews: the clinicians whose programs were profiled in Chapter 8 – Miriam Ratner, Ed Silverman, Anne Hahn, James Spira, and Gerald Koocher; former Linda Pollin Mentors and Fellows who provided background on their counseling activities—Mentor Fawzy Fawzy and Fellows Steven Passik and Mark Schultz; and Suzanne Mintz, co-founder and co-director of the National Family Caregivers Association.

My deepest thanks to Reid Wilson for his invaluable comments on an early draft and his consistent support. I am also grateful for the wisdom and generosity of my colleague Susan K. Golant, who with Irene Pollin wrote *Taking Charge: Overcoming the Challenges of Long-Term Illness* for people with chronic illness and their families. This professional book, and I personally, have reaped many benefits from their ground-breaking collaboration. My thanks, too, to Irene Goldstein for her spirited and high-quality editorial assistance, and to Roz Gordon, Mrs. Pollin's assistant, for many forms of administrative support. Our Norton editors, Susan Barrows Munro and Regina Dahlgren Ardini, deserve special thanks for their skilled and sensitive guidance in bringing this project to completion.

Finally, I want to acknowledge my family, who every day help me know what it means to live to the fullest.

Susan Baird Kanaan, M.S.W.
Washington, D.C.

Introduction

Many health professionals today are well aware that chronic conditions affect every facet of life for their patients as well as their families. Some health care providers even understand that patients facing long-term illness may need special psychosocial interventions to support their adjustment to long-term illness.

No such insights informed the health care practices of the 1950s and 1960s when my husband and I were caring for two children with serious congenital heart defects. Our family's medical crises occurred at a time when technological capabilities had outpaced, or even temporarily eclipsed, the health care system's capacity to offer psychological support. Most medical and even mental health professionals seemed unaware of the emotional needs of people facing a medical crisis. At best, they were unsure of how to minister to those needs.

Although our son, Kenneth, died at age 15 months, medical technology enabled our daughter, Linda, to live to age 16 years—long past what her prognosis would have been without heart surgery. But the professionals responsible for our medical and psychiatric care failed to help our family cope with the emotional and psychological traumas that accompanied these medical circumstances.

Our years of worry and grief were immeasurably worsened by this failure to perceive our distress as a natural result of a medical crisis, and to help us deal with it in that light. The experience left me determined to help fill the void in specialized mental health care for people affected by long-term illness. After Linda's death, I trained as a clinical social worker and, beginning in 1976, developed a psychosocial treatment model that I called "medical crisis counseling" (MCC). Personal experience informed my initial efforts to anticipate the needs of medical patients and their families; over time this schema was confirmed and extended through clinical experience with many hundreds of patients.

The central concepts of MCC can be summarized in a few sentences. Even the most mentally healthy individuals face serious psychosocial challenges as they confront living with a lasting medical condition. Some need professional help to make an adequate adjustment. Of these, most can be significantly helped by a structured, short-term intervention that focuses on the eight "expectable issues" engendered by chronic illness: control, self-image, dependency, stigma, abandonment, anger, isolation, and death.

There are three crisis points when intervention is most effective: diagnosis, release from hospitalization, and exacerbation. Rather than seeking to change coping mechanisms, medical crisis counseling affirms and reinforces patients' strengths. The clinician and patient work together to identify concrete goals. Such intervention can help the patient avoid psychiatric complications, and reduce physical symptoms. Family members also benefit from this counseling. In my experience, even when one member of the family is in treatment, the entire family gains.

The MCC model is brief (typically ten sessions or less) and focused, making it accessible to persons and families who might otherwise lack the time or money to seek counseling. But most important, the patient would have a sense of closure as the treatment reached its successful conclusion— this as opposed to the open-ended nature of the chronic illness itself. Its short time frame and complementarity with medical treatment make it feasible as part of today's overburdened and cost-conscious health care system. Patients have the option of seeking episodic treatment, which is still based on the short-term structured model.

Since 1976, my clinical staff and I have used the MCC model to treat thousands of patients—medical patients and family members—in three Washington, D.C. outpatient clinics that I founded and directed. In those settings, I worked closely with medical professionals from many disciplines, treating patients with a wide range of conditions including multiple sclerosis, lupus, heart disease, cancer, and kidney disease.

As our patients thrived, I realized the necessity of teaching the MCC model to others. This book is the result of 18 years of refining, focusing, and attempting to articulate exactly what I did and why.

Medical Crisis Counseling: Short-Term Therapy for Long-Term Illness begins with an introductory chapter that discusses the personal and social burden of chronic illness and the limits of psychological care available today. The book has two major sections. Part I (Chapters 2 through 7) presents the MCC clinical model. Chapter 2 gives an overview of treatment, and the assumptions and theoretical systems that underlie it. Chapter 3 reviews the steps in getting started with a patient. Chapter 4 uses extensive case material to illustrate the therapeutic objectives and intervention techniques for each of the eight issues of chronic illness (control, self-image, dependency, stigma, abandonment, anger, isolation, and death). [1] Chapter 5 is a lengthy case profile covering all eight issues. Chapter 6 discusses the family perspective—how the family is affected by the lasting illness of one of its members, and the various ways that the medical crisis counselor can work with family members, individually or in combination. Chapter 7 describes the group modality for MCC, using several actual groups as examples.

Part II then examines the administrative aspects of establishing and running an MCC program. Chapter 8 profiles nine medical counseling programs—seven of them actual, and two, hypothetical. It then discusses the principles and steps involved in setting up a program, whatever the setting and whatever the program's relationship to the health care institution. Chapter 9 considers both practical and qualitative aspects of the relationship between MCC and medical care, and suggests ways to cultivate that alliance. Finally, Chapter 10 surveys the sustaining links that both counselors and patients should develop with the community, and also identifies many useful resources.

Since the early development of MCC, there has been unquestionable progress in health care in general and in long-term care in particular. An entire field of health-related counseling (variously named) is emerging, advanced by capable and dedicated professionals. The dramatic expansion of medical technology is tempered by the public's growing awareness of its limits and understanding of the critical distinction between lengthening life and maintaining or enhancing its quality. There is growing insight into the complex interactions between mind and body, and new recognition of the health-promoting roles of psychosocial interventions and social support.

Yet these conceptual and practical advances still are not embodied in the standard practices of contemporary health care. Sadly, the professional and institutional resources are not in place to provide the care that could, and should, be available to people with long-term illnesses and their families. It is time to bring our professional practices into closer alignment with our insights into health and healing.

In recent years, I have worked in a variety of ways to widen the availability of MCC, recognizing that an effective treatment model is of limited value without trained and sensitized specialists who know how to use it. In 1988, my husband and I founded the Linda Pollin Foundation in our daughter's memory to support the training of mental health professionals in MCC. The Foundation will have supported more than two dozen postgraduate Fellows by the end of the 1994–95 academic year. The training effort is expanding with the establishment in 1994 of the Linda Pollin Institute at Harvard Medical School. The Institute will provide training and course development for medical students, sponsor continuing professional education courses, and sponsor postgraduate Fellows in the field of medical crisis counseling.

Clinical research is a related priority that is now receiving attention. In 1994, the Linda Pollin Foundation reached agreement with a central Massachusetts HMO, The Fallon Health Care Plan, to undertake a clinical trial of MCC, measuring the impact of counseling on four variables: psychiatric symptoms, quality of life, consumer satisfaction, and cost offset. The Foundation also has joined with the National Institute of Mental Health to sponsor three conferences on MCC; the first was in 1989.

All of these activities have the same objectives as this book: to stimulate awareness of the emotional, psychological, and interpersonal consequences of long-term illness; to share what I have learned about addressing these consequences; and to increase the number of professionals able to provide appropriate, cost-effective counseling. I hope that this book will reinforce efforts to help individuals and families facing serious long-term illness to live their lives and develop their capacities to the fullest extent possible.

These efforts will take many forms: Health care administrators and policy makers can establish counseling programs as adjuncts to medical treatment; individual medical professionals can use the services of medical crisis counselors; community health agencies can direct patients and families to medical crisis counselors and integrate the principles in their counseling services.

The single most important outcome of this book, however, will be for mental health professionals to use some aspect of MCC in their existing practices with patients who are dealing with long-term illness. These patients and their families may not comprehend what they are experiencing. It is my hope that what I offer will increase professionals' understanding of their patients' reality and how they can help ease the burden. From personal and professional experience, I know the longing for understanding in this long-neglected area.

NOTE

1. The cases profiled in this book represent a cross-section of a typical MCC practice. Taken together, they illustrate the types of patients and the variety of ways in which issues surface and are addressed. Most of the people profiled participated in ten or fewer MCC sessions. A few required episodic treatment over a number of years, either to resolve underlying personality issues interfering with their adjustment or to respond to new crises. (Of course, patients' names and identifying characteristics have been changed to protect their privacy.)

IMPACT OF
CHRONIC ILLNESS
ON PATIENT

CHAPTER ONE

The Challenge
of Long-Term Illness

Stephen Hawking begins *A Brief History of Time* with this acknowledgment:

> Apart from being unlucky enough to get ALS, or motor neuron disease, I
> have been fortunate in almost every other respect. The help and support I
> received from my wife . . . and children . . . have made it possible for me to
> lead a fairly normal life and to have a successful career. I was again fortunate
> that I chose theoretical physics, because that is all in the mind. So my
> disability has not been a serious handicap. [1]

This statement is a fitting beginning to a book on the psychosocial impact
of long-term illness. It reminds us of the great variety of human responses
to illness and the vital importance of "help and support."

Yet we cannot appreciate such a triumph without recognizing what has
been overcome. Rollo May has used the vivid phrase "dissolutions of self" [2]
to describe the way an illness can challenge a person's sense of meaning
and human integrity. The basic terms of identity and relationships are
threatened. Formerly self-reliant individuals feel out of control and struggle
with their new dependence on others. A self-image and reputation that
were once taken for granted feel shattered. Normal human fears of abandonment and death have suddenly lost their distance and abstractness, and
have become immediate and plausible.

In short, life has permanently changed. The image of shattered safety
glass on the opposite page illustrates the far-reaching effects of chronic
illness on the entire system in which the person is embedded. The patient
remains intact, but the illness affects virtually every aspect of his or her life.

Long-term illness forces a radical restructuring of expectations and daily
life, both upon those with the illness and upon their families. What society

1

defines as abnormal becomes normal. Physical changes result not only from the illness, but often from the aggressive treatments that become a routine part of life. Social relationships change as the patient loses mobility or encounters society's prejudices and barriers. Daily routines are altered. Disability can impart a sense of powerlessness, at least temporarily, as the person comes to depend on others for survival. Disfigurement may set him or her apart in a society that places inordinate value on health, good looks, and physical prowess. The illness disrupts and changes family and work roles. The ability to earn a living and pay the costs of medical care—in a word, money—often becomes a pressing concern. Fear and loss undermine the person's self-image and existential reality.

While acute illnesses raise fears of pain, body-mutilation, and death, long-term illnesses create additional fears, such as of an imposed new lifestyle, changed social patterns, lowered self-esteem, and, quite simply, the future. Most of these fears center on losses, both actual and anticipated. In addition to health, the losses may include body parts, sexual function or desirability, cherished relationships, job, home, security, former self-image, and life itself. Psychological equilibrium is threatened not just by the fear of dying but by the fear of living with fundamental changes.

These psychosocial issues of long-term illness compound the many practical problems that the patient must face from the outset. The following challenges are part of living with a chronic condition: medically managing the illness; controlling symptoms; carrying out prescribed regimens; coping with social isolation; adjusting to physical changes; normalizing a new lifestyle; and dealing with financial consequences.[3]

To make matters worse, such practical and emotional concerns can be difficult for medical patients to discuss with family members, who may themselves be feeling overwhelmed. And regrettably few health care professionals understand or know how to help.

For their part, family members have their own urgent needs and issues, and must make profound adjustments. It is estimated that 70 to 95 percent of the daily care for people with chronic conditions takes place in the informal, noninstitutional sector.[4] For the most part, these caregivers are family members, usually women. In addition to the myriad practical and financial demands imposed by chronic illness, families must cope with emotional and psychological pressures such as burnout, dependency, and loss.

Like their medically ill relative, family members must deal with the challenges of uncertainty, role changes, and isolation. Besides playing an active part in caring for the patient's daily physical needs, they also may be responsible for carrying out demanding treatment procedures such as injections or kidney dialysis. Meanwhile, they also may be confronting the possibility of catastrophic economic prospects as well as their own lost opportunities for occupational advancement, recreation, and travel.

These and other psychosocial ramifications can be at least as serious as the more tangible physical effects of long-term health conditions. Most people manage the adjustment to long-term illness, but some adaptations are more constructive than others, and even the most resilient individuals can find the challenges of serious illness overwhelming.

A PUBLIC HEALTH PERSPECTIVE ON CHRONIC ILLNESS

The related terms "chronic illness," "long-term medical condition," and "disability" encompass an enormous diversity of conditions. Each has a distinct set of stages and consequences. The most obvious way to categorize chronic medical conditions is by their physical impact. Some long-term conditions are degenerative, such as multiple sclerosis (MS), Parkinson's disease, and amyotrophic lateral sclerosis (ALS). Some are protracted and normally lead to either recovery or early death—heart disease and cancer, for example. Some are progressive but normally not life-threatening (arthritis, lupus), while others (such as AIDS and cystic fibrosis) drastically shorten life.

Chronic conditions also vary in the cause and the timing of onset. They may be the result of disease, congenital anomalies, developmental conditions, or injuries. Some conditions, such as congenital malformations and cerebral palsy, begin at or before birth. Some have a gradual onset, while others are the sudden result of illness or injury, such as stroke and paraplegia. The salient characteristic of chronicity is duration, but that too varies as the condition may be static, progressive, or intermittent.

The definitions used for chronic illness in the health and human services field are as varied as the conditions themselves. In the broadest terms, chronic illness is associated with one or more of the following characteristics:

- It is long-lasting or permanent.
- It leaves residual disability.
- It requires special training of the patient for rehabilitation.
- It can be expected to require a long period of supervisory observation or care.

One effect of illness and impairment is disability, which has been defined as "a limitation in the person's ability to perform tasks, activities and roles to levels expected within physical and social contexts."[5] The Americans with Disabilities Act has brought new attention to the fact that society has a role in either facilitating or impeding people's use of their capacities, whatever their impairments. One aspect of society's influence is the degree of support or stigma associated with different conditions, as illustrated by the differing social attitudes toward cancer and AIDS.

Much has been written about the upsurge of chronic conditions in this century and the reasons for it. A major reason is that public health measures and medical advances have virtually eliminated infectious diseases and many other causes of acute illness and death in the United States, with the notable and troubling exception of AIDS. These measures have reduced infant mortality and prolonged the lives of persons of all ages, including those with severe illnesses. Resulting increases in longevity, together with reduced birth rates, have led to a marked and growing increase in the average age of the United States population. Together, these factors have led to dramatic increases in the number of Americans who are living with functional limitations and chronic health conditions. Chronic illness is now the nation's number one health problem, accounting for 66 percent of all visits to medical specialists.[6] Both psychosocial and biomedical clinicians can expect to see chronic conditions among growing numbers of their patients in the future.

Despite the predominance of chronic illness, however, its full magnitude remains elusive. This country's traditional focus on acute care, together with the plethora of programmatic definitions of chronic illness, have resulted in scant data on the subject. Chronic illness has emerged as a major public health issue without adequate information with which to define the patient population and identify its needs. But even without firm numbers it is clear that disabilities, long term illnesses, and congenital conditions have taken on immense significance—not only for the millions of individuals who are directly affected by them but also for society as a whole.

Epidemiologists point to survey data as the best indication of the extent of chronic illness in the United States. The 1991 National Health Interview Survey found that 14.3 percent of the population (some 36 million people) must limit their activity because of a chronic condition. Of all Americans, 4.3 percent (more than 10 million) have a functional deficit severe enough to prevent them from carrying out their major activity (e.g., school or occupation). As the population ages, such conditions are likely to have an ever greater impact: Chronic illnesses affect people of all ages, but the severity and number of conditions they experience increase with age. The rates of impairment from a chronic condition in the 1991 survey range from 5.8 percent of those under 18 years old to 39.4 percent for those age 70 and over.[7]

Prevalence numbers for specific conditions also convey the public health impact of chronic illness. Some 56.5 million Americans have one or more forms of chronic cardiovascular disease. Two of every three families will have a member diagnosed with cancer, and two-thirds of people initially "cured" of their cancer will experience a recurrence of the disease. More than 7 million people are severely disabled from arthritis. One in every 2,000 babies is born with cystic fibrosis, another treatable but currently incurable disease. Diabetes mellitus, a major chronic disease affecting all age groups, has become the sixth leading cause of death, killing 40,000 people each year. More than 500,000 Americans have MS. In addition, millions are coping with nonfatal but limiting conditions such as chronic pain, hearing impairment, and asthma.

As important as they are, these numbers only partially capture the phenomenon of chronic illness. Largely invisible, for example, are those who live on the margin between health and illness after a life-saving transplant or other heroic measure. Such measures may extend life, but they also can seriously compromise its quality. In a more positive sense, there has been a basic shift in thinking about illness in recent years. Whatever their health problem and however long they expect to live, Americans today are emphasizing living and surviving. The attitude may be best exemplified by those who are HIV-positive or have AIDS and the communities that support and care for them. For all its deadliness, even AIDS is regarded as a chronic condition that people combat and live with as fully as possible and for as long as possible.

THE NEED FOR CARING

Chronic conditions cannot be cured. The task of the person with the condition is not recovery but adaptation. He or she must adjust physically, psychologically, and practically to living with limitations that are some-times severe and uncertainties that may never be resolved. Correspond-ingly, the primary task of the health care system is caring, not curing. Such caring only happens when people's medical problems are addressed within the broad context of their lives.

George Engel illustrates this perspective with his biopsychosocial model (see Figures 1.1 and 1.2), which places the person in a systems hierarchy with the following dimensions: two-person dyads, the family, the community, the culture-subculture, the society-nation, and the biosphere. Engel points out that each of these dimensions has an influence on health, and all must be taken into consideration by the clinician. He also chides his medical colleagues for their tunnel vision:

> [T]he neglect of the whole inherent in the reductionism of the biomedical model is largely responsible for the physician's preoccupation with the body and with disease and the corresponding neglect of the patient as a person. This has contributed importantly to the widespread public feeling that scientific medicine is impersonal, an attitude consistent with how the biomedically trained physician views the place of science in his everyday work. For him "science" and the scientific method have to do with the understanding and treatment of disease, not with the patient and patient care. [8]

The dramatic advances in medical technology are to be celebrated for virtually eliminating infectious disease, arresting many acute conditions, and extending life for so many. But we must also acknowledge that these measures have created profound personal and social issues by compromising the quality of many patients' lives even while extending them. Equally serious, the emphasis on curing and heroic medicine has fostered a mind-set that makes it difficult for some physicians to "merely" care for those they cannot cure. Failure to recognize these developments has effectively resulted in the emotional abandonment of people with chronic illness by a biomedically dominated health care system. Oliver Sacks laments the preoccupation with physical matters at the expense of emotional needs in *Awakenings*:

> In present-day medicine . . . there is an almost exclusively technical or mechanical emphasis, which has led to immense advances, but also to intellectual regression, and to a lack of proper attention to the full needs and feelings of patients. [9]

Many years after the influential writings of these physicians, it remains true that those with the most knowledge about a patient's physical condition — physicians and other medical professionals — are rarely able to offer needed emotional and practical support. Their expertise is aimed at ameliorating the physical effects of the condition. However great their empathy, they are limited by skill, training, time, and institutional mandate in their ability to help patients address the many nonphysical effects of their condi-

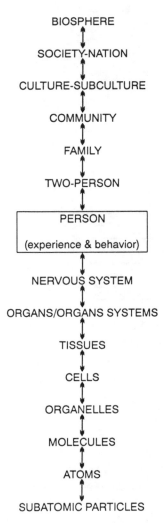

SYSTEMS HIERARCHY
(LEVELS OF ORGANIZATION)

BIOSPHERE

SOCIETY-NATION

CULTURE-SUBCULTURE

COMMUNITY

FAMILY

TWO-PERSON

PERSON

(experience & behavior)

NERVOUS SYSTEM

ORGANS/ORGANS SYSTEMS

TISSUES

CELLS

ORGANELLES

MOLECULES

ATOMS

SUBATOMIC PARTICLES

FIGURE 1.1. Hierarchy of natural systems. From *American Journal of Psychiatry,* *137*(5). ©American Psychiatric Association. Reprinted with permission.

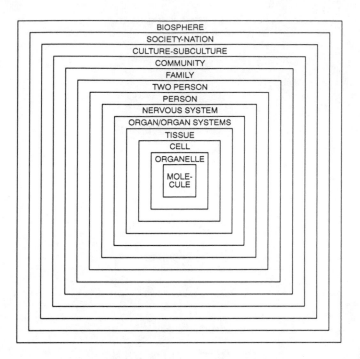

FIGURE 1.2. Continuum of natural systems. From *American Journal of Psychiatry, 137(5)*. ©American Psychiatric Association. Reprinted with permission.

tions. Stories still abound of appalling callousness on the part of physicians.[10]

For their part, most mental health professionals, too, are ill-equipped to help chronically ill people cope with psychosocial problems with a medical origin and focus. Most mental health professionals have been trained to identify and address—and more importantly to assume the existence of—underlying psychopathologies. Psychotherapeutic techniques are aimed at drawing out insights about early childhood, unconscious forces, and long-term psychological themes in order to bring about basic change in personality and interpersonal dynamics. Mental health training typically does not equip students to assume a healthy ego and defenses, or to relate to a medical crisis as the driving force, the salient issue, in a person's emotional life. Thus, like their medical colleagues, few mental health professionals today have the knowledge, vocabulary, and techniques to address the concerns raised by long-term illness and disability.

It is unrealistic to expect physicians to expand their perspective and clinical techniques to meet the psychosocial needs of their chronically ill patients, given the complexities and pressures of today's health care environment. What is needed to complement medical treatment are specialized mental health professionals who understand the impact of chronic illness and who can help patients anticipate and adjust to its demands.

Having such specialists available to chronically ill patients would not reduce medical professionals' duty to be attentive to their psychosocial needs. It would, however, focus their responsibility on assessing patients' need for psychosocial intervention, assuring that specialized help is available, making effective referrals, and being receptive to input from the counselor about psychosocial factors.

THE STATUS OF PSYCHOSOCIAL TREATMENT

The good news today is that the changes called for by Engel, Sacks, and others are underway. The health care system is far more attentive to psychosocial needs since the advent of high-technology medicine. The mind-body dichotomy that has divided medical and mental health care is breaking down, and a multifaceted health-related counseling field is evolving. Specializations oriented to the psychosocial aspects of illness are growing within such disciplines as psychology, psychiatry, social work, and nursing.

The fields of family therapy and family medicine have been a fertile common ground for psychosocial and medical approaches. From that vantage point, Donald Bloch, M.D., editor of *Family Systems Medicine*, wrote in 1993 of

> an intellectual and technological movement:
> - toward holistic approaches in medicine that conceptually unite mind and body
> - toward ecosystemic approaches that conceptually unite the individual with his or her significant social contexts.
>
> . . . This process is substantially changing medicine and its institutions. It is significant, I believe, that workers from many disciplines are involved and make up the psychosocial medicine community: psychology and psychiatry, primary care and family medicine, public health, general and specialty nursing (including nurse practitioners and psychiatric nurse specialists), social workers, family therapists and counselors, and family researchers amid a host of social scientists. [11]

However, despite the existence of cutting-edge programs such as these, health-oriented counseling services are still rare relative to the need for them. The programs that do exist are financially out of reach for many patients, especially those with no insurance coverage. Many programs can serve only a few patients, making it necessary to limit care to those who are in greatest distress or most at risk. Some programs only help patients late in the course of their illness, or family members after the death of a sick relative. Moreover, many health-related counseling programs are confined to a specific condition such as cancer or AIDS. Thus, even when a psychosocial program exists in a given medical setting it may only assist people in a few medical categories. A consequence for the field is lost opportunities for cross-fertilization and the inability to search for common themes across disciplines and disorders.

Many psychosocial programs for people with health conditions are tied to research projects, and this creates another set of problems. For example, research programs typically require a control group that does not receive treatment, thus excluding patients who qualify for treatment. Another shortcoming is that research projects that use a long-term treatment model have limited relevance for the short-term approaches required by many payment programs.

Voluntary organizations are currently the most widely available source of support and psychoeducation for people with chronic illnesses and their caregivers. Such organizations include self-help groups, health-related associations, and visiting and "friend" programs. Typically, these organizations have limited funding and carry out their outreach and support functions through volunteers. The amount and quality of training for volunteers in these vital roles varies greatly from program to program.

WANTED: BRIEF, STRUCTURED, FOCUSED PSYCHOSOCIAL TREATMENT, APPLICABLE IN DIVERSE CLINICAL SETTINGS

The upshot of all of these factors is that relatively few Americans coping with chronic illness are fortunate enough to meet all three of the following conditions: to have primary care providers who recognize their need for counseling; to have access to specialized mental health professionals for such counseling; *and* to have health insurance coverage that will pay for it. Each of these conditions represents a separate arena in which progress is needed.

Affecting all three of these arenas—which, in economic terms, represent demand, supply, and payment—are the reforms currently underway in the health care system. Although the long-term effect of these changes cannot be predicted, some trends are already clear. For one thing, the emphasis on brief treatment is growing. Second, the shift from inpatient to outpatient treatment is continuing and even intensifying. Third, the demand for clear and positive treatment outcomes and for accountability on the part of providers is increasing. And fourth, policy makers may be more willing to invest in prevention and early intervention than in the past.

All of these developments are hospitable to MCC, which derives its special contribution from its structure, brevity, and adaptability. The education of medical and mental health professionals has begun to incorporate MCC principles, notably that the psychosocial sequelae of long-term illness deserve equal attention with the physical ones, and that such sequelae are normal, not pathological.

I have found that the MCC model can be incorporated into the training of new medical and mental health professionals, as well as into the clinical techniques of those who are already in the field. This treatment approach can be integrated into varied clinical settings: outpatient or inpatient, independent or affiliated with a medical institution. It is a brief, structured intervention that is relevant to the needs of people in medical crisis as well as those of the health care institutions and professionals that care for them. Finally, MCC will enable professionals already working with this patient population to do so more effectively, and give those who wish to begin such work the skills and insights for doing so.

NOTES

1. Hawking, S. W. (1988). *A brief history of time* (p. vii). New York: Bantam.
2. May, R. (1977). *The meaning of anxiety* (p. 193). New York: Norton.
3. See Strauss, A. et al. (1984). *Chronic illness and the quality of life* (2nd ed.). St. Louis: Mosby.
4. Edwards, R. (1987). Professional and family caregivers: A social work perspective. In J. Nottingham & J. Nottingham (Eds.). *The professional and family caregiver—Dilemmas, rewards, and new directions* (p. 49). Proceedings of the 1987 Inaugural Conference of the Rosalynn Carter Institute for Human Development. Atlanta: Nottingham & Nottingham.
5. National Institute of Child Health and Human Development (1993). *National Center for Medical Rehabilitation Research report and plan* (Report No. 93-3509). Washington, DC: U.S. Government Printing Office.
6. Hymovich, D., & Hagopian, G. (1992). *Chronic illness in children and adults: A psychosocial approach* (p. 82). Philadelphia: Saunders.

7. Adams, P. F., & Benson, V. *Current estimates from the national health interview survey, 1991* (p. 106) (Vital Health Stat 10 [184]). Hyattsville, MD: National Center for Health Statistics.

8. Engel, G. (1980, May). The clinical application of the biopsychosocial model. *American Journal of Psychiatry*, 535–543.

9. Sacks, O. W. (1983). *Awakenings* (p. xii). New York: Dutton.

10. The *Washington Post* of July 12, 1994, reports on a finding that 71% of a random sample of malpractice suits were "over a doctor's poor communication with the patient and family." It quotes the researchers as saying that "the most common complaint was 'the feeling of being deserted and feeling alone.'"

Two examples:

• Placing a stethoscope on the chest of a man in critical condition after an aneurism, a resident remarked to the observing interns, "This is the *best* aortic insufficiency I've ever heard."

• A 16-year old girl struggling with a recent diagnosis of lymphoma was told by an internist, "Please don't cry in my office. I just don't like to hear people sniffling."

One patient's response: A college student hospitalized for cancer treatment kept a water gun near his bed and "shot" any provider who referred to him in the third person in his presence.

11. Bloch, D. (1993). Editorial: Family and psychosocial medicine. *Family Systems Medicine*, *11*(3), 231–232.

PART I

Clinical Issues

CHAPTER TWO

Overview, Special Issues, and Underlying Concepts

Medical crisis counseling focuses on three critical and interacting arenas in patients' lives:[1] the illness and its treatment, emotions and coping skills, and family relationships. The demands of the medical condition always frame the counseling goals. The overarching goal of MCC is for the patient to integrate the illness and live as fully as possible. The counselor pursues this goal by validating fears and concerns and enhancing positive coping and communication skills. Often, improved teamwork among all those responsible for treatment and care—including the person with the illness— is a byproduct of this process.

Four assumptions lie at the heart of MCC:

- *The medical condition is the focus.* MCC defines a medical crisis as a time of unusual emotional distress or disorientation caused by the onset of, or a major change in, the medical condition. Typical crisis points are the initial diagnosis, discharge from hospitalization, and exacerbation. These are optimal points of psychosocial intervention. MCC stresses that in a medical crisis, the medical condition is the governing factor. It, rather than any inherent pathologies or dysfunctions in the person's psyche and relationships, determines the issues to be dealt with in treatment. The counselor takes it for granted that strong emotions such as depression, fear, and anger are normal reactions to serious illness. This normalization gives the patient permission to express feelings that may have been suppressed or denied. To be sure, some patients enter MCC carrying psychological burdens in addition to those imposed by their illness. Nevertheless, because it is a brief and focused modality MCC confines itself to effects of the medical condition. It deals with coexisting problems only to the extent that they interfere with the adjustment to the illness.

- *Medical crises are temporary and offer opportunities for learning.* A person may be facing permanent illness and impairment, but with proper support the state of emotional crisis it engenders can be temporary or at worst episodic. A crisis is a time of intense learning, the insights from which can be helpful throughout life. MCC helps the patient take advantage of this opportunity for learning.
- *The adjustment issues faced by people with chronic illness can be predicted.* People with lasting medical conditions typically encounter the same issues, and generally in a similar order. Understanding and knowing how to cope with these issues strengthens the patient's ability to deal with the many physical, practical, emotional, and interpersonal challenges that can be expected.
- *People have strengths and capacities that can be built upon.* Human beings possess inherent survival mechanisms and common sense. Even while facing a serious medical condition, people can learn to cope with difficult problems and preserve the quality of their lives. Their ego strengths and capacities are important here, not their deficiencies and handicaps. MCC assumes that a way exists for the individual to adapt to crisis, and it facilitates that adaptation process.

MCC differs from traditional psychotherapy in several key ways that stem from its tight focus on the effects of the medical condition. Barring evidence to the contrary, MCC patients are assumed to have the ego strength to adjust to a life-long physical condition. The usual open-ended approach of psychotherapy is unnecessary because the therapeutic focus of MCC is already established. Lengthy reflection on personality issues is inappropriate; the object of therapy is to reinforce patients' strengths and coping abilities and to maximize their adjustment to long-term illness.

WHO, WHEN, WHERE, AND BY WHOM

The Patient

MCC is intended for people with lasting medical conditions, their family members, and other informal caregivers. It often is most effective when both patients and caregivers participate. The breadth and flexibility of the model, which evolved out of experience with a wide range of disorders, make it relevant to most, if not all, chronic conditions.

Occasionally, medically ill persons or family members contact the MCC counselor directly after learning about MCC from sources such as self-help groups. Most often, though, patients and family members are referred by either the primary care physician or a specialist. If the MCC program is related to hospital services, the referral may come through the hospital's social work department.

Roughly a third of the patients in a typical MCC practice are informal caregivers, usually family members. Although this book generally talks of the primary MCC patient as the person with the medical condition, the intervention is also appropriate for caregivers, who experience a version of all the principal issues of chronic illness. Family members are often seen as adjunct MCC patients when their ill relative is the primary patient. Family issues are noted where appropriate throughout the book, and discussed in depth in Chapter 6.

Timing

Medical Crisis Counseling is so named because in the course of a long-term illness, at least three points, marking new stages in the disease, constitute a medical crisis. They occur at the time of (1) receipt of diagnosis, (2) discharge from the hospital, and (3) exacerbation of symptoms after a remission. These are the points at which an intervention is most needed and can be most effective.

I have generally found that the earlier counseling is received, the greater its effectiveness. Whether suddenly struck by injury or serious illness or diagnosed with a chronic disease that will take years to ramify, the individual is likely to react with strong emotions of fear, despair, and a sense of losing control. Some patients and family members engage in extreme denial, or experience what has been called "frozen fright," the inability to react at all. At that vulnerable time, the physician may be unable to provide crucial comfort and support. This is a strategic time for preventing the onset of patterns of adaptation that could turn temporary emotional crises into long-term states of anxiety, depression, and family disruption. The medical crisis counselor's timely intervention can reduce the likelihood of dysfunctional adaptations and speed the process of adjustment. The same reasoning applies to intervention at the other crisis points of release from hospitalization and exacerbation: the sooner the intervention, the better.

My experience has been that the psychosocial intervention is usually initiated by the patient's physician, who recognizes that it is normal for serious physical problems to have emotional ramifications. Ideally, the physician will not only make a referral but prescribe it as adjunctive therapy, thereby establishing a critical link in the patient's support network.

By making a distinction between medical and psychosocial issues and ensuring that the patient has expert help with the latter, the physician can give more freely in his or her area of expertise while the patient learns to be a more constructive partner in treatment.

Where and By Whom

Mental health professionals can use the MCC model in a variety of health-care-related capacities, including consultation-liaison psychiatrists, behavioral medicine practitioners, medical psychologists, nurse clinicians, and clinical and medical social workers. They can offer counseling in conjunction with inpatient care in hospitals and nursing homes, in outpatient clinics or physicians' offices, in the counselor's office, or in patients' homes. Medical crisis counselors can serve as salaried staff members or consultants for health care institutions, or they can be independent practitioners. Part II of this book contains information on setting up MCC programs in different treatment settings.

The patient populations of most independent mental health practitioners are likely to include people coping directly or indirectly with a serious health problem. MCC can increase these counselors' ability to help their patients in these situations. The MCC model can also be adapted by support group facilitators in voluntary health organizations, pastoral counselors, and the staff of caregiving organizations such as hospices. In the medical care arena, physicians and those responsible for health care planning and administration should be familiar with MCC because it provides a valuable service and has the potential to enhance the efficacy and cost-effectiveness of health care.

THE TREATMENT PROCESS IN BRIEF

MCC can be offered in a variety of formats and time periods, depending on factors such as the severity of the patient's concerns and the mode and context of service delivery. In my experience, the optimal format involves ten one-hour sessions, once or twice a week over two or three months. The process begins with an initial consultation and ends with a final review and summary. Between these two framing sessions, the number of intervening counseling sessions can range from two to eight. The intervention is approached as a mutually agreed-upon contract, albeit a very flexible one. Changes can be made in the course of treatment as needed. Some people require only a single consultation with a medical crisis counselor, while others need to return for brief episodic treatment over a period of years.

Following is a brief overview of treatment, which is described in detail in Chapters 3 and 4.

The Initial Consult

The first MCC session is a structured interview that establishes the framework for treatment. The counselor gathers information about the medical condition, personal and family resources, and known coping mechanisms. The patient expresses his or her major concerns and problems and explores the feelings caused by the illness. If he or she agrees to come in for treatment, the counselor and patient then establish a treatment plan that centers on a concrete and realistic goal set by the patient. This consultation is the pivotal event, in that it creates the conditions that help patients take charge of their lives.

In fact, the consultation gives some patients all they need for the time being: an assessment of the situation, identification of concerns, affirmation of skills and resources, and assurance that more professional help is available if needed. This "one-time-only" alternative is an entirely appropriate outcome of the consult, as the clinical experience of many people in this field attests.

Counseling Sessions

In the ensuing sessions, the medical crisis counselor uses a loosely structured format to help the patient address concerns, identify and reinforce coping strategies, and achieve therapeutic short-term goals. The counselor's conceptual framework for guiding the counseling process is the issues that are known to arise as a result of chronic illness: control, self-image, dependency, stigma, abandonment, anger, isolation, and death. These eight issues usually become salient in the order listed, although they may surface at any time and in some cases appear and reappear. Control issues usually arise at the outset because from the time of diagnosis a patient struggles with a feeling of losing control of his or her life. Typically, self-image is the next issue to emerge, as the patient grieves losses and works toward a self-image that integrates the profound emotional and physical ramifications of the medical condition. The "external" corollaries of the first two issues are dependence and stigma—representing the emergence of concerns about relationships with others. Anger and fear of abandonment usually surface when the other issues have been addressed and the hard reality of chronicity must be faced. The troubling prospects of isolation and death may be on the patient's mind from the outset, but these concerns are usually less immediate than the others.

At the time that they are addressed in MCC, the issues will almost certainly vary in the degree to which they arise out of the patient's experience or his or her imagination and fears. Some issues (for example, control and self-image) may already have been experienced as "real-life" problems caused by the illness. Others will exist for the patient as fears about the future—for example, fears of abandonment, isolation, or severe impairment. Which concerns arise out of experience and which are fears about the future depends primarily on the stage of the disease at which the patient enters treatment.

I want to stress that these are not mechanical clinical steps, but rather naturally arising concerns to be addressed in roughly the order indicated. The MCC framework provides a kind of "soft" order, with ample allowance for individual variations. Differences among individuals in the significance and urgency of these issues are a function of many factors, including the nature and stage of their medical condition and developmental, personality, and family characteristics. These factors come together to form a unique dynamic for each individual. While they may vary in intensity and order, all issues are addressed in the course of treatment. The MCC structure is useful because it assures that no critical issue is missed.

The very specific concerns and experiences that patients bring into treatment from their daily lives fit naturally into this framework. Confronting fears and concerns in the concrete terms of personal experience helps them integrate the medical condition. The process is given focus and a sense of direction by repeated reference (explicitly or implicitly) to the personal goal set in the first session.

The objective of this brief and focused treatment program is not to resolve these complex and far-reaching issues once and for all, although that sometimes happens. Rather, it is to help patients internalize an adjustment process that will work for them over the "long haul" of a chronic illness.

The Final Session

MCC is concluded when the patient achieves the short-term goal set in the first session. Normally, he or she accomplishes this within the standard ten-session format of the treatment program, or sooner—a satisfying achievement that depends greatly on the clinician's skill in guiding the patient's choice of a realistic goal. In the final session, the clinician reviews with the patient his or her accomplishments, stressing the ability to deal realistically with the consequences of the illness.

A fraction of MCC patients (perhaps one in ten) finds it necessary to return for further treatment at later stages of the illness. This possibility of episodic treatment should be mentioned in the consultation, to relieve any mistaken sense of having to "get it right" in a brief period of time. Follow-up treatment is also brief and focused, for the same reasons that apply to the initial intervention. An alternative to further individual treatment is for MCC patients and family members to join MCC groups, a treatment modality discussed in Chapter 7.

ELEMENTS OF THE MEDICAL CRISIS COUNSELING APPROACH

To apply the principles and accomplish the goals of MCC, counselors can draw on a wide range of clinical models and techniques, including cognitive, behavioral, and brief psychodynamic therapies, in individual, family, and group treatment settings. Useful techniques include anticipatory guidance, supportive confrontation, role playing, visualization, and educational interventions.

The medical crisis counselor takes an active, dynamic role – guiding goal-setting, asking focusing questions, and drawing out salient issues. Counselors with an eclectic approach to treatment are best equipped to meet the diverse and changing needs of chronically ill patients. Their willingness to be flexible and creative is essential, for it is often necessary to use several techniques with a patient, possibly in more than one setting. The more theories and techniques at the counselor's disposal, the greater the chance of finding the right means of applying MCC principles.

This is a transparent, demystified process. The counselor is straightforward about the process and techniques being used. The object is to help patients maintain mental and emotional control, even as they face diminishing physical control. At the outset, the counselor describes (in nonthreatening lay terms) the structure of treatment and the concepts underlying it. As treatment proceeds, this straightforward approach promotes the MCC goal of helping patients to be constructive and practical members of their health care teams.

Several other themes and principles underlie this counseling approach. Fundamentally, MCC is a process of *cognitive restructuring*. The cognitive work encourages individual solutions and takes for granted the patient's inherent good sense, ability to cope, and desire to get the most out of life. Experience has shown that people with this grounding are able to determine for themselves what they need to do and make personally authentic changes in behavior and attitudes. The underlying assumption is that a wide range of adaptive responses are appropriate.

The counselor's first task is to identify the strongest elements of the patient's personality. For example, the individual's sources of strength might be a close family, religious faith, a resilient sense of humor, creative outlets, strong links to a supportive community, or a meaningful and sustainable occupation. With the counselor's guidance, such resources become the bedrock on which an adaptive process can be built. Patients are helped not so much to learn new skills as to become aware of the ways in which they are already coping, and to strengthen those that are most positive.

I have found it useful to ask patients about difficult experiences that have called upon their coping skills in the past. This review of coping styles and experiences begins as part of the consultation. It may indicate some of the ways they can adjust to the current medical crisis. There are clearly limits to the predictive value of the exercise: People who have not experienced a crisis of this magnitude know little about how they will cope with a lasting medical condition. Its value is in suggesting that having coped with difficulty in the past, they can do so again—even if they doubt that capacity at the present time.

Even in the absence of comparable experience, however, such a review can help the patient focus on the notion of coping, become more aware of personal style, and understand that there are many ways to cope. The exercise also reinforces the key MCC principle that people need not develop new capacities when they are affected by a medical condition; rather, their task is to discover and develop the capacities they already possess. This insight comes as a relief to patients.

The counselor cannot promote individual solutions without being aware of the many variables that affect the patient's experience of the medical condition. Obviously, health issues do not exist in a vacuum and psychosocial treatment interacts with a host of factors besides the patient's physical condition. In addition to the effects of the disorder, there are other physical characteristics such as age, gender, and coexisting health/mental health conditions. The counselor also must be attuned to educational, socioeconomic, cultural, developmental and other influences on the patient.

Goal-setting has a pivotal role in MCC. With the counselor's assistance, the patient sets a realistic, achievable goal in the first session. It is then a reference point against which progress is tracked in subsequent sessions. Treatment is considered complete when (and only when) the patient's short-term goal is achieved. One of the counselor's first, and most critical, interventions is therefore making certain that the patient sets an attainable goal. The goal provides a frame of reference for treatment from session to session, and its achievement can help restore a badly needed sense of control. Setting a single goal keeps the prospect of working toward it from being too daunting.

Listed below are a few examples of appropriate goals; others will be noted in the case descriptions throughout the book. Typically, patients' goals become even more focused in subsequent sessions.

- To adjust to a new home
- To find new sources of social support
- To improve family relations
- To reduce tension at work
- To become more comfortable talking about one's disease
- To find a constructive approach to decisions about nursing care

Changing conditions and uncertain outcomes are the hallmarks of chronic illness, and the source of much of its stress. Some stress precedes rather than follows threatening events — beginning, for many people, with the agonizing search for a correct diagnosis. MCC is in part a strategy of *anticipatory guidance,*[2] which helps patients not only think through their current concerns but also prepare for future challenges. Patients gain mastery by examining their feelings about and planning for the likely future effects of the illness, facilitated by the medical crisis counselor within the framework of the eight issues.

Even if these measures do not wholly eliminate stress, they can desensitize patients to the power of feared events and increase their ability to adapt to them. The counselor must help patients understand the speculative nature of this process: Even if the typical course of the medical condition is known, its manifestation in that individual, including the exact nature, severity, and timing of its effects, cannot be predicted. Surprise outcomes are always a possibility.

Because extreme emotional distress can exacerbate the symptoms of a medical condition, MCC maintains a *careful balance between support and confrontation,* with body awareness as an explicit dimension. Patients learn to recognize their physical reactions to emotional stress and acquire techniques for managing them. Awareness of the interactions between thoughts, emotions, and physical symptoms enables patients to monitor them not only during therapy, but also at other times. If special treatment is indicated to help the patient manage stress, the counselor can either provide it or refer to a specialist such as a biofeedback practitioner. Anticipatory guidance is itself a means of managing stress: By helping patients anticipate emotionally charged issues, it prepares them to deal with those issues when they arise in the future.

MCC pays considerable attention to interpersonal factors, including but not limited to those within the family. Four of the eight issues (stigma, dependency, abandonment, and isolation) explicitly concern interpersonal relations. Because the chronically ill person's interaction with caregivers and others is so important, MCC treatment places great emphasis on strengthening *understanding and communication*. The patient clarifies current patterns of communicating and expressing emotions, considers alternatives, identifies existing skills and those needing improvement, and practices new approaches. Work on this area may involve one or more sessions with family members, either singly or together.

A cornerstone of MCC is the priority attached to *good communication between the counselor and key medical caregivers*. This communication begins at the time of referral, and ideally (with the patient's consent) launches a process of information exchange and consultation that continues throughout treatment. This interaction should not be time-consuming for either party. My experience, like that reported by many other counselors, is that the benefits of a psychosocial intervention are greatly enhanced by links between medical and mental health care. This dimension of MCC is discussed in Chapter 9.

SPECIAL ISSUES

Family Versus Individual Treatment

The counselor must make several key decisions at the outset, in consultation with the patient. A critical one is whether to see the individual alone or with one or more family members. I have found that in the early stages of treatment, most patients derive the greatest benefit from individual counseling. People with serious medical conditions need a setting in which they can speak freely and openly of their darkest fears, such as about pain, disfigurement, abandonment, physical deterioration, role changes, economic changes, dependence, and death—fears that might upset or frighten their families and friends. Individual sessions afford the chance to express fears such as these and to receive validation and support for feelings that may have seemed difficult to safely express elsewhere.

Family members have many of the same fears, which they may feel constrained about revealing lest they upset their ill relative. They, too, need a chance to air emotionally charged concerns in the supportive privacy of counseling. For medical patients and family members, venting such concerns and exploring how to broach them with each other can avert a breakdown of communication. Medical patients often need a chance to talk about the very person who brought them to the counselor's office, especially if that individual is the principal caregiver. To open up, patients need assurance that they are not "talking behind the person's back" but rather trying to improve a deteriorating relationship that is causing everyone pain. Despite their reluctance to do so (and after being assured that the office is soundproof), they usually are able to ventilate long-suppressed feelings that desperately need airing.

Often, a family member brings the medically ill person to counseling sessions. This opens the possibility of family or couples therapy, which actually may be requested by the patient. If asked, I usually tell patients that it is important to see one or both of the members of the couple individually to assess the situation. Sometimes after beginning treatment with individual sessions, I will see the couple together for one or more sessions. Occasionally, the process happens in reverse. I have often arranged for the ill person and the spouse (in most instances the primary caregiver) to have back-to-back sessions, waiting the hour for each other. Their joint travel time gives them an opportunity to share experiences and insights.

Couples often present their marriage as the focal problem when in fact the medical condition is the primary cause of marital difficulty. For this reason, medical crisis counselors should immediately begin to heighten awareness of the illness as a causal factor. Patients need to understand the normalcy of their feelings, recognize the illness as the source of much misdirected anger, and learn how to redirect it. Addressing marital concerns in this manner often significantly reduces the hostility between partners and enables patients to turn to more fundamental issues. The counselor should also, of course, be aware of major dysfunctions in the relationship that predated the illness.

If family relations do prove to be a major impediment to coping with the illness, couples or family therapy is in order for some or all of the remaining sessions. Chapter 6 discusses the ways in which MCC addresses family issues while keeping the focus on the medical problem.

Some people may wish to continue brief counseling after they complete a series of MCC sessions. This may be desirable, for example, to work on a personality trait that is interfering with the individual's adjustment to the medical condition. In that instance, counseling would move beyond the standard boundaries of MCC. Whatever the focus of follow-up treatment, the basic principles are still followed: a limited number of sessions, a clear treatment contract, and short-term goals set by the patient.

Some MCC patients choose to enter an MCC group after completing individual treatment, to reduce their sense of isolation and continue normalizing their experience. Group treatment is discussed in Chapter 7.

Working with Hesitant Patients

Some people who come to a medical crisis counselor at the behest of their physician or a family member are tentative, at best, about their need for counseling. While acknowledging the growing stress in their lives, they may insist that they are handling the challenge well. They may assert that they came only out of respect for the doctor or consideration for a family member, implying that it was not their decision to consult with the medical crisis counselor.

Counselors need to keep several things in mind when working with hesitant patients. The first is that hesitancy in this context is qualitatively different from "resistance" in standard psychotherapy. There are a number of reasons for this difference. For one thing, medical crises often necessitate a psychosocial intervention at a far earlier stage of patient readiness than is typical for other kinds of mental health problems. People often live with a psychological problem for years before seeking therapy. When referral to MCC takes place soon after diagnosis, as I have recommended, it is quite normal for patients to be hesitant or ambivalent about it. Even at a later stage, the medical condition may force patients and family members to confront a crisis before they have grown comfortable with the idea of consulting a mental health professional. The common social stigma against "craziness," and thus against psychotherapy, is often a mitigating factor.

I chose the name medical crisis *counseling* to minimize people's misgivings by avoiding the word "therapy." This type of intervention, which bridges the medical and mental health worlds, may be unfamiliar to patients and need some explanation. A central principle to be conveyed is that MCC is for "normal" people and a source of valuable support for the adjustment to life-changing illness. In this vein, MCC can be described as an adjunct to medical care. (Ideally, the referring professional has stressed these points when recommending counseling to the patient.)

Patients may feel hesitant for reasons other than a lack of emotional readiness or concern about stigma. The enormous demands on patients' time and money have been noted, and the simple prospect of dealing with another treatment regimen can be daunting. One of the counselor's first tasks, therefore, is to describe the MCC process and stress that treatment is short, structured, and goal-oriented. Unlike the illness, the end of this intervention can be seen. As I have noted, the process is also straightforward so the patient knows what to expect from it.

Whatever they may say about their reason for being there, however, patients need to recognize that they are motivated by more than a desire to comply with a physician's advice or placate a family member. It is important to point out to hesitant or ambivalent patients that they made a free choice to come to the consultation. This choice indicates that they are in control of their lives and at least mildly curious about counseling, if not yet committed to it. Once they agree—and they usually do—they can then be drawn into discerning or acknowledging what they are seeking.

If patients begin to show some interest in counseling but are reluctant to commit to an entire course of treatment, it may be helpful to remind them that they always have control over termination. If necessary, a special short-term treatment contract (perhaps three sessions) with a narrowly defined goal can be suggested. Some people simply need time before they can fully take responsibility for the decision to seek help. In the meantime, if viewing the decision as a fulfillment of someone else's request—perhaps the doctor or a friend or relative—helps to ease them into personally accepting treatment, then it can be done this way, as well. This form of denial of "neediness" is adaptive for some individuals, at least initially.

It is also possible, of course, that the patient will decide not to return for further treatment. Some individuals remain unconvinced about the need for counseling; others get what they need from the single consultation. In both cases, patients can be reminded that the counseling service is always available to them if they need it. The discussions of the "one-time-only patient" on pages 19 and 46 review the benefits of a single session.

When a Child Is Ill

The heterogeneity of chronic illness is most striking among children. Conditions caused by injury, disease, or congenital factors may be severely disabling or impose only a few limitations. Some children look forward to relatively normal life expectancy, while others face imminent death. Whatever the timing and nature of onset, the trajectory of children's chronic illness looks quite different from that of adults, the majority of whom contract their condition in adulthood.

As the major informal caregiver, the family of the chronically ill child plays the pivotal role in MCC. Chapter 6 discusses the family's experience of chronic illness and the various ways the counselor can work with family members to enhance communication, provide support, and clarify roles. That discussion applies in particular to families of older chronically ill children.

When the ill child is very young, counseling focuses on key family members (usually one or both parents). A crucial objective is to improve communication and strengthen mutual support between the parents. In her seminal book *Chronic Illness in Children: Its Impact on Child and Family*, Georgia Travis stresses, "Enabling the parents to love and sustain the child is an obligation of those who would prevent later psychic distortions."[3] Families also need support to ensure that the needs of other members, particularly children, receive adequate attention.

Counseling a chronically ill child calls upon the clinician's full knowledge of child psychology and development as well as some familiarity with the medical issues involved. These areas of knowledge and expertise serve as a lens through which MCC principles are understood and applied. Those principles, outlined at the beginning of this chapter, apply equally to working with children: keeping the focus on the medical condition; viewing medical crises as temporary and as opportunities for learning; framing treatment in terms of the eight expectable issues of long-term illness; and mobilizing preexisting capacities.

Naturally, the intensity and salience of each of the eight issues depends on the medical condition as well as developmental and psychological factors of both the child and other family members. The nature of the intervention also varies depending on the age and capabilities of the child. Travis uses Erik Erikson's life cycle model in a detailed discussion of the interaction between illness and developmental issues[4] — specifically, the ways the illness disrupts the basic tasks of childhood.

Travis acknowledges that her book "addresses itself primarily to an understanding of the problems that chronic illness creates, not to the art of helping."[5] That subject, the art of helping, is ably treated in another fine resource that examines the partnership among professionals, young patients and their parents. The authors of *Building the Healing Partnership: Parents, Professionals, and Children with Chronic Illnesses and Disabilities*[6] bring together the insights of scores of families. Parents of chronically ill children offer experience-based advice for health care professionals on such subjects as conveying painful information, collaborating on a treatment plan, and dealing with grief. The authors' goal is to strengthen the *caring* in health care through mutual respect and effective communication among all the participants in the healing partnership.

An important aspect of life for chronically ill children is the large number of institutional sectors that influence their well-being and care. These services suffer from regrettable fragmentation. In addition to the school system and numerous health care providers, the helping institutions include public and private social service agencies concerned with such matters as financial support, transportation, rehabilitation, respite care, and home care. The medical crisis counselor faces a challenge in maintaining a systems perspective that is broad and dynamic enough to encompass all the critical players.

IMPORTANT THEORIES

Three theories are especially relevant to MCC, each involving a different but related notion of crisis as well as a unique view of development. Erik Erikson's life cycle theory of human development sheds light on the interactions between chronic illness and the developmental processes of those it touches. Crisis intervention and bereavement theories enhance understanding of patients in crisis and how they can be helped.

Erik Erikson's Life Cycle Theory of Human Development

Erik Erikson's theory[7] provides a useful context in which to understand the patient's reactions to chronic illness. Understanding the current developmental tasks of the patient and family members, given their ages, aids the counselor in predicting the major issues and identifying coping skills and defenses as well as deficiencies. It also suggests which losses will be most acute for the medical patient and for each family member.

Looking at chronic illness from this developmental perspective, we see that while the patient may have proceeded along the developmental path relatively uninterrupted until the onset of the medical condition, now the trauma of the diagnosis marks an interruption in the developmental process and the introduction of a new and permanent challenge. The illness not only interrupts the person's normal developmental tasks, but also imposes a new set of tasks that must be resolved, either instead of or in addition to those that are a normal part of the life cycle. This is the case whether the individual is 17, 47, or 74 years of age.

The medical crisis also heightens the normal tension between the developmental issues of various family members.[8] An example of such tension is the case of a paraplegic teenager thwarted in her drive for independence and her distraught parents torn between the impulse to be protective and the desire to support their child's natural struggle for independence. These parents also may be ashamed of their very natural regret at being denied the independence normally enjoyed by the parents of young adults.

Medical patients' and family members' experiences of each of the eight issues are greatly influenced by their developmental status. Erikson's life cycle model should therefore function as a kind of backdrop for the MCC model, aiding the counselor in assessing patients' responses to stress and in developing an effective treatment plan. The theory helps to individualize the MCC model – clarifying each patient's ability to confront and resolve crisis, illuminating major developmental issues, and indicating which tasks will be especially important. Ultimately, the goal of MCC is the same as Erikson's culminating developmental task: integrity rather than despair.

Crisis Intervention

Crisis intervention concepts and techniques[9] are relevant to the experience of people whose coping mechanisms are challenged by dealing with the consequences of a medical condition. As a crisis, chronic illness has special complexity: Not only does the loss of health create abnormally high stress levels, but unusually high stress can itself undermine health. Some of the stress of the medical condition is anticipatory, first as the diagnosis is awaited and then as the condition progresses. Physical changes create the need to adjust to impairments and losses. The pervasive element of uncertainty can heighten the stress; many conditions take years to ramify, with many possible outcomes. A major characteristic of chronic illness is waiting to see what will come to pass.

MCC is in essence a method of crisis intervention that addresses fears, reduces stress, and mobilizes coping strategies. It begins by identifying the most urgent source of stress so that it can be a focus of treatment and the basis of its central goal. The patient's ability to adapt constructively is a function of his or her success in reframing the crisis as a challenge.

The analysis of adaptive coping is especially useful in this context. Crisis theory holds that a healthy response to a crisis involves:

- A clear perception of the situation
- Management of affect through awareness of feelings
- Verbalization of feelings (leading to a release of tension)

- Seeking and using help
- Using interpersonal and institutional resources

Applied to chronic illness, that list would translate into the following components:

- Having accurate information about the condition and processing it without distortion
- Expressing feelings, consistent with one's personality
- Communicating clearly with others about needs
- Establishing trust, especially with medical caregivers
- Knowing what social support systems can be counted on
- Marshaling financial, medical, and family resources
- Staying flexible as medical and other conditions change

Initially, MCC follows the same road as crisis theory, using the guideposts of brevity, focused and limited goals, and an active role for the counselor. Then the road splits. Chronic illness differs from many other crises in that its challenges are ongoing and often cumulative. Crisis intervention is most often used to help patients deal with a crisis that already has ended—for example, a fire or an earthquake. Its goal is to restore the patient's functioning to its level prior to the crisis. In contrast, the goal of MCC is to bring the patient to a new level of functioning in order to cope with a future of recurring crises.

Another contrast between MCC and crisis intervention lies in the extent to which the two approaches seek to promote change in the individual. Most people with chronic medical conditions are forced to plan for the future and to develop new adaptive strategies. MCC strives to minimize the amount of change expected of individuals who are already highly challenged. It concentrates on identifying and reinforcing preexisting coping mechanisms—strengthening familiar strategies and realistically anticipating how to use existing capacities to cope with future medical crises.

MCC applies four principles of crisis intervention:

1. *It reviews precipitating events to give the patient an intellectual understanding of the crisis and its ramifications, and of the specific factors that led to MCC treatment.* Faced with a medical crisis, the patient often does not comprehend the full implications of his or her condition. Adjustment depends on a realistic assessment of his or her status and prognosis.
2. *MCC helps the patient accept that the stress and his or her emotional reactions*

are normal. Each person has a unique set of responses and coping mechanisms. This realization reduces anxiety, fear, and guilt, and encourages the expression of feelings that have been repressed and the reinforcement of individual strengths.

3. *It explores the defense mechanisms and adaptive coping strategies that the patient relied upon in the past to deal with crisis.* Once these are identified, the patient can use them to his or her advantage in the present and future. The process also helps to objectify and "unlink" this crisis from prior ones, so that problem-solving can be approached more rationally.

4. *MCC helps the patient identify social, financial, and other support resources such as those in the family and community.* Unless absolutely no resources exist, which is unusual, this assessment leads to a greater sense of comfort and security and points the way to specific actions to mobilize resources.

To these approaches, MCC adds the critical element of *goal-setting,* which maximizes the individual's sense of control in the face of an uncertain future.

Bereavement Theories

The word "bereavement" is normally associated with the death of a loved one, but its broader meaning applies equally to the loss of health and capacity. "Bereave" is from the Middle English word for "rob" or "plunder." *Webster's New Twentieth Century Dictionary* (1983) defines it as "to deprive; to strip; to leave destitute; to deprive, as by death." "Bereaved" is defined as "deprived; stripped and left destitute; having lost a friend or relative by death." Thus it is appropriate to consider how bereavement theories can be "bent" to apply to people facing the deprivations caused by serious health conditions.

Ever since Elisabeth Kübler-Ross brought concepts of death and dying to the attention of the medical profession and the lay public, much has been written on bereavement.[10] Few writers, however, have applied those insights to the losses associated with chronic illness, despite the fact that adjusting to it is very much a matter of grieving losses. The literature on grieving should not start at the point of death. I hope that this subject will begin to receive more attention in the future.

People with long-term medical conditions usually fear life in a diminished or diminishing capacity far more than they fear death. They must adjust to living with change and uncertainty. The "life-related losses," which are cumulative, can include income, mobility, social life, a sense of efficacy, spontaneity, companionship, control over one's life, independence, and even relationships with loved ones.

Each of these life-related personal losses calls for its own kind of grieving. Patients can find compensations for some of them, an impossibility when a loved one is lost. But while the "normal" grieving process is akin to healing, gradually restoring a sense of equilibrium, chronic illness seldom allows time for this slow process to take place before sending up a new challenge. Grieving and letting go are recurring tasks for those experiencing chronic illness, either their own or a loved one's.

In the grieving process related to chronic illness, the patient identifies losses as well as those assets and capacities that can be built on and expanded. Limitations in one area may push the person into other, undeveloped areas. (British physicist Stephen Hawking has said that his disease impelled him to stop being a "lazy student.") Ego-oriented support from the counselor can promote this process.

The experience of anticipatory loss involves a range of emotions that can include denial, separation anxiety, anger, and guilt as well as heightened intimacy and appreciation for life. By focusing on and facilitating anticipatory loss, MCC aids in release from the valued and imperiled characteristic or capacity so that detachment is easier when the anticipated loss occurs.

I want to stress the importance of helping patients distinguish between outcomes that are *certain* or at least likely to occur (such as a surgical procedure or a particular impairment) and outcomes that are *possible* and may not occur at all (such as death in a given period of time due to cancer, or blindness due to diabetes). Physician and writer Bernie Siegel[11] has challenged the common medical practice of telling people with a serious illness that they have a given amount of time to live. He argues that this is not only unscientific but, more seriously, could become a self-fulfilling prophesy for an overly compliant patient.

In a similar manner, current thinking on disability is helping to unlink the physical aspects of pathology and impairment from false notions of inevitability about their consequences. Disability theorists and advocates stress the role that social attitudes and structures play in the progression from pathology to impairment to disability, and conversely the role that "buffers" (assistive devices, medical equipment, social support, attitudes) can play in retarding or even preventing that process.

Armed with insights such as these, medical crisis counselors can help patients challenge assumptions—personal ones and those of others—about the consequences of their conditions. This places the grieving and adjustment process in a more realistic, and more hopeful, context. Besides challenging faulty assumptions, counseling reinforces positive attitudes, strengthens social supports, and stimulates patients' resourcefulness.

THE BRIEF, STRUCTURED APPROACH

MCC uses a tightly focused structure and a brief time frame because that approach has proven effective in helping people adjust to chronic conditions. There are several reasons that a brief, focused intervention is appropriate for this patient population. First, no time is needed to surface issues, because the therapeutic focus is on adjustment to the illness rather than unknown psychopathologies or deep-seated complexes. Second, the medical condition is imposing enormous demands on the patient's time and money, so that an unstructured, long-term treatment approach could make counseling prohibitive. Third, structured and focused sessions with a clear end point are an oasis of manageability for people who foresee no end to their destabilizing illness. Patients know they always have the option of revisiting the counselor, as needed, for further counseling.

Today, economic and other pressures are stimulating the establishment of many short-term (6–10 weeks) mental health treatment programs. Interestingly, however, few short-term psychotherapy models are directed at chronic illness. And conversely, until very recently few of the models developed for treating chronic illness have been structured within a short time frame. Yet, my experience over more than two decades has convinced me that brief structured therapy is an excellent modality in which to help patients integrate their medical conditions. Like the general population, most patients have healthy personalities and strong defense systems that simply need to be adapted to the challenges of their illness. My clinical experience has also shown that for most patients, 10 sessions provide ample time in which to learn the principles of an adjustment process they can then use on their own.

In an excellent book on brief therapy,[12] Simon Budman and Alan Gurman note the proliferation of brief treatment models, stimulated primarily by the dominance of managed care in today's healthcare marketplace. They point out that economic conditions are causing most psychotherapy to be brief, but often only by default. In contrast, they offer a model of "planned brief therapy" that has as its central elements an emphasis on the patient's strengths, the establishment of a clear therapeutic focus, constructive use of the periods between treatment sessions, and a high level

Table 2.1
COMPARATIVE DOMINANT VALUES OF THE LONG-TERM
AND THE SHORT-TERM THERAPIST

Long-term Therapist	Short-term Therapist
1. Seeks change in basic character	Prefers pragmatism, parsimony, and least radical intervention; does not believe in the notion of "cure"
2. Believes that significant psychological change is unlikely in everyday life	Maintains an adult developmental perspective from which significant psychological change is viewed as inevitable
3. Sees presenting problems as reflecting more basic pathology	Emphasizes patient's strengths and resources; presenting problems are taken seriously (although not necessarily at face value)
4. Wants to "be there" as patient makes significant changes	Accepts that many changes will occur "after therapy" and will not be observable to the therapist
5. Sees therapy as having a "timeless" quality and is patient and willing to wait for change	Does not accept the timelessness of some models of therapy
6. Unconsciously recognizes the fiscal convenience of maintaining long-term patients	Fiscal issues often muted, either by the nature of the therapist's practice or by the organizational structure for reimbursement
7. Views psychotherapy as almost always benign and useful	Views psychotherapy as being sometimes useful and sometimes harmful
8. Sees patient's being in therapy as the most important part of patient's life	Sees patient's being in the world as more important than being in therapy

From *Theory and Practice of Brief Therapy* (p. 11), by S. H. Budman and A. S. Gurman, 1988, New York: Guilford. Reprinted with permission.

of counselor activity. As in MCC, the authors stress the appropriateness of subsequent return visits by patients, if needed, in what they call a "primary care/family medicine" model.

Table 2.1 lists the contrasting characteristics of long-term and short-term therapy, according to Budman and Gurman. While some long-term therapists may take issue with certain characterizations in the left-hand column, the other column provides a useful outline of key aspects of short-term therapy. The table is reproduced here because each of the short-term elements listed is present in the MCC model—not in response to market forces, as these authors imply, but because the approach is highly effective with chronically ill individuals and their family members. It is worth noting that MCC even has a "leg up" on other short-term therapy situations in that it always begins with a preestablished therapeutic focus: the illness and its consequences.

Today, as Budman and Gurman have recognized, the healthcare field is moving rapidly toward brief, structured, and focused therapy. A variety of factors, including research showing the efficacy of psychosocial interventions, has made the healthcare environment more hospitable to short-term programs.

NOTES

1. In this book, the term "patient" refers to the MCC patient or client. This individual may also be the medical patient or may be an informal caregiver, probably a family member. When necessary to avoid ambiguity, the person with the medical condition is referred to as "the medical patient." (Some readers may favor the term "client," but I prefer to use the term that is most commonly used among health care professionals.)

2. See Caplan, G. (1964). *Principles of preventive psychiatry*. New York: Basic.

3. Travis, G. (1976). *Chronic illness in children: Its impact on child and family* (p. 2), Stanford, CA: Stanford University Press. Although written more than 20 years ago, this book has not been surpassed in scope and depth on the subject.

4. Travis, 57–64.

5. Travis, 2.

6. Leff, P. T., & Walizer, E. H. (1992). *Building the healing partnership: Parents, professionals, and children with chronic illnesses and disabilities*. Cambridge, MA: Brookline.

7. Erikson, E. (1968). *Identity: Youth and crisis*. New York: Norton.

8. John Rolland describes the family's experience of clashing developmental tasks in "Anticipatory loss: A family systems developmental framework, in *Family Process*, September 1990.

See also Pollin, I. (1976, February). The dying adolescent. *Clinical Proceedings Children's Hospital National Medical Center*, 32(2).

9. For example:

• Parad, H. (1965). *Crisis intervention: Selected readings*. New York: Family Service Association of America. (In this collection see especially Rapoport, L. The state of crisis: some theoretical considerations, pp. 22–31.)

- Rapoport, L. (1970). Crisis intervention as a mode of treatment. In Roberts, R. W., & Nee, R. H. (1970). *Theories of social casework.* Chicago: University of Chicago Press.
- Lindemann, E. (1956). The meaning of crisis in individual and family living. *Teachers' College Record, 57,* 310–315.
- Lindsay, R. (1975). *Crisis theory: A critical overview.* Nedlands: University of Western Australia.

10. Dr. Kübler-Ross has written seven books on the subject, including *On death and dying* (1969) and *Living with death and dying* (1981). New York: Macmillan. Other writings on bereavement are listed at the end of Chapter 4.

11. Siegel, B. (1990). *Love, medicine and miracles: Lessons learned about self-healing from a surgeon's experience with exceptional patients.* New York: Perennial.

12. Budman, S., & Gurman, A. (1988). *Theory and practice of brief therapy.* New York: Guilford.

CHAPTER THREE

Getting Started

Ideally, medical crisis counseling would be offered as a routine and early part of treatment for chronic illness. Soon after diagnosis, every person with a serious long-term condition would have at least one session with an MCC-trained counselor. Clinical experience has shown that even a single well-formulated consultation is valuable; it gives the patient an opportunity to articulate concerns, review resources, and confirm coping abilities. MCC becomes one of those resources. The consultation also allows the medical crisis counselor to assess the individual's need for and receptivity to further counseling.

Since it is hardly possible to offer MCC to everyone with a chronic condition, the referring health professional (e.g., physician, medical social worker, or nurse) is in the position of determining whom they will refer. Important factors to consider in identifying patients include their current emotional state, living situation, social supports, access to and ability to use community resources, as well as the status of their illness. Prime candidates generally have limited social supports (note that some people who live alone actually have good supports); their affect is either suppressed or agitated; the medical condition either is already in a serious state or has a serious prognosis; their culture or language is different from that of medical caregivers; and they have limited ability to use community resources. Changes in financial resources are almost always a complicating factor, although by themselves they are seldom decisive.

Another deciding factor for the referring professional is the patient's potential receptivity to treatment and ability to use MCC. It has been my experience that one or more of the following characteristics predict counseling success: The person has already had successful psychotherapy; he or she initiates the consultation or is openly appreciative that the doctor saw a potential problem and cared enough to make a referral; and/or the

38

patient gives evidence of having a strong ego. Risk factors and predictors of counseling success are summarized in Table 3.1.

As one is considering the possibility of referral, it is important to remember that MCC has the focused objective of enhancing the patient's adjustment to the medical condition. It does not aim to modify personalities or repair basic family dysfunctions. People with underlying psychiatric conditions can usually benefit from this counseling, as long as expectations for their progress are based on the highly focused goals of MCC treatment. The decision as to whether to work with individuals with coexisting psychiatric conditions rests with the medical crisis counselor. Some patients should be referred for psychiatric treatment, either after completion of MCC or in lieu of it.

Table 3.1
RISK FACTORS AND PREDICTORS OF SUCCESS FOR MCC

The referring professional can acquire the following information through observation, the patient record, interview, informal discussion, and/or patient self-assessment.

The following characteristics indicate special need/high risk:
- Serious long-term medical condition (either life-threatening or disabling, at present or projected)
- Suppressed or agitated affect
- Suicidal ideation
- Inadequate cognitive assimilation of the illness (failure to seek information or make necessary decisions)
- Inappropriate behavior in respect to health care needs
- Inadequate communication with medical caregivers (due to language, culture, educational level, or attitude)
- Limited social supports (family or other)
- Difficult living arrangements (physical setup and/or location)
- Limited financial and other practical resources
- Limited knowledge of/ability to use community resources

The following characteristics suggest the ability to benefit from MCC:
- Presence of a medical crisis
- Capacity for normal cognitive functioning
- Previous positive experience with psychotherapy and/or receptive attitude toward counseling
- Evidence of ego strength

THE REFERRAL

As has been noted, most patients do not seek MCC on their own, but are referred by their physicians. The nature of that referral process depends largely on the relationship of the MCC program or counselor to the health care setting. Early consultation and intervention are most easily accomplished when the MCC clinic is an integral part of, or a close adjunct to, the medical treatment setting. I discuss this arrangement and other possible relationships between MCC clinics and medical treatment settings in Chapters 8 and 9.

Usually, physicians are motivated by two things when they refer their patients to MCC: the desire to prevent or minimize emotional crises stemming from chronic illness and the hope of increasing the efficacy of medical treatment. Whether the patient is referred at the time of diagnosis, release from hospitalization, or symptom exacerbation, the ideal is for the counselor to see the patient soon after the medical crisis occurs. The optimal time for counseling is the earliest, diagnosis; this is the stage at which patients are generally most vulnerable and most receptive. Counseling at this early stage can cultivate the understanding that emotional and psychosocial issues are a natural dimension of coping with serious illness. Once internalized, this understanding can help patients adjust to future exacerbations.

The medical crisis counselor is often in a position to advise medical colleagues (if they are receptive) about the most effective way to talk with patients about MCC treatment. The referring professional should stress that emotional and interpersonal issues are a normal byproduct of chronic illness. He or she can express confidence in the counseling as a helpful resource for the adjustment process, facilitated by a specialized mental health professional who understands what the patient is experiencing.

Even if the physician has done all of the above, a referral to counseling may still create confusion or resistance in patients who do not fully understand the reasons for it. This may be due to their having been too anxious to hear everything the physician said on the subject, or perhaps to feeling that their defenses are threatened. In spite of this hesitancy, however, patients often do as their physicians suggest out of trust in their professional judgment. As a result, the counselor must be prepared for patients who have mixed feelings about counseling. Chapter 2 suggests some approaches to hesitancy in patients.

Some individuals will seek MCC without a professional referral, having learned of it through a self-help group, the media, or a friend or family member. Such patients can be assumed to be more receptive to therapy.

THE CONSULTATION

The initial session between the medical crisis counselor and the patient is a crucially important hour. The clinician gathers essential information about the patient's medical history and psychosocial status, and establishes the tone and focus of treatment. The counselor has several interrelated goals for this meeting:

- To set the therapeutic focus on the psychological, social and practical ramifications of the medical condition;
- To gather brief essential information on the patient, including medical history, chief concerns, basic personality structure, adaptive capability, family characteristics, and experience with psychotherapy;
- To reduce the patient's anxiety and promote an understanding of the normalcy of emotional reactions to medical crises;
- To describe MCC as the patient would experience it;
- To have the patient decide whether to enter MCC treatment; and if so,
- To jointly set a treatment goal and treatment contract.

These goals are approached through three clusters of discussion topics, beginning with the patient's medical and personal history and the particular concerns and expectations he or she brings into treatment. For clarity, they are presented below as three discrete segments; in practice, however, the interview is likely to go back and forth between the first two topics (obtaining the patient history and explaining MCC) until the essential information has been gathered and the counselor and patient are ready to focus on the treatment plan.

Although this chapter focuses on the information-gathering and decision-making that take place during the consultation, it should not obscure the fact that the consultation elicits the release of powerful emotions. Whether they have known about their illness for a week or ten years, patients come into MCC with strong emotions of grief, fear, anger. The simple act of telling their story begins to release these feelings. The process of sharing information thus has a therapeutic function for the patient, helping to separate and illuminate tangled emotions and fears and to make them seem less overwhelming.

Obtaining Patient History, Profile, and Assessment

For both medical patients and family members, the counselor establishes a basic profile and assessment that focuses on the medical problem and its psychosocial consequences, as well as on areas of particular difficulty. A critical question is, why is the patient seeking or being referred for MCC at this time?

The pivotal event in the patient profile is the medical diagnosis. The counselor gathers information in order to establish what the person was like prior to the onset of the illness; what changes the illness has brought about; and his or her current status. This eliciting of the all-important "illness narrative"[1] helps focus the patient's attention on the illness as a distinct and powerful influence in his or her life. This is one of the key premises of MCC treatment.

Table 3.2 lists the information to be gathered in the initial interview and subsequent sessions. Because of the number of topics that must be covered in the consult, the clinician must decide what information must be obtained and what can be deferred to subsequent sessions.

Explaining Medical Crisis Counseling

The second cluster of discussion topics concerns the expected course of treatment. After taking the history and hearing the patient's special concerns, the counselor briefly describes how they will be approached in MCC treatment. This description sets the tone for treatment by reflecting an upbeat, calm, and objective approach. The goal is to make the patient's concerns seem less overwhelming and more amenable to problem-solving.

Briefly, the counselor explains that people with chronic conditions encounter certain expectable and normal feelings. The purpose is to assure the patient that what he or she is feeling is felt by others as well. The counselor then describes some of the clinical techniques that may be used, such as role playing and visualization. The description of treatment is meant to demystify the process for patients who may fear it. Knowing what to expect and feeling more in control helps them put their trust in the therapeutic relationship.

In this first session, it is also important for the counselor to begin cultivating awareness of the relationship between psychological stress, physical symptoms, and health. This awareness of mind-body interactions will be developed as treatment progresses.

The counselor also can ask the patient to recall ways in which he or she has coped with crises (both medical and nonmedical) in the past. Patterns of behavior will probably emerge which suggest whether the patient is a "confronter" or an "avoider." For example, the counselor might ask whether the person feels better after coming face to face with problems as soon as possible, or prefers to let things happen without speaking directly

Table 3.2
SUGGESTED PATIENT PROFILE

It is useful, if possible, to record the patient's responses in his or her own words; let the patient know you will be taking notes. These initial comments can serve as valuable references in later sessions.

Basic Data
- What is the patient's name, age, birth date, gender, religion, race/ethnic group?
- What are the names, ages, and health status of parents, siblings, and children?
- What are pertinent addresses and telephone numbers?
- What is the patient's appearance, reactions, mannerisms, emotional tone?

Source of Referral and Attitude to Counseling
- Who suggested that the patient come for counseling, and why? *(If the patient is self-referred, determine how he or she learned of MCC.)*
- How does the patient feel about coming for counseling?
- What does the patient expect of counseling?
- What are the patient's previous experiences with counseling?

Presenting Problem
(Allow the patient to tell his or her story with minimum interruptions, but encourage him or her to stay "on target.")
- What does the patient consider to be the main problem?
- Why is the patient seeking counseling at this time?
- How does the patient describe his or her experience with the medical problem, beginning with the earliest symptoms, the reaction to them, the diagnosis, the current status, and the prognosis? *(Get dates. Chronology is important here because dates of medical crises can be matched to other events at the same time in the patient's life.)*

Brief Personal and Family History
- How does the patient describe his or her marriage, children, and other close personal relationships, including close friends?
- What changes, if any, have occurred in these relationships since the time of diagnosis? *(Patients are unlikely at this point to see such changes as the result of the illness.)*
- How much support (emotional, practical, financial) does the patient feel he or she is getting?

Personal Strengths and Weaknesses
- How does the patient feel he or she handles crises, in general? What has helped in difficult times in the past? What were those difficulties? How do they relate to this one?
- How does the patient feel he or she is handling this crisis?
- In what area(s) of life does the patient feel especially vulnerable? How does the illness affect that? *(At this point, begin helping the patient understand that the illness can be the cause of many problems.)*

about them; if the patient wonders whether one mode is better than the other, the counselor can reply that both approaches are viable.

Creating A Framework for Treatment

Finally, the patient decides whether to enter MCC. If the decision is positive, the patient and counselor conclude the consultation by establishing a treatment plan and contract. (The decision not to enter treatment is discussed below.) The counseling contract is verbal and flexible, and framed in terms of the patient's expectations for treatment. It provides the informal framework for counseling, consolidating information about baselines and goals that will be used to evaluate progress as treatment proceeds. Changes are made to the treatment plan as the patient's needs change (for example, if the counselor determines that the patient and spouse should be seen together).

Goal-setting is a central event in the consultation, as has already been noted (see Chapter 2). It is important to help the patient identify treatment goals that are not only realistic but also attainable. These goals are based on what patients see as their central problem. They should be concrete, such as "getting back to work" or "improving my relationship with my daughter," rather than amorphous, such as "achieving peace of mind." The patient's emotional concerns, which are likely to be highly diffuse, can be translated into viable goals in such areas as work, social life, marriage, sex life, children, education, housing, and finances. Reference to practical, attainable, and specific goals is a positive theme throughout treatment, and the backdrop for a sense of accomplishment when the patient achieves them.

The final topic of the consultation is the relationship between the counselor and the patient's physician(s). When patients have been medically referred, the counselor affirms the referring physician's good judgment in suggesting counseling. It is explained that the physician can be kept informed about the patient's progress in counseling, if the patient so desires. If ongoing communication is acceptable to the patient and the physician, the counselor is also in a position to alert the doctor to areas of particular concern. The counselor can ask those who were not referred by a physician if they wish their physician to be contacted and sent case reports.

Such communication is standard procedure for referred patients, and should be recommended for all patients. It can enhance both medical and psychosocial treatment, and give the patient a strong sense of support. Counselors should not report on counseling sessions, however, if their patients are opposed to it. Of course, some physicians are not interested in communicating with medical crisis counselors about shared patients. Counseling certainly can still be effective without this periodic contact between counselors and referring physicians.

The consult ends with the standard discussions of future treatment appointments, fees, and insurance responsibility.

Depression brought Marta Simpson into MCC two years after she was diagnosed with cancer. A handsome woman of 55, she had left her long-time teaching job and hometown after her husband's death from chronic renal failure. Soon thereafter, she was diagnosed with lung cancer, and within months of treatment for that condition learned that she needed a second course of chemotherapy for a pelvic tumor. She had recently purchased a condominium near her eldest daughter, Barbara, and was receiving treatment at a nearby clinic. Marta's emotional needs had become too great a burden for Barbara, who was coping with the serious illness of one of her children. She sought counseling at Barbara's suggestion.

It was clear from her brief description of her life prior to getting cancer that Mrs. Simpson was a capable woman, accustomed to making her own decisions and happiest when doing so. She had cared for her husband and handled his renal dialysis at home for seven years while holding down a full time job. Now, having placed herself in a position of dependence on her daughter, she needed to recover her sense of competence.

As she told her story, Marta repeatedly apologized for rambling and being "disconnected." Recognizing her longing to feel organized again, I assured her that I would keep her on target. Because she displayed such discomfort with feeling out of control, I decided to use the consultation itself to focus attention on her attitude toward the decisions affecting her. Marta resentfully believed that her daughter had "made" her come to the MCC session. We examined this assumption, and I helped her understand that the decision had actually been her own, and not Barbara's. This shift of responsibility astonished her; the interpretation had never occurred to her. But the recognition that she had indeed made the decision to come helped Marta begin to regain a sense of control. If she was responsible for coming to this session, she could also identify and change other distressing things about her life. She agreed to commit to brief MCC treatment.

We were then ready to set treatment goals. Marta began by reviewing the general problems she was now facing: her poor health, her age, the changes in her life, her depression. With prompting, she began to shift her focus to her primary and most immediate concern: her feeling that she was not getting enough attention from Barbara. Marta had not taken responsibility for her decision to move because she was feeling vulnerable and wanted to have someone else make the decision. Now she was project- ing anger about her illness and the move onto her well-meaning daughter. The parallel with the decision to come for the MCC consult was clear to both of us. She then resolved that her goal in treatment would be deciding whether to stay near Barbara or move near her younger daughter.

Marta left the consultation with a renewed sense of her capacity to take charge of her life. This confidence and sense of responsibility laid the groundwork for the crucial decisions she would make later in treatment.

ONE-TIME-ONLY PATIENTS

It is rather common for patients and counselors to decide at the end of the consultation that treatment will not go forward. They discover that they are coping and they have a resource in the future. In this case, the counse- lor can point out that if needed, he or she is always available.

This single consultation session actually serves a number of therapeutic purposes for the patient. Reviewing the precipitating events increases the person's understanding of the crisis and gives a measure of objectivity about it. Recognizing the normalcy of stresses and reactions can reduce anxiety and guilt. Simply being able to express fears and emotions in a safe place to someone who understands can lower the stress level. By identifying defenses and coping patterns with the counselor, the patient begins to recognize strengths as well as weaknesses. Even a brief inventory of social, financial, and community resources—including the option of later MCC treatment—can help the patient feel less isolated and more supported. Even in one hour, many patients reach a sense of their ability to cope with their situation. They also have found another resource.

NOTE

1. Kleinman, A. (1988). *The illness narrative: Suffering, healing, and the human condition.* New York: Basic.

CHAPTER FOUR

The Eight Issues of Chronic Illness

The eight issues that are the subject of this chapter form the framework for medical crisis counseling because they arise naturally out of the daily experience of chronically ill patients. The counselor uses them as a template, watching for signs of each issue and for subject matter on which to draw the patient out about it. As a result, they are addressed in concrete and experiential terms. These issues should be confronted with care. MCC patients need their defenses to meet both the physical and psychological challenges in front of them, and the counselor should respect this healthy need. As each issue is addressed, the fear of confronting it is diminished. It may not be completely resolved, but counseling introduces the idea that the fears and issues are normal, and that the person can confront them without falling apart. If the issues return after counseling is completed, as is likely, they will be less overwhelming.

How does the counselor recognize these issues? A variety of nonliteral cues may surface to suggest the presence of an issue. For example, if the patient says, "I'm afraid I'm getting on my wife's nerves. How long is she going to put up with me?" his fear of abandonment is surfacing. If this is an appropriate time to pursue this issue, the counselor can respond with a question such as, "What is your worst fear about getting on her nerves?" Before asking this question, however, the counselor should assure and reassure the patient that talking about a feared eventuality will not bring it about. Indeed, confronting the fear can reduce its intensity. The counselor's office is the safest place for the patient to explore frightening feelings, once it is clear that he or she is ready emotionally to do so.

Some issues raised by patients are better left for a later session to maintain the immediate treatment focus. In such instances, the counselor can acknowledge the patient's concern and state that there will be a chance to pursue it soon. A notation can be made in the patient's record of the context in which the issue arose.

The guiding principle here is that all of the eight issues are implicitly present at all times, and will appear and reappear. To handle them effectively, the counselor must address them in depth, one at a time. Because treatment is brief and focused, little time will elapse before the patient has a chance to deal with each major concern. If a particular issue does not surface again in a subsequent session, the counselor can raise it at a more appropriate time.

The best example of this principle is the issue of death. Fears about death usually surface early in treatment; but patients will be far better able to explore and resolve their concerns about it later when they are more bonded with the counselor and have become accustomed to exploring other fears. Even terminally ill patients benefit from addressing other issues first.

With some individuals, one issue remains dominant throughout treatment. In such cases, that issue often becomes the central focus of the patient's treatment goal. Several of the cases described in this chapter illustrate the use of treatment goals to deal with a dominant issue—for example, lupus patient Bob Smithson's struggle to recover a sense of control over his life while making life-saving changes in the way he lived. Even when one issue dominates the work, however, it is essential that all other issues be addressed in the course of treatment.

Just as one or more of the eight issues may dominate, some issues may be of relatively minor importance to patients. Variations in personality, environment, home situation, and the illness itself all have an effect on their intensity. As has been suggested, the function of the template of issues is to help the counselor make sure that nothing serious is overlooked. If upon examination an issue proves to be unimportant, the counselor and patient can move on.

Variations such as these do not alter the fact that all eight issues are almost always present in some form for patients. They may simply be manifested differently in different individuals. For example, for some patients, the issue of abandonment may be so charged that it defies direct confrontation and may require a more subtle approach. It may need to be revisited several times, in different ways, until it can be dealt with directly. Another variable is that the timing of counseling may make a particular issue moot. Consider, for example, a patient entering MCC years after diagnosis, completely physically dependent on the care of his or her family. In such a case, the fear of being abandoned may no longer be active.

It would of course be impossible to outline all of the treatment scenarios that an MCC counselor might encounter. I have provided several variations to make the point that the medical crisis counseling model must be applied with flexibility and good judgment, guided by careful attention to the specific needs expressed by each patient.

Control

I'm tired of this. I want my life back.

Lupus is controlling my life.

OBJECTIVE: TO REESTABLISH CONTROL

The fear of losing control of one's life is probably the most powerful issue for people with a chronic illness. This is usually what brings patients into treatment; and even when mastered, it remains a challenge throughout the course of their lives. People with long-term medical conditions have the same goals as everyone else: to live fully and to function optimally. They must attempt to do so while adjusting to the fears, emotions, and physical limitations imposed by their medical condition. This is an enormous challenge, demanding both physical and mental energy. The ongoing power struggle between the illness and the patient must be framed in such a way that the patient can achieve mastery.

Control issues surface almost immediately upon diagnosis. Walking out of the physician's office, the patient's head swirls with questions, one overtaking the other. The feeling is one of being adrift in a sea of uncertainty, with all anchors gone and previous points of reference rendered meaningless. Maintaining control of emotions and thoughts about the future is a struggle.

Mary felt that the world had collapsed around her. "I heard the doctor say that it definitely was cancer. Then he went on to say something about causes and treatments and outside chances. He was using medical terms. But by then I had stopped listening. When he said the word 'cancer,' I knew my life had changed forever."

Sitting by her side, her husband had a comparable experience. "I was paralyzed. I kept sitting there looking at the physician, afraid to glance at Mary because I might begin to cry. Then I found myself thinking that the doctors were wrong, that the test results belonged to someone else, that a nurse would come into the room and say there had been a mistake. I don't remember what the doctor said. Then suddenly I found myself in a state of panic. Questions I couldn't answer rushed to the forefront of my thinking. 'If anything happened to Mary, how would I manage? Oh, my God, why am I thinking these terrible things?' I finally just shut down."

Diagnosis always comes as a shock, even when patients and families have anticipated it. The diagnosis arouses feelings of disbelief, disorientation, denial, hope for a miracle. Along with these emotions can come the terrifying recognition that one's sense of self and well-being have been shattered. Emotional paralysis may follow. In response to this emotional crisis, the person's attention narrows dramatically. It seems impossible to think of anything but the medical condition. The overwhelming feeling is of having lost control of one's life.

Forty-year-old Annette recounted the days following her diagnosis with lupus. While there were few debilitating symptoms at this point, her physician had explained that the disease would eventually incapacitate her. "A million things washed across my mind. I wanted to cry, to scream. I wanted my husband to hold me. I felt sick. I denied that this was happening to me. I became angry. Yet all I could do was sit and stare silently out of the window. My husband, who was sitting next to me, tried to talk; but all I could do was stare. I wept a little but I just couldn't tell him what I was thinking. There were just too many feelings, and they overwhelmed me. I couldn't do or say anything."

Another patient, Angela, described her feelings when she received her diagnosis of multiple sclerosis (MS): "My physician was wonderful. He explained the problem, and what I should expect as I grew older. He told me how the disease might progress. He explained how remissions and exacerbation would come unexpectedly, and would last for unpredictable amounts of time. I tried to imagine what it would be like to feel good for long periods of time, years maybe, and suddenly wake up one morning and feel worse than ever. And there wouldn't be anything I could do to control it! It would just happen to me. I felt that my life was being shaped by something—or someone—else. I have never felt more like a helpless victim than I did that afternoon."

Often, at the point of diagnosis, life actually has not changed to a great extent. Symptoms are just emerging. And even if the symptoms or disability have already been experienced, the patient has not yet felt the full impact of living with the condition. People in this position do not fully comprehend what their futures will be, but many assume that the condition will progress in the worst way imaginable, and frame their thinking and actions accordingly. At that point, a therapeutic intervention can be strategically important in bringing the patient back to the present reality. A constructive adaptation process can begin when "worst fears" have been identified and stress is reduced.

As time goes on, many problems of daily living are added to the chronically ill person's initial swirl of concerns: daily encounters with pain, physical limitations, medical regimens, and, most difficult of all, uncertainty about outcomes. The person must live with the knowledge that the disease or injury may never be cured, and that little can be done to change the situation. During times of exacerbation, the battle for control becomes particularly strong and discouraging.

Desperate to maintain control over their destinies, some people make life decisions prematurely. One young woman gave up her job and moved to a country town to live with her grandmother as soon as she learned she had MS, a disease that can take decades to seriously interfere with daily living. Paul Tsongas gave up a senatorial career when he learned he had cancer. Did he dream at that time that years later he would run for president?

Some people faced with a long-term illness seek any form of control available, including ineffectual or even potentially harmful forms of alternative "treatment." One MS patient knew very well that changing her diet would not cure her condition. She did it anyway, however, saying that it gave her something to do, "to keep myself going."

Some patients unintentionally cede control to others and then feel resentment at being controlled. As we saw in the previous chapter, Marta Simpson's anger at her daughter was due to her perception that Barbara was making decisions for her. Counseling helped Marta see that she had given over this control.

ROLE AND STANCE OF THE COUNSELOR

The counselor's goal in respect to control issues is to reinforce the patient's confidence in his or her own ability to cope with the demands of the medical condition. To this end, one of the counselor's first tasks is to help the patient give expression to his or her feelings of loss of control and identify specific areas where he or she feels powerless. Normalizing the patient's fears and emotions, which may seem overwhelming to him or her, begins the process of establishing a sense of control.

A candid review of the patient's situation helps him or her clarify and objectify problems. One important aspect of this process is distinguishing actual, current problems from possible future ones, as well as from fearsome specters that may never come to pass. After realistically reviewing the situation, the counselor can help the patient identify areas in which control is possible. Some areas may have been overlooked as a result of extreme stress. The counselor helps shift the patient's focus from overwhelming challenges to specific, achievable tasks.

This process is illustrated in the story of Terry Fernandez, an unmarried law student in her late twenties who was referred by her neurologist for MCC a month after being diagnosed with MS. Terry's immediate concern was whether she had enough stamina and concentration to pass her bar exam the following week. Passing the exam would be the culmination of four years of hard work; failing would mean the first serious loss as a result of her illness. She feared she was not physically up to the two long days of examinations.

I had to work quickly to help Terry overcome her feelings of helplessness, get a grasp on this event, and get through it. We moved promptly into the details of her impending challenge. I asked her to describe the conditions of the exam: Where would it be held? What was the room like? How many people were taking it with her? Would there be breaks? How long? Where could she go for the break? Could she bring food or drink into the room? Did she have to stay all day? Each of these questions suggested ways for Terry to control her situation. I also briefly gave her some tips on how to relax during the exam, using deep breathing and taking short walks away from her desk.

Terry successfully took the bar exam the following week. This was the first time since her diagnosis that she had experienced some control over her life.

Medical crisis counselors have a variety of ways to help patients reassert control. Reviewing the illness and its manifestations helps pinpoint specific areas that need to be mastered. Forecasting problems that lie ahead can help patients plan for inescapable realities. Simple actions such as rearranging the home environment can be concrete ways to ease functioning and exercise control. (For instance, Terry related how she repeatedly fell over a chair near her front door. It was a constant, chilling reminder of her disability, but one she had been unable to remedy. I asked if she could move the chair a foot out of the way—a suggestion she responded to as though it were a gift of gold.)

In addition to practical problem solving, the patient needs to reassess his or her attitude toward the medical condition in order to regain control. Verbalizing fears and feelings around the illness helps reduce their intensity and bring them under control. It also helps the patient understand that emotional reactions are temporary, and subject to conscious adjustment. Even when they cannot control their bodies, people can change their attitudes and assumptions.

Patients can be expected to fit across a continuum in terms of their notions of control. At one extreme of the continuum are those who derive their self-definition from others, believe in an ultimate rescuer, and tend to be compliant and to fuse with the counselor. This group may have difficulty assuming responsibility for coping with a problem they see as beyond their control, and for which they hope to receive an externally driven solution.

The other extreme of this continuum is occupied by those who derive meaning and self-definition entirely from their own interpretations and feelings, and who tend to be obsessively self-reliant. This group may attempt to control the counselor-patient relationship, possibly denying the realities of the medical condition. Such patients can have difficulty accepting the counselor's suggestions. These two extreme attitudes clearly call for different strategies for dealing with control issues.

For some people, paradoxically, conscious relinquishment can create the conditions for a greater sense of control. The individual faces up to what is being lost and makes conscious decisions to give up longings that cannot be fulfilled. He or she lets go of old habits that can no longer be sustained.

Bob and Sally Smithson were in their early thirties when they entered MCC treatment. Bob was very ill with systemic lupus erythematosus, a sometimes fatal autoimmune disease. Having managed the illness for ten years, he was now experiencing serious exacerbations, and had been told he had just six months to live. Sally, a psychiatric nurse, recognized the need for professional help and asked his physician for a referral. She called to appeal for an MCC appointment on the day before Bob was scheduled for decisive tests for a reassessment of his condition. Could they come on the way to hospital? I hurriedly rearranged my schedule in order to meet their needs, and the next day we met for a consultation. We discussed the frightening prospects they were facing, and agreed to meet again the following week.

When she called a few days after the consultation to confirm our first counseling appointment, Sally told me that Bob's prognosis had proved to be less serious than they had feared. Nevertheless, he was still quite ill and had been told he would have to completely alter his lifestyle to survive.

In our first session, Bob expressed his fears about the anticipated changes in his life, his work, his income. He lamented having to give up his work as an engineer, a source of pleasure and prestige, and he expressed discomfort with having to depend on his wife. He described his feelings laconically: "Lupus is controlling my life."

From now on, Bob's life would have to be entirely different. Control issues became the essence of Bob's treatment goal. He had to wrest control from his disease and take charge of his life again.

Treatment began with methodically pinpointing the areas where the illness was forcing changes—his diet, minimizing the amount of stress in his life, getting enough rest, shifting work and income-earning roles with Sally—and exploring what these life-style alterations meant to him.

As we addressed each challenge, Bob found ways in which he could reassert control. For example, although he grieved giving up his career, Sally was eager to begin working in the field in which she had been trained, and he was happy to cook and care for their son. They would have much preferred to make these changes for other reasons, but shifting roles in itself did not prove too difficult for them. He quickly found another way to be useful and creative.

Bob still had to grapple with the possibility of an early death. As he did so, his major concern was leaving Sally alone without family support. (She had been estranged from her family since marrying Bob, a member of a different ethnic group.) He attached great importance to identifying potential sources of support for Sally in the event of his death. The two of them spent considerable time in an early counseling session pursuing this question. The couple was close to his parents, who were divorced, and they were the first to be considered. As we explored the parents' ability to provide support, however, it became apparent that his father was unavailable because of constant travel, and that his mother was too easily unnerved. Bob and Sally did not even feel comfortable having her baby-sit their four-year-old child.

After they reviewed and rejected each option within the family, the Smithsons' search led to an interesting solution. They realized that the people on whom they could depend most were their neighbors, who had been responsive in emergencies in the past. Once they realized this, Bob and Sally experienced a great sense of relief about the future.

This young couple made good progress in their accommodation to new roles until a new crisis brought them to an MCC session in great distress. Bob's doctor had strongly advised against their annual summer beach vacation. This was an event that they had eagerly anticipated for many months. Now, because Bob's medication made it dangerous for him to be in the sun, it seemed impossible for them to go. They were crushed. This was not just a vacation, but a cherished annual ritual shared with their closest friends—two refreshing weeks of good food, conversation and to-getherness. The holiday was particularly important to them now; with a tenuous future, they were wisely investing in the pleasurable events that were near at hand.

There was no doubt about the significance of this activity, nor about the threat that its possible loss posed to the couple's hard-earned equilib-rium. As they spoke, I searched my mind for a way they could continue the summertime tradition without endangering Bob's fragile health. It occurred to me to ask Bob if he could accept going to the beach but staying indoors during the day. I asked, "What is it about this vacation that is most important?"

At first he did not seem to understand my question. But after a long pause he responded, "What I care most about is being with my friends in the evenings, not being on the beach. During the day, I can rest and pursue my love of cooking by preparing dinner for the group." The couple left the session with renewed hope and plans to propose this idea to Bob's doctor.

They arrived at their next MCC session in high spirits: The doctor had agreed to let Bob go to the beach, with the stipulated precautions. This triumph convinced them that they could indeed manage his condition. The task also provided an opportunity to introduce Bob and Sally to a process that they, like all MCC patients, would have to undergo repeat-edly: identifying what was of greatest value in their lives, and finding ways to preserve it.

Several years later, I received a letter from the Smithsons. Inside was a photo of a wonderful beach house that they had designed and built. Clearly, lupus was not controlling their lives; they were.

As we have seen, the medical crisis counselor not only promotes a realistic review of the patient's situation and validates his or her fears and concerns, but also helps identify concrete issues that need addressing. These may include decisions to be made (such as whether to find a less stressful job); relationship issues to be confronted (such as a spouse's seeming insensitivity); and information to be acquired (such as treatment alternatives). On this basis, the patient is able to consider real options and make plans.

One important way for patients to assert control over their medical condition is to gain knowledge about it. Such knowledge enables them to be active members of their treatment teams, to participate fully in decisions, and to engage in as much self-care as possible. Medical crisis counselors can support this process by recommending educational material and encouraging patients to become informed about their conditions. They should also encourage patients to ask questions of their medical care providers, and not to be intimidated.

Chapter 10 discusses community resources that may be useful to patients, and the major national health organizations are listed in the back of the book. Many of these groups publish excellent booklets, brochures, and newsletters with information on the latest treatments as well as practical suggestions for self-care. In addition, a wide variety of books for lay persons about an array of health topics are available in libraries and book stores.

Self-image

I'll never be the same.

I'm damaged goods.

OBJECTIVE: TO GRIEVE LOSSES AND REDEFINE THE SELF

After control issues, self-image is usually the most pressing concern for people adjusting to chronic illness. The medical crisis counselor addresses this issue by first determining what the patient's sense of self was prior to the onset of the condition. This becomes the reference point for identifying losses and grieving them. The goal in respect to this issue is for a different self-image to emerge that integrates all of the new realities in the patient's life.

Self-image issues, which are in part a function of one's developmental stage, act as a backdrop against which the illness plays. The counselor must ask what the patient was like before he or she was diagnosed, and determine how the limitations imposed by the illness will affect this current stage of life. Physical conditions that occur either at birth or at an early age can gradually become integrated into the personality as the individual develops. Supportive family members can help soften the blows. People learn to compensate and adapt: One of my muscular dystrophy patients, at age 14, learned to "dance" and cheerlead. The blind writer Ved Mehta says he has "read" hundreds of articles and books. In contrast, when the diagnosis comes later in life, the blow to self-image can be more devastating and more difficult to integrate. The longer someone has lived with a particular identity—"strong," "quick," "healthy," "invulnerable"—the harder it is to give it up and replace it with something equally gratifying.

A person's self-image encompasses his or her beliefs and values, personal capacities, social roles, and body image. When any of these is challenged, he or she feels disoriented and devalued. Abruptly or slowly, medical conditions can strip away qualities that were central to an individual's self-definition: speaking, writing, athletic or artistic prowess, physical beauty, or quick wit, for example. In contemporary society, a high premium is placed on good health and physical appearance. If there is diminishment in these areas, it can be difficult to feel attractive, competent, valued, and loved. Even if the effects are invisible, the patient feels changed, even damaged. Soon after diagnosis, the individual must begin to cope with the fact that he or she will never be the same again, physically or psychologically. The loss of valued attributes raises the question of who he or she is now.

The family's perception of the medical patient, and of the family itself, is also affected. Family members cope with strong feelings of loss, and possibly even disorientation, when a relative is changed by illness. They must also cope with the patient's diminished self-confidence and vitality, and with fear-based projections about the loss of the family's love and regard. One young woman had great difficulty adjusting to her father after his stroke. He changed from the proud, independent, and powerful parental figure she had known and relied on to a fearful, dependent old man.

ROLE AND STANCE OF THE COUNSELOR

A change in self-image is not only inevitable, but also necessary for the chronically ill individual's adjustment. The ease of the transition to a self-image that integrates the illness depends greatly on his or her self-image prior to the illness. If the ego is strong, the patient is more open and flexible. Patients with more limited egos undergo the same adaptation process, but have fewer personal resources to draw upon.

Work on self-image begins with the counselor asking the patient what life was like before the illness. This leads to an exploration of the subjective meaning and importance of the losses experienced since then. This is a full-blown grieving process, in which the patient painfully reviews what has been lost and will never be regained. The process can be facilitated by confronting these losses either verbally or on paper. One method is for the patient to compose an inventory of valued qualities and abilities. These are divided into two categories: those that cannot be recovered, and those that remain. Attention can then be focused on strengthening the attributes that remain. The emotional dimension is critical to this process. As the patient reviews his or her losses, the counselor should encourage the expression of the very normal feelings of sadness, disorientation, and anger that are aroused. This process is extremely difficult for most patients, but necessary.

It is important to understand that the self-image that emerges out of this grieving process is not new, but rather a modified version of the original. The patient can capitalize on traits and capacities that remain, while consciously relinquishing those that have been lost. The desired result is an identity that encompasses the medical condition and draws on the untapped potential still available to the patient.

When I met 67-year-old Frieda, she had already undergone four surgical procedures for a benign meningioma of the spinal cord. Her physician had told her there was a good chance it would return within 10 years. She entered my office in a severely depressed state. Indeed, she came quite reluctantly, but nevertheless agreed to complete 10 sessions.

Physically, the Frieda I met was dramatically different from the person she had been prior to her meningioma. She described herself as she was then, just three years before, as a healthy, vibrant woman who "felt 45." Her husband added that she had been beautiful, with gorgeous legs which she always proudly showed off with high-heeled shoes. In contrast, when I first saw her, she was thin, gaunt, and leaned heavily on a cane. She wore low-heeled, lace-up shoes. Her short hair was wispy and grey. She had lost feeling on one side of her tongue, and one of her hands was quite weak.

Frieda's self-image had taken quite a jolt. Where would I begin with this lady who had lost so much of what she and her husband had valued? What did she have that she could use to carry on? I began treatment by asking her to identify the most important things she had lost, and to explain what they meant to her. I also had her consider which aspects of her self were completely gone and which were retrievable. This was an extremely painful process for her. During the three years after her diagnosis, she had not even begun to confront these issues. She and her husband still fantasized that one day she would become her "old self" again.

In fact, they not only fantasized, but Frieda and her husband were determined not to accept her current state. I pointed out to her that being a battler could work in her favor, provided she directed her energy toward what was realistic and what she could recover.

In searching for ways that she could feel useful and important again, Frieda recognized that she could be helpful to her husband as a driver. This was important for many reasons: It not only gave her a sense of independence and control, but also allowed her to be valuable to her husband, whose poor eyesight prevented him from driving. Frieda was delighted to realize that in spite of her impairments, she could still drive. Once she identified the importance of this role, she focused on recovering the ability to perform it.

In this way, Frieda's pre-illness identity and self-image were critical elements of her post-illness self-image, as they are for all patients. Although it seems a simple goal, recovering her capacity to drive strengthened Frieda's now fragile sense of worth. Her adjustment was aided by a vital support network that included her husband, son and daughter-in-law, sister, and many old friends. Together, her basic ego strength and social supports created the environment in which she was able to restore her positive self-image, despite her drastically changed physical condition.

A medical crisis counselor can facilitate the repair of self-image by exploring the patient's general feelings about impairments and disabilities before he or she became ill. How did the patient feel when he or she saw someone in a wheelchair? What did he or she think of someone whose hands shook? This information brings to light the attitudes that must be addressed in order to restore a positive self-image. People often carry negative images of others who have their condition, and then identify with those negative images. By projecting these attitudes onto others, it is more likely that they will respond as expected. It is therefore important to help patients articulate and understand previous assumptions about the way others regard them. Focusing on these projections often leads to the realization that assumptions about others' attitudes may be incorrect. (Sometimes, of course, others' attitudes are indeed the problem. The issue of stigma is discussed below.)

After grieving losses and examining assumptions, the counselor's final task in respect to self-image is to help the patient strengthen and integrate the newly reorganized sense of self. It is important for the patient to learn that he or she has not lost everything; not all of one's positive attributes are undermined by a medical condition. Those that remain can be reinforced.

In our initial consultation, MS patient Terry Fernandez uttered a statement that became the major theme for the rest of her treatment: "I'm damaged goods! I belong in a bargain basement!" Her self-image issues came through loud and clear. I knew that this statement reflected assumptions that would impede her adjustment to MS and that it called for major work. As soon as we had addressed her first priority—getting through her bar exam—we turned to the self-image issue.

None of Terry's relationships with men had ever succeeded. Now, with MS to limit her energy and attractiveness, she was convinced that no man would ever want to make a commitment to her. Marriage and children, a central part of her dream for the future, now seemed completely out of the question to her. She was devastated.

We began our work on this issue by exploring the ways in which she had related to men in the past. Terry had always felt that in order to attract a man she had to provide all the care, from cooking gourmet meals to arranging tickets for events. As we explored further, the source of her perception of herself as "damaged goods" came into focus. Terry had grown up in a stable and loving family, but had never felt as feminine as she perceived her mother to be. She felt she could never match her mother's ongoing sex appeal to her father. Since her parents were very close, Terry and her brother often felt "left out." Always anxious to please her parents, she had compensated by "being good," a role she had carried over into her adult relationships. This served her well in her other social relationships, but not in her relationships with men. Her mother's constant efforts to "teach" her how to relate to men as she did only succeeded in making Terry feel more inadequate.

Gaining perspective on these relationship problems was vital to Terry. In therapy she worked on changing her self-defeating behavior toward men. Many strengths worked in her favor: She was bright, charming, and successful in school and at work. She had many friends, was active in a number of community organizations, and was deeply religious. As her understanding of the roots of her low self-esteem grew, so did her estimation of her own value and her choices.

With this foundation, she was able to consider alternative behaviors.

An important one was withholding information about her MS, so that her male companions could get to know her as a person rather than as "an MS patient." This was difficult for her, given her instinctive openness and candor. In therapy, we discussed sexual dynamics and the differences between her intimate relationships with men and those with family and friends. After all, a man might be considering marriage, and MS would be a factor in his life as well as hers. This subject of MS thus needed to be dealt with sensitively.

Meanwhile, Terry was still having negative experiences with her dates. In one instance, soon after meeting a wheelchair-bound young man in an MS peer group she began pressuring him to marry her. Fortunately for both of them, he correctly perceived that one source of attraction was his inherited wealth and the secure future it represented. He sent her away. In another traumatic experience also borne of desperation, she became pregnant following first-date sex with another man. She made the decision to have an abortion, which was extremely upsetting to her: She was deeply religious, she wanted a child, and she feared that she might never marry and that the MS would decrease her capacity to have children.

This last trauma brought Terry back into episodic treatment after a hiatus. Recognizing the severity of the problem, I began systematically coaching her in her relationships. We explored the ways in which her recent behavior had been self-destructive. Happily, soon after we began this exercise she met in her church book club an attractive lawyer who shared not only her religion and sense of values, but her intense interest in politics. She was terrified that she would destroy this relationship, as she had the others. Our primary task was to determine how she could tell him about her MS without driving him away.

We planned a step-by-step strategy. I stressed that she must allow this man to get to know her as a person before telling him of her MS. I explained that while she knew enough about herself and the condition to put the information in perspective, he did not—knowing too much too soon could be confusing as well as shocking. I advised her to wait until he knew he loved her and then tell him in a way that would not frighten him.

While Terry waited for the right moment to share this difficult information, we carefully rehearsed her words. I stressed that when the time came, she should allow him to ask questions and then give him time to digest the information rather than pressing him for a reaction. Ultimately, she did as we had planned, and then anxiously endured the wait for his call. But call he did, and with a proposal of marriage. Before long, I was enlisted to help

Terry's fiance plan how to tell his parents about her MS, using the same approach of first giving them time to know and love her. A few years later, I received a birth announcement from the happy young couple.

Terry created a fulfilling life despite her MS because of her ego strengths—most of which she had not recognized prior to counseling. Ironically, her sense of personal value actually increased as a result of her MS. We had resolved a problem that had originated well before her MS but was brought to the fore by her condition. Her desire to improve her life impelled her to seek counseling, address her longstanding self-image issues, and find a basis for a modified self-image. Treatment reinforced her ego strengths.

Dependency

I've always been independent; I have a hard time asking for help.

Since he got sick, my husband just won't do anything for himself.

OBJECTIVE: TO COMBINE MAXIMUM SELF-RELIANCE WITH ACCEPTANCE OF A LEVEL OF PHYSICAL DEPENDENCE

Threats to independence can cause a depression deep enough to prompt thoughts of suicide. Dependency issues surface soon after diagnosis, when the individual realizes that he or she will be a patient forever. Even ambulatory patients must face the fact that their condition may require lifelong medical care and supervision. Whether daily life has already changed drastically or very little, persons with serious chronic conditions know that adjustments lie ahead to accommodate a changing physical reality; they cannot avoid dependence on the medical establishment and other caregivers.

Like many other issues, dependency concerns are usually a mixture of objective appraisals and fears. They vary considerably with different personality types. Patients who are too willing to become dependent present one kind of challenge for caregivers and the counselor. In them, self-reliance must be cultivated, obviously within the limits of their capacity. But for those who have always valued their independence, becoming dependent is a deeply fearsome prospect. The concern is twofold: The person fears not only the loss of personal independence, but also becoming dependent, a burden to the family. These individuals need assurance that fears about dependency are normal.

For patients who are or have been hospitalized, dependency issues are complicated by the fact that the dependent role actually serves a necessary function during hospitalization. At that time, medical treatment requires a dependent posture. Family caregivers may encourage this attitude, hoping to reduce the patient's stress and promote recovery. But after hospitalization, the patient's role is redefined and expectations change.

Professional caregivers now encourage the individual to take more responsibility for his or her own care, and family members may wish for a return to former roles and responsibilities. It is at this transitional point that those who are inclined to stay in a dependent, sick role need encouragement to become more self-reliant, and those who have difficulty asking for help must learn how to solicit support.

A critical aspect is the actual availability of help. The patient needs to identify people whom he or she can comfortably approach for help, including those who can be depended upon for assistance and care—a friend, spouse, child, parent. Knowing that there are people to count on is enormously important. In fact, research has shown that not having such support can actually contribute to illness.[1]

Dependency issues are affected by many variables. A key one, of course, is the type of disease or injury involved. This factor determines whether dependency needs emerge gradually, as through a progressive disease, or suddenly, perhaps as the result of a stroke or accident. Family members' capacities for caregiving also vary greatly, and the counselor must carefully assess this factor.

The gender of the patient is another important variable, given the strong (albeit increasingly flexible) sex roles dictated by social convention. Another factor is the individual's age and level of psychosocial development: A 16-year-old who is just achieving independence will respond to the loss of independence very differently than an active 40-year-old executive or a 70-year-old retiree. By the same token, the parents of a disabled 16-year-old will react differently than the spouse of the mid-life executive or the adult children of the retiree.

The counselor must remember that there are various kinds of dependence—emotional, physical, financial, and so on. Patients may be highly independent in one sphere and thus create the mistaken impression that they are the same in other spheres, when in fact they may need considerable help and support in some areas. For example, they may not wish help with physical tasks, but need a great deal of emotional support and companionship. Conversely, they may be emotionally quite independent but require considerable physical assistance.

Dependence and independence are important variables in close relationships such as marriages, and obviously these dynamics will affect the nature and approach to these issues in MCC. In some marriages, dependency is part of the unwritten contract between the partners. Each party expects certain behavior of the other, and both are comfortable in their respective roles. If the dependent spouse becomes ill, roles may not change significantly; but if the independent spouse becomes ill and dependent, the potential for problems is high.

Even if a relationship is flexible enough to sustain greater dependence by one partner, this change in roles will inevitably subject it to substantial stress. The nature of the dependency issues that arise will be a function of the importance that each person attaches to independence, as well as the nature of the relationship prior to the illness.

Of all the issues, dependency may be the most symmetrical for the patient and caregiver as they share the burden equally but from opposite perspectives. Both parties experience a loss of independence—one through becoming dependent, and the other through being depended upon. It is for this reason that counseling often entails meeting with both partners.

Obviously, the family's material resources and social supports have a major effect on the gravity of this issue. A family that can afford nursing care, or that can call on a large group of friends, a giving family, and/or a community, such as a religious congregation, for support will not feel this issue as acutely as those who lack such resources.

ROLE AND STANCE OF THE COUNSELOR

The treatment goal in respect to dependency combines two seemingly contradictory facets: maximizing the medically ill person's self-reliance while strengthening his or her ability to ask for and accept help. To accomplish this, counseling involves a delicate balancing of objective realities, cognitions, personality factors, and family relations.

The counselor will need to know a good deal about the medical patient and family caregivers in order to assess the dynamics among them around dependency issues. What was the degree and type of independence of each party prior to the illness? How troubling is dependency to each of them? How easy or difficult is it for the ill person to ask for help? How easily is it given by others? What forms of interdependence exist in the family in other areas? What are the practical demands of this situation?

For the reasons noted above, this inventory of dependency needs and attitudes must be conducted in at least three distinct areas—emotional, physical, and practical (for example, finances and transportation). Once this information is elicited, the counselor's role is to facilitate forms of problem solving that are compatible with individual and family styles and values. Individual solutions will vary widely, as usual, influenced by all of the above-mentioned factors. Whatever the solutions are, they should be encouraged as long as they are not destructive.

Twenty-four-year-old Katie had great difficulty adjusting to her loss of independence as a result of MS. Prior to her illness, her need for independence was exceptionally strong. She had chosen a husband who was not only supportive of her desire to pursue her career goals but who was also emotionally dependent.

This fierce independence depended in large part on Katie's abundant energy. Indeed, she took pride in getting along on three or four hours of sleep a night. Now, she could no longer count on that energy, and she became terrified at the prospect of having to rely on a husband whom she viewed as fundamentally weak. She instinctively knew that although he was a caring person, he would not have the resilience to handle her increasing physical dependence. This fear was expressed in a vivid dream in which he struggled to push her wheelchair through a revolving door while she tried to hold onto the hands of their children (who existed only in this dream).

As Katie's counselor, my job was to help her rationally address these concerns. First, we talked about the couple's relationship prior to the onset of MS. I then had Katie assess her current and anticipated needs and her sources of support. I also made sure that the couple was talking openly about their changing situation and roles. I met with the husband for one session, and his passivity was consistent with Katie's reports to me about him.

Ultimately, Katie made the difficult decision to divorce her husband while she was still relatively strong and self-reliant. The decision was based on her understanding that he would never be able to handle his increased caregiving responsibility. This was her way of maximizing her independence in the short run, and preparing for the time when she might require more help.

Coaching by the counselor can strengthen the medical patient's skills in respect to dependency concerns. He or she can teach the patient not only how to ask for and graciously accept help, but also how to decline unwelcome offers. It may be useful to role-play such scenarios. In this manner, the patient can rehearse different ways of responding and see which feels most comfortable. In the process, he or she can identify emotions such as anger that could interfere with communication.

The counselor may need, as well, to help the patient recognize the needs and emotional responses of caregivers, and understand the effect of his or her behavior on them. An important objective of MCC is for the patient and family to discuss and negotiate their changing roles. How will they handle these changes? What are the patient's legitimate needs for help? Does he or she feel guilty about being a burden to the family? Do family members feel resentful or confused as they assume new roles and responsibilities? Are their needs for respite and appreciation being met?

Every family establishes a unique balance of dependence and independence among members. This changes when a member becomes chronically ill. As the family informally negotiates shifting roles, the counselor can help members be more attentive to one another's needs, perceptions, and fears. What works for one may not work for another; the key element to be cultivated is mutual respect. In general, the goal is for the ill person to be as self-reliant as possible, and for the caregivers to receive the appreciation and respite they deserve. To set the tone for addressing these sensitive issues, the counselor acknowledges each person's capacities and limitations, and is straightforward about their needs.

To adjust to these demands, family members need to understand the full impact of dependency issues on their lives, including the extent of the patient's present and future helplessness and each person's feelings about it. Their task—possibly done with the counselor's help—is to realistically assess their ability to minister to the patient's needs. Counselors may need to help caregivers discern whether they are inadvertently contributing to helplessness—a dynamic that is difficult to recognize from the "inside."

Before suffering a serious stroke, Marian Davies was an energetic, self-reliant 70-year-old. Active in her community, she was a frequent public speaker. In the three years between her stroke and referral for MCC, she had recovered most of the use of her stricken right arm and leg, but she continued to speak haltingly and with a strange sound in her voice. This impairment as well as other limitations were the source of a long and deep depression. Her husband, Larry, had retired to care for her; but instead of becoming more active as she improved physically, she became more reclusive.

Larry's way of encouraging Marian to persevere in her rehabilitation was constantly to push her to do more and to try harder. Yet despite what they both saw as his active encouragement, she was becoming increasingly depressed. By the time I saw her, she had ceased virtually all activity and effort. She refused to leave the house, talk on the phone, or carry out routine household chores.

Larry, concerned about their increasing isolation and Marian's seemingly intractable depression, insisted that they enter counseling. A psychiatrist who had been unable to bring her out of her depression referred them to me for counseling.

In the consultation, I could see that Marian's strength lay in her essentially gregarious nature and strong ego. Based on that assessment, I assured her that while her personality might be weighted down by depression, this strong ego was still there for her to tap into. Nothing, not even the stroke, could take that away. Assessing and reactivating her ego strength became the foundation for our work together.

The question was how to get this basically outgoing woman to rejoin the world she loved. One of my first steps was to see each member of the couple individually, to give Marian the chance to speak for herself. Because she had become shy about the sound of her voice, she had allowed Larry to speak for her in the consultation and the world-at-large. This was just one of the unconscious habits the couple had developed that were maintaining her status quo. Private sessions forced Marian to speak to me directly; and although she was concerned that I might not understand her, I told her I had no problem in doing so.

Marian's first idea for a goal was to gain "peace of mind," but I knew that this unfocused attempt would inevitably fail. In contrast, talking on the phone and speaking to a saleslady were achievable goals. Success with them would motivate her to undertake larger tasks.

We began treatment by allowing Marian to grieve her losses: her ability to speak, type, chop wood, garden. She mourned the pleasure she had derived from their home. Once we had worked through her grieving, she was able to focus on a series of small, easily accomplished tasks through which she regained her energy. One of her first breakthroughs was making a telephone call to a repairman. She described it to me in detail. Soon thereafter, she went shopping for a new dress and spoke to a salesclerk without Larry's help (she had him hide around the corner).

My work with Larry was at least as important as that with his wife. Gradually, he came to understand that his unrealistic expectations and pressure had promoted the opposite of what he had wanted. He actually *was making Marian less self-accepting and more reliant on him. Without intending it, he had pushed her in areas in which she knew she would disappoint him. For example, after three years of trying she knew she would never be able to type his work as she had before. Marian believed, understandably, that Larry was unable to accept her with her limitations.*

Larry also needed help with his reluctance to let Marian grieve for her losses. When she talked about her limitations, his usual reaction was to minimize them, believing that accepting them amounted to "giving up." All of his previous caregiving efforts had focused on restoring Marian to her former self—one that was physically strong, verbally quick, and independent. In his sessions, he worked through his own inventory of losses, which included missing her quick wit and the repartee he looked forward to after work each day. This grieving enabled him to discard unworkable expectations for Marian and begin to accept her limitations.

As Larry stepped back from his role as protector and caretaker, Marian began to take more responsibility for herself. Her spirits were lifted when she understood that he loved and accepted her despite her limitations; and paradoxically, this enabled her to go beyond them. She began to assert her old forms of self-expression and independence, and to recover old skills. Indeed, she became more comfortable with public-speaking, despite her awkward voice, and moved into a leadership role in a self-help group.

The relationship between Marian and Larry illustrates the critical role the caregiver can have in promoting or impeding self-reliance. For them, dependency issues were closely linked to self-image. Their story shows how unresolved self-image issues can increase a patient's dependency on the caregiver, and, conversely, how an overprotective caregiver can undermine a patient's self-confidence.

One of the counselor's important contributions in respect to dependency issues is helping patients with reality-checking. If a patient has been independent and is now having difficulty accepting help, the counselor may be able to stimulate some cognitive restructuring. Why does the patient consider himself or herself a burden? How does this perception correspond to the reality of other people's attitudes? How would the situation be handled if it were reversed? What views do the family members hold of one another, and how have these views changed? What courses of action are called for, given the realities of the situation?

People with progressive illnesses tend to prepare themselves for the worst, but the situation may not be as bad at a given stage as they imagine, and indeed it may never become that bad. As a result, the objective needs for care at a given stage may not be as great as the patient, or perhaps the caregiver, fears. The counselor should encourage the patient to be as self-reliant as possible, in order to maximize a sense of competency and minimize caregivers' resentment or overprotectiveness. An understanding of each person's behavior and emotions promotes these objectives.

Even under the best of conditions, however, caregivers may be ambivalent about how much independence to expect or encourage. They do not want to give the impression that they are burdened by the patient's needs, nor that they are insensitive to his or her frailties. Every family must establish its own balance, recognizing the needs of each member. Since most caregivers cannot handle all of the physical and emotional needs of their charge, the counselor should encourage them to find support, either from other members of their family, friends, caregiver support groups, or respite programs. Thoughtful analysis of the patient's needs may make it possible to distribute responsibility among several caregivers.

Of course, approaches that work at one stage of a chronic condition may be less effective as the disease progresses. Dependency relationships are a changing aspect of life for persons with long-term illness. (They will be revisited from a different angle in the context of abandonment and isolation issues.) If the condition worsens over time, this cluster of issues may become less a matter of fears and more a matter of difficult and unavoidable practical choices. Addressing dependency issues at an early stage teaches the practice of realistically assessing needs and options. This should lay the groundwork for the difficult decision-making that may be needed at a later time. It may be necessary, for example, to decide about a move to a nursing home or a risky treatment procedure. If the work on these issues has been successful, the family can reach decisions with the full participation of the chronically ill person. Earlier work sensitizing the patient to the perspectives of others should help him or her to keep them in mind as new decisions are made. The story of Ben and Sarah Petrovsky (page 76) illustrates the consequences when such a foundation is lacking.

In the face of very natural concerns about growing dependency, it is crucial that the medical crisis counselor and other caregivers not adopt a patronizing attitude that demeans the medical patient. Instead, needs and strengths must be acknowledged, without condescension. Within the bounds of his or her personality as well as given resources and physical constraints, the person should be encouraged to be as independent as possible. Effective counseling can help even the most physically dependent patient to maximize autonomy and cooperate with caregivers with dignity and sensitivity.

Eric, a 21-year old epilepsy patient, had never gone out alone in the seven years since his seizures began. Although a seizure was possible at any time despite strong medication, he was eager to experience a measure of independence. One way was for him to come to my office on his own, rather than having his mother drive him. I helped Eric plan to take the bus to my office. We reviewed several scenarios to prepare him in the event of his worst possible fear—a seizure on the bus (which in fact never occurred). Planning for himself was entirely new to Eric, and he was thrilled with the idea. We knew it would also give his mother a much-needed respite. Later, participating in an MCC group further strengthened his identity and sense of competence.

Stigma

Everywhere I go, I feel that people are staring at me.

People at work are avoiding me.

OBJECTIVE: TO DEVELOP THE
SELF-ACCEPTANCE AND SOCIAL SKILLS
NEEDED TO DEAL WITH OTHERS' ATTITUDES

Thanks to patient advocacy, new legislation, sensitive media attention, enabling medical devices, and other factors, people with impairments are now increasingly active and visible. As a result, society's concept of "normal" appearance and behavior is widening and social stigma is a less powerful constraint than in the past.

Nevertheless, there remains a natural human tendency to avoid or label persons who appear different or vulnerable. Those who have, or anticipate, visible manifestations of their condition need to become reconciled to stigma, and need to develop ways of dealing with it. This will enable them to "take on" the outside world. Depending on their condition, they may have to deal with avoidance, discrimination, hostility, fear, disgust, condescension, or simple curiosity.

The experience of stigma is influenced by the type of impairment or disfigurement caused by the medical condition and by its significance to the individual. Other factors are the person's gender and the stage of life at which he or she acquires the condition. Women with disabilities tend to be regarded as less "heroic" and more "damaged" than men (although social conditioning may make self-image issues more difficult for men). Persons of both sexes who are impaired later in life may feel particularly uncomfortable with people whom they knew before their impairment. A visible change forces them to face people's reactions and redefine roles and relationships. Marian Davies, for example, broke off all contact with family and old friends out of shame about her strange new voice.

Some conditions, such as paralysis from a stroke, cause an immediate, visible change; many others have a long period of latency before finally becoming visible and forcing openness. The slow development of a condition can raise questions about the best time to share information about it and whether, or how long, to keep it a secret. Carrying such a secret can cause the patient enormous stress. It can lead to breakdowns in communication, and even exacerbate physical symptoms. Each patient should weigh the costs and benefits of revealing this information, and decide on the best time to share it and with whom. Taking charge of how and when to convey this information is one way of exercising control.

ROLE AND STANCE OF THE COUNSELOR

MCC's therapeutic goal with stigma is to strengthen self-acceptance and promote the understanding and skills to confront stigma constructively. The counselor's work with the patient on this issue builds directly on the groundwork already laid in respect to self-image. These two issues are closely related: Self-image concerns people's sense of themselves, while stigma concerns other people's attitudes toward them. The inevitable tendency of people to project makes it difficult sometimes to distinguish the two, although it is clinically important to try. Individuals who have integrated their medical condition and its limitations into their identities are better able to handle others' unfavorable attitudes. If they wish to manage their lives successfully and live in society, it is important that they learn to manage the stigma they will inevitably encounter.

The best way to begin addressing this issue, and simultaneously to continue strengthening the patient's self-image, is to identify the personal prejudices that the patient may unconsciously be projecting onto others. Examining one's own attitudes gives insight into others', and it can create a greater sense of objectivity about them. Having the patient recall his or her previous attitudes toward people who are "different" can promote greater tolerance for the normal human tendency to retreat from the unfamiliar. It also can provide clues about how to deal with such attitudes when they are encountered.

Patients may need reminding that while projections are their responsibility, stigma is a reflection on the other person and not on them. Their task—far from an easy one—is to determine how to deal with such attitudes. Doing so can be an overwhelming prospect until it is understood that "society" is generally dealt with one person at a time, and in a manner over which the individual has considerable control. Stigma is most often challenged through person-to-person encounters with a sales clerk, a relative, an old friend, a neighbor, a real estate agent. Taking on all of society would be overwhelming.

The patient may find it helpful to consider the behavior of highly visible people with disabilities such as Stevie Wonder, Itzak Perlman, and Barbara Jordan. Interviews, biographies, or autobiographies describing the experiences and attitudes of such public figures can be a source of insight and inspiration. They are almost certain to reveal the growth process—one that probably involved considerable struggle—behind the confident persona that is presented to the world. The counselor should draw attention to the element of struggle. Perhaps the patient is acquainted with exemplary individuals who can serve as models. (This, of course, is one of the great benefits of self-help groups.)

Once the patient's own attitudes have been brought to light and possibly revised, the counselor can use anticipatory guidance to help plan responses to stigma. Visualization and role-playing are useful tools in this process. The most effective techniques for confronting stigma are those that are consistent with the individual's basic personality. Some people use humor, while others overtly challenge inappropriate behavior. Some choose to ignore it, and others use an awkward situation to gently or firmly educate the other person. One of my patients, bald from chemotherapy, favored almost outrageous forms of behavior and dress, such as attending formal occasions without a wig or other head covering. This was her way of forcing people to deal with her differentness on her terms. Another patient, who lost one of her legs due to cancer, painted flowers on her crutches; rather than hide her amputation, she drew attention to it, causing people to comment. Another young patient, disabled by muscular dystrophy, placed herself unabashedly in the spotlight by becoming a cheerleader in a wheelchair.

The medical crisis counselor can be especially helpful to patients who need to share information about their condition with others. This is the context in which self image and stigma issues are most difficult to disentangle. As they anticipate this difficult revelation, patients must distinguish their personal fears and shame from the reactions they can expect from others. After examining personal attitudes, the counselor can guide patients through careful decisions about whom to tell, and about when and how to do so. The counseling session can provide an ideal setting for selecting and rehearsing ways of revealing information and imagining the other's response.

In the 9 years in which 32-year-old Todd had known of his MS, he had sworn his wife, Kelly, to secrecy and insisted that they reveal his condition to no one. When his neurologist referred them for MCC, the two were suffering from profound anxiety, depression, and growing estrangement.

Todd had always been a leader, particularly in athletic activities, which were the core of his social life. He attached great importance to his relationships with his sports buddies. Ever since learning of his MS, he had feared that his friends and family would reject him if they knew of his weakness. But now, his gait was becoming unsteady and he could no longer conceal his condition simply by declining invitations to play basketball or join colleagues for lunch. Todd's usual coping measures no longer worked; he had to find a way to relieve his rising tension and anxiety. In the consultation, he decided that keeping the secret was costing too much physically, emotionally, and socially. One way or another, he would have to begin telling people about his condition. It was not going away.

In order to take that step, Todd needed to understand the exact nature and source of his fear. With focused, careful questioning he searched for his reasons for hiding his illness. What did he value in himself? What did he think others valued in him? What was his view of people with disabilities? What was his worst fear about revealing his condition? Through this exploration, it emerged that Todd harbored his own prejudice against "weak" men, and was terrified that others would see him in this disparaging light when they knew he had MS.

Fortunately for him, Todd was also intensely uncomfortable with pretense. He recognized that hiding was causing him severe stress and depriving him of strong sources of support from family and close friends. The new insights garnered in counseling readied Todd to reveal his secret. The decision then was whom to tell first, and what to say. When I asked whom he most wanted to know about his condition, Todd answered quickly: his 10-year-old daughter, Sara. If that went well, he would then approach his parents, his wife's parents, and his friends and colleagues.

Once these decisions were made, we began rehearsing what Todd would say. Playing the role of his daughter, I asked him every question I imagined she might ask, particularly those he would find painful. He wept as we practiced, releasing emotions that had built up over years. Searching for the words that would elicit the desired response from Sara, he came to the realization that his key question was, "Will you still love me?"

After this preparation, Todd felt ready for the conversation. He decided to go on a picnic with his daughter. He reported the results of that meeting at the next counseling session. Sara had responded to him in exactly the way he had hoped: She reassured him of undying love. He also learned that she had already suspected that something was wrong, watching him turn down his beloved basketball games week after week. Now, his uncharacteristic behavior made sense to her.

With a counselor's support, Todd felt an enormous weight—the fear of stigma—lifted from his shoulders. His exchange with his daughter filled him with new energy. Almost immediately, his depression lifted and his physical symptoms subsided. His relationship with his wife also improved considerably. Having put this first difficult step behind him, he found it easier to tell everyone else. Each time, he discovered that others' feelings for him did not change as a result of the confession. What he had feared so much simply never came to pass.

Discomfort in the face of social stigma leads many people to seek out support groups of others with their condition. Counselors should encourage patients to join such peer groups, which can be an excellent source of social support. They should also, however, urge patients not to limit their associations to these groups to the exclusion of others, and to beware of groups that promote unhealthy isolation and preoccupation with the disorder.

Like medical patients, family caregivers may need encouragement from the counselor to keep their involvements broad, as well as help in building skills for coping with stigma. It may seem easier to socialize only with those who understand their situation, avoiding those who do not. Family members struggle with a welter of personal feelings including shame, guilt, pity, self-pity, and anger as well as uncertainty about how to constructively deal with others' attitudes. In coping with these and other feelings, self-help groups have the same benefits and pitfalls for family members that they do for medical patients.

One manifestation of stigma is discrimination, something with which disabled people are all too familiar. Medical crisis counselors can help patients recognize and contend with discrimination in areas such as employment and housing. Where relevant, they should encourage patients to become familiar with the rights of disabled people and the legal and advocacy resources for confronting abuses, and also to take appropriate actions in their own defense. The Americans with Disabilities Act has significantly strengthened protections against discrimination for disabled people. National organizations concerned with specific health conditions are good sources of information and support in this area.

Abandonment

I'll have no one to take care of me.

My son has deserted me in this nursing home.

I couldn't live with myself if I didn't care for my husband myself.

OBJECTIVE: TO BE ABLE TO FACE DIFFICULT DECISIONS WITH REALISM AND SENSITIVITY TO OTHERS' NEEDS

The specter of abandonment is one of the most terrifying and primitive, echoing fears from earliest childhood, and for some people exceeding even the fear of death. This fear resonates most strongly for those whose disorders are progressively or suddenly incapacitating. Such conditions impose a severe burden on the caregivers as well as on family finances, and create psychological and interpersonal stress. They also can necessitate the kinds of decisions that may be perceived by the patient as abandonment.

Because the fear of abandonment is so profound, issues that evoke it are especially difficult for families to address. Nevertheless, they are forced by some chronic illnesses to do so. It is important to recognize the powerful and contradictory feelings surrounding this issue. The patient fears abandonment, but also regrets being a burden. He or she wants and needs care, but is aware of the hardship this imposes. Indeed, he or she feels distress at being the cause of the caregiver's problems. The caregiver wants to provide care and comfort, but may also wish to be "rid of the problem." While guiltily rejecting this thought, his or her behavior may sometimes betray the exhaustion and frustration inherent in this role—perhaps snapping at the patient for requesting yet another trip up the stairs. Both the patient and the caregiver have difficulty acknowledging these powerful and heart-rending feelings to anyone, possibly even to themselves. What they may fail to understand is that it is the illness, and not the other person, that is the problem. Such conflicting and disturbing feelings are often the cause of a deep and serious communication breakdown.

As with so many other issues in MCC, timing is a crucial factor with abandonment. If the counselor sees the patient soon after diagnosis, the specters of total disability and abandonment can be confronted as fears, not imminent possibilities. Early intervention will make difficult subjects, such as the need for nursing home care or the possibility of the family caregiver's relinquishing or seeking a paying job, easier to discuss. The counselor can help the caregiver as well as the medical patient confront painful issues, consider options, and make plans. In doing so, it is vital to keep each person's needs and perspectives in mind. Decisions considered at this early stage may never be acted upon, but there is benefit in considering the possibilities: It creates a greater sense of objectivity about such decisions, discharges emotional overtones, and leaves the family with a set of options to choose from or amend when the time comes.

At a later stage in the illness, abandonment issues are often what drive caregivers or patients to seek MCC. By then, however, resentments have accumulated, options have dwindled, and the counselor's ability to be of assistance is limited. At this point, all that may be possible is to achieve a few concrete changes that help reduce stress.

In the four years following her diagnosis with amyotrophic lateral sclerosis (ALS, a progressively crippling illness also known as Lou Gehrig's disease), 37-year-old Sarah Petrovsky had deteriorated to the point that she would not survive without being placed on a respirator. Her husband, Ben, who had cared for her at home until then, left to Sarah the decision as to whether to prolong her life in that way. They never discussed where she would be cared for after this decisive change in her health status, and they approached it with quite different expectations. Sarah and Ben had been a devoted couple and excellent communicators who shared family decisions. But coping with the disease had exhausted them both and eroded their communication. They were simply unable to face this critical juncture together.

While Sarah was in the hospital being placed on the respirator, Ben reached the long-delayed decision that he could no longer care for her at home while also supporting the family at a demanding job and caring for their three children. He reluctantly arranged for her to be moved to a nursing home upon discharge, rather than back to their home as she had expected.

Sarah and Ben's story (which will continue below) illustrates the vital importance of prevention and early intervention—an urgency to which all primary care providers should be sensitive. When Sarah's neurologist recommended counseling at the time of diagnosis, the family physician advised against it. The couple had a good marriage, and he viewed them as emotionally strong enough and felt they communicated well enough to cope with the illness. Their neurologist, however, had a more realistic sense of the long-term impact of this devastating disease. By the time I met Sarah and Ben, their anger and estrangement were so entrenched that there were real limits to what I could accomplish. I recognized the limits but wanted to do what I could to help.

As happened with the Petrovskys, caregiver burnout and worsening communication due to guilt and anger are often what lead to the very abandonment the medical patient dreads. Differing perceptions, conflicting needs, and above all an inability to discuss these differences can contribute to stalemates that prevent effective and mutually acceptable decision-making.

Another family's story illustrates the counselor's role in helping patients come to terms with unavoidable decisions.

A young doctor consulted me in great distress at having placed his mother, who suffered from Alzheimer's Disease, in a nursing home. He and his wife had considered all other alternatives and reluctantly concluded that it was no longer possible or safe for them to care for his mother at their home. Because of her cognitive impairments, they could not discuss the decision with her. She was inconsolable about this outcome, and insisted that her only son had abandoned her.

My brief therapy with the son focused on reviewing both the process and the content of his decision. We examined his real options, given the illness and strains in the relationship between his wife and mother. He had no alternative but to recognize that by visiting his mother daily and tracking her progress in the medical charts, he was doing everything he realistically could for her. Our work in counseling relieved him of his guilt about being unable to do more.

ROLE AND STANCE OF THE COUNSELOR

A central task in MCC is to facilitate communication between caregivers and medical patients—something that is especially crucial when addressing abandonment issues. Under ideal conditions, the patient and caregiver are open to each other's feelings and desires, but such conditions are rare. In their absence, when communication seems impossible around painful subjects, the counselor can serve as an interpreter of each person's point of view to the other.

The counselor's role is to help patients and families separate the practical decisions necessitated by the medical condition from their powerful emotional overtones. Abandonment issues are often grounded less in a specific set of conditions—housing, nursing care, inclusion in family activities—than in the quality of relationships, communication, and planning in which the patient is involved. Chronic illness can severely limit options and call for painful, undesirable decisions. The patient can avoid a sense of abandonment, emotional as well as physical, by being an active, empathic participant in these decisions.

The difficulty of clear communication and joint decision-making should not be underestimated: They are extremely difficult to achieve and often require the assistance of a counselor. This process should begin as early as possible and include even the most difficult questions. It often begins by meeting separately with each party to broach painful subjects and give each one a chance to vent. Discussing sensitive issues with each party enables the counselor to discreetly "represent" them to each other. Having aired strong feelings and difficult issues privately in an atmosphere free of accusation, guilt, and value judgment sometimes creates enough openness and trust for the parties to then engage in dialogue about their points of view. This is extremely difficult to accomplish, especially when issues have become charged over time. Even if open communication on the sensitive subject is not achieved, the effort will probably increase each person's awareness of the other's perspective. It may also help them see ways in which they can act on their own to ameliorate the situation.

Here as elsewhere, the most effective measures are preventive. In particular, the counselor should do everything possible to prevent caregiver burnout, for example, by acknowledging sacrifices and urging that respite be built into his or her routine. (Some communities have helpful respite services and support groups for caregivers, although the former are still in short supply.) Besides directly supporting the caregiver, the counselor should also sensitize the medical patient to the caregiver's need for respite. The patient must understand that taking time out not only does not constitute abandonment, but may even prevent it. Attention to the caregiver's needs in these ways helps prevent the patient's fears of abandonment from becoming a reality.

Communication is the key to dealing with these issues—and chronic illness places a severe strain on this ability. To deal with their frustration and anger, both patient and caregiver may need to be reminded again and again that the medical condition is "the villain" in this drama: It is not the patient whom the caregiver wishes to be "rid of," but the illness. Once they understand this important fact, the patient and caregiver can unite in shared anger at their situation rather than projecting their anger onto each other.

Jack Goldman was referred by his neurologist when he was 42 and his MS symptoms were exacerbating after some 20 years of being relatively symptom free. Family relations were pivotal for Jack and his wife, Marilyn. Their four children ranged in age from 10 to 18, and all six family members were deeply affected by Jack's illness and shared in his caregiving. Jack was reluctant to enter MCC treatment, but agreed to try a few sessions.

At the outset, Marilyn reported having frequent thoughts of suicide because of the derisive way that Jack directed his anger and frustration at her, his devoted caregiver. As his MS progressed and his dependence intensified, Jack increasingly tested his wife's commitment. He taunted and criticized her. His fear of abandonment, together with a driving anger, was causing him to "flirt" with the very outcome he most feared. When Marilyn seemed tired or overwhelmed, he would angrily ask her why she didn't just put him in a nursing home. She always gave him the answer he wanted to hear, but it was beginning to sound less convincing. In fact, she did many times seriously consider moving her husband to a nursing home.

In MCC, Marilyn grew in her understanding of Jack's anger and need for support, and was thus buttressed in her role as primary caregiver; Jack grew more sensitive to Marilyn's needs for appreciation and respite. Instead of removing him from the household, she was able to manage a very complicated daily routine with the help of their children. The Goldmans averted abandonment through greater mutual awareness and improved communication.

The medical crisis counselor has several interrelated goals in respect to abandonment fears: for the patient to maximize self-reliance as well as sensitivity to the needs of the caregiver; for the caregiver to empathize with the patient's needs, feelings, and desires; and for the two of them to communicate as openly and realistically as possible about their situation.

Cognitively, it is useful for medical patients to understand two things: that abandonment is more a fear than a likelihood, and that they can have a major effect on the outcome by being sensitive to the caregiver's needs. The counselor's role includes cultivating the understanding that rationally chosen outcomes—even painful ones such as moving to a nursing home—do not necessarily constitute abandonment. Sometimes they are simply the best that the family can do in a difficult situation.

Working toward this kind of cognitive adjustment and supporting problem-solving within given constraints were the most I could offer to Sarah Petrovsky and Ben. To continue their story (begun on page 76), I began to work with them at the request of an attorney several months after Sarah was moved to the nursing home. Hurt and angry and determined to reestablish some control over her life, Sarah was considering a lawsuit to force her way back home. Two days after the lawyer's phone call, I was on my way to the nursing home knowing I faced an enormous challenge.

I found a frail young woman lying motionless on her bed. The only sound was the pumping of her respirator. Knowing she had 24-hour coverage, I waited for a nurse to come in and introduce us. Sarah communicated with her by means of a letter board above her bed, blinking or moving her eyes to indicate the letters that spelled out her message.

My first challenge was to establish communication. Sitting next to her bed and making eye contact with her, I decided to use the nurse as an interpreter because I did not wish to take up valuable time learning the system. This arrangement also gave me a few moments to think and record her responses. I asked the nurse to sit behind me so Sarah and I would not be distracted, and to make no personal remarks. Our consultation session gave Sarah a chance to describe the situation and declare her intention to move—ideally to her home, but definitely out of the nursing home.

In the weeks that followed, I spent as much time in my office with Sarah's husband as I did with her in the nursing home. Ben explained that he had simply reached a point of no longer being able to meet his wife's physical and psychological demands. He and their three children had badly needed some respite. As he spoke, it became clear to me that under no circumstances would he allow Sarah to return home. I continued to visit Sarah on a weekly basis, and learned that she was just as determined as Ben: There were no conditions under which she would stay in the nursing home. Both of these anguished individuals had made up their minds; my job was to help them adjust to this reality.

Although Sarah was determined to go home, she slowly began to understand that whatever she threatened, her husband realistically could no longer handle her care. Finally accepting this reality, she reluctantly chose to move to an apartment. This seemed to me a daunting prospect. How would she manage her three shifts of nurses? What if there were an emergency and no nurse was available? She was unable even to use a telephone. Nevertheless, recognizing her determination and sensing her ability to organize nurses and find an apartment, I helped her evaluate the feasibility of her goal. Her energy and attention were now redirected to the details of preparing for her move. Interestingly, I often forgot the extent of Sarah's incapacitation. Our eye contact overcame my awareness of her mode of communicating.

In a matter of weeks, Sarah secured commitments for her nursing care, found an apartment, and arranged for her move. She had accomplished her goal of getting out of the nursing home. I visited her in her apartment several times, and we gradually discontinued treatment.

Throughout this period, I continued to meet with Ben to help him work through his own anger and grief. He described their lives together: He had been very much in love with Sarah, and he talked about her warmth and generosity as a wife and mother. He was angry and deeply hurt at her response to his decision, and at her family's failure to support him. Why didn't she understand his exhaustion? (He did get emotional support from his parents, but they lived in another city.)

We discussed the conditions that had led to Ben's decision, including his desire to meet his children's needs. He always took responsibility for decisions on his wife's behalf and saw to it that she had weekly contact with their children, despite his anger at her and her family for not understanding his actions. Attempting to resolve family conflicts and to give Ben more support, I also met with other family members, including their children, Sarah's parents, and her brother.

In time, Sarah moved (at least intellectually) toward accepting that Ben had not emotionally abandoned her by moving her to a nursing home. She tried to understand his position and his feelings. I assured her that he loved and respected her and shared her anger at what the disease had done to their lives. He had simply "burned out" as her primary caregiver. Even though living alone was not her initial goal, getting out of the nursing home relieved her of some of her anger and resentment.

My ability to help Sarah and Ben was limited because of the late stage at which they received treatment. Had this capable and caring couple received help from a medical crisis counselor soon after diagnosis, they might have been able to jointly arrive at a mutually acceptable solution.

Ben would not have been pressed to make a decision that was essentially against his basic caring instinct, and Sarah would have been more consider-ate of her husband's physical and mental condition.

Anger

I have a scream inside me just waiting to get out.

OBJECTIVE: TO IDENTIFY AND REDIRECT ANGER, AND THEREBY RELEASE CONSTRUCTIVE ENERGY

It is natural to assume that anger is one of the first responses to the diagnosis of a lasting medical condition. Yet most people become aware of this emotion only after processing many others. Usually, in the early stages of the disease people are preoccupied with fears about losing control and becoming dependent. They struggle with changes in self-image and fear of abandonment. Eventually, they come face to face with their anger.

Anger often manifests itself in ways that are not immediately obvious. Patients may simply be aware of intense feelings of sadness, hopelessness, and frustration. They may notice physical symptoms, such as fatigue and a general malaise, which they may mistakenly attribute to the medical condi-tion. Sometimes they may find themselves expressing intense sarcasm or shouting outright. This leads family members to believe their personalities have changed.

People's responses to anger vary, affected by upbringing and culture. Some people suppress this emotion because their upbringing enforced an injunction against feeling or expressing it. Others may deny their anger because they see it as irrational; still others have witnessed so much anger that they recoil from it.

Unrecognized anger can be a signpost for depression. The patient may be aware of feelings of lassitude, frustration, and hopelessness, but be unable to recognize the seething anger that underlies and causes these emotions. Getting to its source and finding ways to ventilate and redirect anger can release trapped energy, relieve physical symptoms, and lift the mood of the patient to a degree that he or she might have thought impossible. This is a vital part of MCC treatment.

Even while refusing to admit that they are angry, some people misdirect their free-floating anger: at the health system, at doctors for not finding a cure, at spouses for not paying enough attention to them, at friends for being insensitive, at the grocery clerk for being too slow. This confusion is understandable, given the fact that anger cannot be meaningfully directed at its real but abstract source—the medical condition. After all, how can one be angry at cancer?

Anger is a normal response to frustration, and thus a natural one for someone whose future has been radically changed by chronic illness. A cancer patient described her feelings this way: "I have a scream inside of me just waiting to get out." In "Anger: The Hidden Part of Grief,"[2] Cerney and Buskirk assert that "the resolution of grief depends, in major part, on the willingness . . . to recognize, own, and resolve feelings of anger." Grieving losses is central to the adjustment to chronic illness, as was noted in Chapter 2 and in the discussion of self-image.

Cerney and Buskirk also weave in another thread of MCC theory. They note that because the need for security is a basic human drive, the fear of abandonment arouses intense anger: "This threat [to a sense of security] can stimulate an unrelenting rage in persons placed in a vulnerable situation." Few situations make one more vulnerable than a lasting and serious medical condition. Regardless of the individual's ability, to accept his or her fate on a rational level, the unconscious self still rages at the losses it represents. This rage is a reaction to threats that constitute "an attack on the omnipotence we experienced as children."[3]

While such anger is both natural and appropriate, it also can have severe physical consequences. Both suppressed anger and frequent temper tantrums create stress on the body, raising cholesterol levels, placing strain on the heart, and lowering immunities. For those with chronic illness, the desire to avoid placing additional stress on an already vulnerable body can be a powerful incentive to find ways of dealing constructively with anger.

When at age 38 Ellen Suzuki learned that the breast cancer she had battled 10 years earlier had recurred and metastasized, a friend encouraged her to seek MCC. When I first saw her, she was intensely angry about the return of her cancer. More destructively, she felt that she had caused it. "I know it's because of my terrible personality," she said. Although she was an outstanding and well-respected professional, Ellen was profoundly unsure of herself. She gained her identity and sense of worth through association with her prominent colleagues.

This was a difficult patient—deeply ambivalent about her feelings for her parents, unwilling to acknowledge the depth and pervasiveness of her anger, and, near the end of her life, verbally abusive toward her husband and son. She was also a deeply insecure and frightened young woman who did not know how to live and did not want to die.

Ellen clearly needed intensive psychotherapy to resolve these deep-seated issues. Because of her severe illness, I saw her intermittently over a period of several years. During that time we did discuss her relationship with various family members, particularly her strong and dominating father, but our chief goal was helping her live with her cancer.

Because of the possible foreshortening of her life, Ellen's immediate goals were to reduce stress and enjoy her family more. In treatment, these goals were translated into specific actions such as changing jobs, taking a trip with her family, and even making peace with her parents. MCC helped her identify and achieve these concrete goals, alleviating some of her distress and bringing her a measure of peace toward the end of her life.

Nevertheless, the deep-seated anger that she carried into adulthood, and from wellness into illness, continued to stand between Ellen and the peace she sought. Her physical condition prevented her from facing her pervasive anger, which she would only address insofar as it pertained to having cancer. It was the cancer that had caused her anger to explode, pushing Ellen to turn on her husband, her parents, and her child.

MCC helped Ellen to stay in the realm of immediate experience and to act constructively. It also led her to one of her final and most life-affirming gestures. Just weeks before her death, she decided to organize a party to share her wedding anniversary with family, friends, and colleagues. I was there to witness her spending a happy and spirited evening, despite being so ill that she could hardly walk. Ellen had created a highly satisfying experience for herself and those she cared most about; she had organized an event at which she bade a symbolic farewell.

More than anything, Ellen's case illustrates the limitations in what brief, focused therapy can accomplish with chronically ill patients. The inexorable course of an illness can prevent or at least limit the patient's development and change, especially of a fundamental nature. Nevertheless, as with Ellen, much can often be accomplished on a behavioral level to give the patient relief from emotional pain.

ROLE AND STANCE OF THE COUNSELOR

The key to a patient's coping with this issue is his or her understanding that it is natural to be angry when one cannot control one's life or one's illness. Acknowledging the feeling and identifying its roots in the illness are the first steps toward finding appropriate ways of expressing it. Doing so will release valuable energy that can be used to physically and emotionally manage the medical condition.

Mental health professionals are well versed in techniques for facilitating this process. With chronically ill patients, they must bear in mind that a good deal of anger can be traced to having the medical condition, regardless of the patient's sense of the cause. Armed with this insight, the patient and caregiver can then work together to find activities that provide outlets for negative emotional energy. These can include such simple measures as joining a peer group, recording feelings in a journal, or working in the garden.

I want to stress that in my experience medication is rarely the best way to manage anger and stress. While a mild medication may be necessary to temporarily relieve symptoms, tranquilizing a patient to suppress anger only delays identification of the emotion and makes its eventual resolution more difficult. Additionally, the patient is at risk of becoming dependent on the medication. Anger diminishes only when the patient identifies its real cause, finds appropriate outlets for it, and uses that energy in a positive way.

Unfortunately, the home is often where people inappropriately vent their anger, sometimes setting off a destructive cycle of escalating ill feelings. This is common because medical patients and caregivers are struggling with frustration. On the other hand, the home is also the setting in which anger can be discussed and understood, and constructive forms of release worked out. Every individual and family has unique mechanisms for dealing with anger. If they are not destructive, these should be respected. There are many mechanisms to deal with anger, including humor, opportunities to vent, quiet talking, being alone, teasing, friendly competitive activities, and disciplines such as the proverbial counting to 10.

Carol Tavris offers a useful examination of anger in her book, *Anger: The Misunderstood Emotion.*[4] She points out that expressing anger can restore an individual's sense of control, provided that (1) it is directed at the proper target, (2) it is expressed through "I-messages," and (3) it produces results. These are difficult conditions to meet when chronic illness is involved, but they remain appropriate goals for MCC. Tavris encourages people to say what they really feel instead of resentfully bearing grudges, and without attacking others' emotional reactions. As we saw in the discussion of abandonment, a counseling session may be an effective and safe place in which to express highly charged emotions. Tavris also advises people to analyze their patterns of anger to illuminate trigger points and characteristic modes of expression.[5] In MCC, the patient's knowing the pattern helps him or her maintain control.

Tavris suggests taking stock of the ongoing positive aspects of life, and this is highly relevant for people with serious medical conditions. Like many other issues of chronic illness, extreme and persistent anger can dull one's awareness of strengths and opportunities, and of life's pleasures that are still available to them. The exercise of looking at the "full" rather than the "empty" portion of the metaphorical glass, even if done mechanically at first, can begin a positive feedback process that restores a sense of balance and hope. This process has already been discussed in other portions of this book (see the sections on control and self-image in this chapter).

For the medical crisis counselor, an added challenge comes from the absolute appropriateness of the patient's anger. It is altogether natural to ask, "Why me?" and to rail against the unfairness of the universe. The counselor's task is to help the individual direct this energy, justified as it is, into positive activities such as political advocacy with a local health organization, helping others, or visiting people who are newly diagnosed. First-person stories abound with examples of chronically ill people lifting their spirits by turning away from their own troubles to other involvements.

The anger of Jack Goldman, the 42-year old MS patient described on page 79, is more typical of MCC patients than that of Ellen Suzuki. His anger was responsive to therapy because it was not embedded in a damaged ego. Counseling with Jack and his wife, Marilyn, heightened their awareness of their contrasting styles of expression. This increasing understanding helped both of them in their desperate moments. Even when words were flying, each knew that the other's support and love were unconditional. They knew why they were angry and what to do to relieve it. This was something, sadly, that Ellen could never do.

Isolation

Why don't my friends call me?

I just want to go off by myself.

OBJECTIVE: TO SUSTAIN AN APPROPRIATE LEVEL OF MEANINGFUL CONTACT WITH OTHERS

Some isolation is almost inevitable for chronically ill persons, and it affects medical patients and family members alike. In the relatively early stages, both may find themselves withdrawing from contact with people who seem not to understand them. Indeed, old friends may avoid them, uncertain of how to behave and worried about saying the "wrong thing." At later stages, the condition may reach a point at which it is physically too difficult to continue with work, normal social life, or other activities. All of these forms of isolation — social, physical, and emotional — can lead to serious depression.

Counseling on isolation normally occurs toward the latter part of MCC treatment, after other issues have been confronted. In some ways, the issue encompasses previous ones. Isolation raises echoes of self-image, stigma, and abandonment issues, and the skills and insights garnered in previous sessions are important resources for facing this challenge.

As with many issues addressed by MCC, isolation can have a direct negative impact on health. Research shows that being cut off from friends and family can double a well person's chance of sickness or death.[6] It is therefore crucially important for medical patients to find satisfying ways to maintain contact with others.

This concern is just as pressing for family caregivers, who have been shown to be vulnerable to disease and reduced life expectancy because of the stress of their roles.[7] This stress and its consequences are only exacerbated by isolation.

ROLE AND STANCE OF THE COUNSELOR

The medical crisis counselor's first task is to help the patient identify the reasons for his or her isolation and ways in which he or she can alleviate it. Counselor and patient should not feel they are looking into a tunnel with no light: It is critically important for patients to understand that they do have options, even in the advanced stages of illness. One MCC patient with late-stage cancer was still making calls from her bed to help friends and neighbors just weeks before she died. A man with advanced ALS continued to play cards every week in his home with his buddies. As we have seen, lupus patient Bob Smithson and his wife found a way, without endangering his health, to continue their cherished beach vacation with friends.

Once options are identified, the patient can set priorities for spending the available time and energy. This process applies the MCC principle of setting attainable goals and finding workable strategies to reach them. Given the opportunity, energy, and encouragement, patients can be highly resourceful and creative about reconnecting with others.

Solutions will vary from patient to patient. Some prefer to limit involvements to a few special relationships and activities, while others may dislike and even fear being alone. Still others actually may choose to spend more time alone. This can be a time to develop or use a writing or artistic gift or other skills that are best exercised in solitude. Such choices should be encouraged and respected by the counselor and family, provided they are made for positive reasons. Counselors must also be alert, however, to the possibility that the patient's withdrawal is motivated by depression or fear of rejection. This impulse can lead to isolation that is not truly of the individual's choosing, and that he or she is unprepared to handle. Once judging it to be healthy, the counselor should understand and support the patient's wish either to be isolated or to be involved with others.

While still in the early, symptom-free stages of MS, Jennifer had com-pletely absorbed herself in a self-help group out of a need for acceptance and a belief that only people with her condition could understand and love her. My major concern about this involvement stemmed from her appar-ent desire to devote all her time and energy to this group while divesting herself of all of her old relationships—family and friends, people who cared about her and whom she loved. This outgoing, sociable young woman was cutting her ties with the "normal" world to avoid experiencing the rejection she anticipated. She had taken refuge in a group in which she believed she could have "real relationships." Jennifer was in danger of being completely cut off physically and psychologically, and was blinded to this fact by her overwhelming need for acceptance.

Exploring this need in therapy, she expressed a life-long feeling of being "different" and a need to "hide." She had always used the facade of heavy makeup to conceal her "true self." Now she was going into deeper hiding, even moving into a basement apartment in her parents' home. She saw the MS group as a way to be with people who also felt different and isolated. Unfortunately, we later discovered one group member was seeking to control and manipulate this naive, frightened young woman.

To combat Jennifer's self-imposed isolation, it was necessary to discern why she desired such a complete break with her past and why she felt a need to hide. We examined the basis of her low self-esteem and her sense that people valued her only for superficial reasons. Finally, she was able to understand that people cared about her "true self," and that she no longer needed a facade. She realized that she still cared deeply about her family and old friends, but more importantly that they loved and accepted her. This single insight removed a burden she had carried all of her young life. As a result of counseling, Jennifer once again became close to her mother,

father, and brothers. Her renewed connection to these family bonds freed
her from absorption in an isolating self-help group.

Medical crisis counselors should encourage the patient to maintain important personal relationships, even when it involves working through
communication barriers. The patient needs these vital relationships now
more than ever. It may be necessary to brave social stigma—what has been
called "the pariah syndrome"—to move about in "normal" society. Early
work on stigma should prepare the individual to deal with avoidance and
real or imagined rejection.

For some, old and familiar relationships can be more difficult than more
anonymous public activity. But those who have integrated their condition
and developed strong coping skills can take the initiative in maintaining
contacts and even modeling the relaxed behavior they want with their
friends. The counselor can use techniques such as role play to help patients
and family members develop the skills to handle difficult interpersonal
situations. The counselor's relationship with the patient serves as a model
of comfortable interaction.

In this context, social supports come critically into play; again, these are
best cultivated in the early stages of a medical condition. Just as lupus
patient Bob Smithson and his wife found a support system among their
neighbors, patients can identify and develop networks that stand ready to
provide support in times of need. These may include a church or syna-
gogue, self-help groups, friends, family, and neighbors.

Isolation was an overarching issue for stroke patient Marian Davies and
her husband, Larry (see page 66). Marian's stroke had seriously limited
her ability to communicate, and a move to a retirement community had
added to their grief and sense of isolation. The couple's isolation was
symbolized and reinforced by their move from a home and garden they
had loved. Although this move may have been necessary in order to relieve
Marian of the responsibilities of managing a large home, it also separated
them from activities that had given them great pleasure. Without foresee-
ing the consequences, the Davies had thoroughly removed themselves from
their old lives.

Marian, in particular, felt this loss. Depressed about giving up her
beloved former home and all that it signified, including being a hostess and
enjoying the physical strength to chop wood, she found herself unable to
take charge of her new home. She was physically capable, but frozen into

inactivity by her depression. Boxes containing the Davies' belongings sat unopened, as they had for the two years since their move.

The Davies' isolation was primarily a function of changeable behaviors and attitudes rather than fixed physical limitations. Marian needed to find ways to break through apparent impasses and to make her way back into the social interactions from which she and her husband had almost completely withdrawn. As we saw earlier, there proved to be many arenas in which she could venture forth and rebuild confidence and connections.

The unopened boxes became symbols of Marian's treatment progress: When she began unpacking them, we knew she was getting better. Eventually she was calling old friends and making trips out of town to family functions. She was becoming one with the world again.

An important part of Marian's recovery was joining a Stroke Club. This support group proved to be a setting in which she not only received support and felt secure, but also rehabilitated some of her old skills. She began speaking publicly at the group's meetings, eventually becoming its president. Toward the end of her MCC treatment, Marian gave a speech to stroke victims in which she stressed the importance of hard work in overcoming impairments. She described the "lift" she had received from "shifting my thoughts and my efforts to something useful."

In confronting her isolation, Marian Davies was fortunate that her chief barriers were within herself rather than in her environment. Changing her attitude thus enabled her to end her isolation. No attitude change, however, will prevent people with movement problems from encountering external barriers to their mobility and social interaction. It is useful to remember that loss of mobility is a function not only of physical impairment, but also of environmental factors in the patient's home, workplace, school, and so on. Often it is the environment that must, or can, be changed, as the law now requires in public places. Assistive medical devices such as wheelchair-friendly vans can open up new vistas of travel and recreation for both disabled patients and their families.

Even given the will and wherewithal to do so, however, solving the problems of physical isolation requires enormous effort, ingenuity, and patience. The counselor must be aware of the patient's physical issues and environmental factors, and must also be sensitive to the effort demanded of the patient. Sensitivity includes being flexible in the event of missed appointments or late arrivals, as well as in initial appointment scheduling. Counselors must also ensure that their treatment sites are easily accessible. In some cases, they may choose to visit patients in their homes.

Many people coping with severe medical problems join a support or self-help group to avoid physical and emotional isolation. Such groups give members a way to interact with others who share their experience. They offer an environment of comfort and acceptance in which members seldom have to explain themselves. The counselor should encourage patients to take advantage of this powerful source of support, but both should be aware of the drawbacks of complete absorption by a self-help group. Rather than solving the problem of isolation, membership can intensify it if group participation becomes a substitute for other involvements. Although the emotional attraction of this haven is strong, the world in which members are involved can shrink without their realizing it. Self-help groups are useful when they truly reinforce the adjustment process and help members retain their involvements outside the group. The counselor should make this point to MCC patients.

In this area, as in others, the counselor's knowledge of the community can be a valuable aid for patients and caregivers. It can help them find community resources, be selective in their choice of a support group, and perhaps create their own group or resource. (Community resources, including self-help groups, are discussed further in Chapter 10.)

Death

What kind of life will I have if I can't function?

I need someone to talk to about dying.

OBJECTIVE: TO PROMOTE EXISTENTIAL ACCEPTANCE WITH AN EMPHASIS ON THE QUALITY OF LIFE IN THE HERE AND NOW

People with chronic medical conditions begin thinking about death long before it is imminent. The nature of death-related issues for patients and their families varies considerably, depending on such factors as the age of the patient, the stage of the disease, personal belief systems, and social supports. Naturally, the counselor's role with a patient who is near death will differ from that with a patient who has been recently diagnosed and for whom death is a distant possibility.

Soon after diagnosis, chronically ill individuals believe they can anticipate the cause of their death and even what the experience will be like. In time, however, most come to worry less about dying than about living with their illness. There are few chronic conditions that drastically shorten life compared to the number that threaten its quality. Because of either a healthy desire to concentrate on life or a more troubling preoccupation with what may lie ahead, seriously ill patients tend to think and talk far more about their lives than about their anticipated deaths.

ROLE AND STANCE OF THE COUNSELOR

Whether death is imminent or a distant possibility, helping people face that prospect means assisting them to live their lives to the fullest. Even with death close at hand, it is possible to remain invested in living. The counselor's task is to support that investment.

MCC is about living—to the final moments of life. Dying is, after all, a continuation of living, with death as the endpoint. The goal of counseling in respect to death, therefore, is for the patient to focus attention on living to the fullest extent possible. This is facilitated by grieving losses, finding meaning and joy in the present, coping as effectively as possible with the medical condition, and getting closure wherever possible.

Anna was a 14-year-old with advanced muscular dystrophy. Her sister, Maria, had died of the same disease a month earlier. She also had a 5-year-old brother, Antonio, who was healthy and vigorous.

I knew that Anna would be in a wheelchair because her mother had already asked if my office could accommodate one. I was also aware that this case would touch on my personal history—a circumstance that was still difficult for me. This was going to be a "heavy" case. Yet, even as I experienced trepidation, I also felt challenged and confident. Helping Anna would take high energy on my part, and I wanted to be involved.

Even though I expected Anna in a wheelchair, I was unprepared for the young woman who greeted me as she rolled herself electronically into my office. Her square form was firmly planted in the sophisticated equipment, which she handled with ease derived from years of practice. It seemed a permanent part of her body. Sitting atop this combination body-machine was one of the most marvelous faces I had ever encountered. Anna smiled and gazed directly into my eyes. Her adolescent expression was filled all at once with pain, resignation, calm, animation, humor, and warmth. She charmed me immediately, and within moments dispelled my concerns about working with her. Indeed, I looked forward to our future sessions.

As Anna spoke, I was amazed at her deep appreciation for life and living. Her zest knew no bounds. She took as much as she could from each moment, each experience. She had lived life to the fullest, and had never shied from a challenge. Her aggressive attitude had brought her into activities such as cheerleading (in her wheelchair!), dancing, and swimming (including a concern about beautiful, sexy bathing suits). She described her "boyfriend," a young priest, whom she had maneuvered into carrying her around. She was clever, cunning, and manipulative—even unstoppable—and I stood in awe of her determination.

I wondered what brought Anna into MCC. After all, she had been seriously ill most of her life, had had many painful surgeries and difficult emotional experiences, and had never required counseling before. Indeed, her mother, Elena, had provided excellent physical care, and clearly Anna enjoyed a high quality of life. As this remarkable girl spoke, I listened for the eight issues and found, as I had expected, that she had addressed and resolved most of them on her own and with the support of her family and a host of caring health professionals.

Anna had been in control of her life. Her self-image was good. She enjoyed "dressing up" for social occasions and confidently sought new relationships. She had learned how to be a good friend, listener, and confidant. She was comfortable being dependent, and everyone liked caring for her. She had long ago overcome stigma, and knew exactly how to handle other's reactions to her. She no longer feared being abandoned by her family, and her anger had long since been redirected into positive energy. She certainly wasn't isolated—her phone rang off the hook. Given what life had dealt her, Anna had coped extremely successfully. She felt loved and supported.

So why was she seeking my help? The answer was clearly the death of her younger sister, Maria. As soon as she began talking about her, Anna's face contorted with pain. Maria had also spent her life in a wheelchair, and the two sisters had been best friends. Now Anna needed help to manage her life, in light of her identification with her sister and the enormous loss that her death represented. Anna knew that her own life span was extremely limited, but her zest for life was so great that she was determined to get through this greatest trauma—facing her own death.

Anna's ego had taken a hit, and my job was to help her regain a sense of control in the face of death—her sister's and her own. I had a lot to work with. Anna had proven over and over that she was an incredible survivor. We needed to build on this solid ego base.

My first task was to help her grieve Maria's death and articulate what it had meant for her. I knew the loss was painful, but almost immediately, I took it further. "What do you want from your own life?" I asked. Time was of the essence, and I didn't waste any. I knew that life was very precious to her. Anna's hope was to continue her current activities for as long as possible with as much vitality as she could muster. I felt confident that I could help her with this goal, and so she came to my office for 10 sessions. We shared a remarkable time together, during which I was able to help her fill the space left vacant by Maria's death.

Anna's mother, Elena, came in for several sessions during those 10 weeks. She was an exceptionally attractive and dynamic person. She had high energy and was unquestionably the source of her children's strength. She had conveyed to them the zest for life Anna displayed—something Elena had in full measure. Her joie de vivre was infectious. Moreover, she had a strong ego, and encouraged her daughters not to fear anything. She described caring for her two disabled daughters without tears or self-pity. She had long before accepted that they would die at an early age. Her task—and certainly she had fulfilled it—was to give them the fullest and happiest lives possible. Indeed, even though she had recently lost one child, her current goal was to keep the others as happy as she could.

Her young son, Antonio, gave her much pleasure. He was healthy, bright, strong, and sensitive to his sisters. She was very close to him and expressed concern about how living with illness would affect him.

Fortunately, Elena and her husband had good financial resources, as well as the ability to recognize and access community programs. She also had household helpers who assisted her in handling her ill daughters' physical needs—bathing, dressing, and so on—and who also provided respite. Elena understood the importance of respite, and felt fortunate to be able to continue working at a part-time job she found enjoyable and meaningful. Like Anna, she was quite sociable, and valued the opportunity to continue her many social contacts that the household help afforded her. The family had managed and coped extremely well, given the daily difficulties they faced.

Like her daughter, she had overcome all eight issues, except this final confrontation with the end. We talked about her future, and the emptiness she would feel after Anna's death. She was extremely realistic. She had been so directed for so many years, she wondered what life would be like for her without her daughters' needs to look after. We crossed that "bridge" soon, for within the year, Anna died, "living life" up to the very last. My treatment objective in this case had been to help both daughter and mother deal with impending death. I was gratified that I was able to do so.

Some patients want to talk to family members about death and a future without them. If they encounter resistance from loved ones who prefer to avoid this painful subject, they may feel extremely isolated. In such cases, the counselor can meet with the caregiver to air the issues privately and determine the feasibility of such a discussion between the caregiver and the patient. If the caregiver continues to be resistant, the counselor can encourage the patient to find others with whom to talk, possibly another relative, a close friend, someone with the same condition, or a spiritual advisor.

The prospect of dying raises many practical issues, and some MCC patients want the counselor's help in addressing them. Resolving practical concerns can clear the way for the investment in living that MCC promotes.

As we saw on pages 53–55, lupus patient Bob Smithson used MCC to help him face death by surveying his important relationships. His worries about how his wife, Sally, would manage without him were put to rest when they identified a support system she could call upon. Bob also reviewed the financial and other practical ramifications of his death, and satisfied himself that Sally could manage without him. Having resolved these concerns and feelings, he turned his full attention to getting the most out of life.

The approaching end of life is an opportunity to clarify priorities and values. The individual seeks a stance that is consistent with his or her sense of self: What is most meaningful about my life? How do I want to be remembered? What do I want to take care of? What can I let go of? Both practical and philosophical explorations, facilitated by the counselor, help the patient stay in control of life until its end.

At her husband's urging, Frances sought MCC treatment as she faced a decision about a second kidney transplant that might prolong her life. In the consultation, she expressed anger and frustration that her family, who insisted that she have the surgery, were denying her right to make this profound decision for herself. It was, after all, her life.

The first step in counseling was to affirm Frances's inalienable right to make this life-and-death decision. This confirmation of her instincts immediately reduced her agitation and enabled us to review her situation more dispassionately. I learned that Frances was weighing conflicting feelings and desires. On the one hand was her reluctance to endure another painful, risky operation; on the other were her desire for relief after a long illness, the impending birth of her first grandchild, and her family's plea

*that she have the surgery—they wanted her to "buy time" for the meaning-
ful life events that lay ahead.*

*Frances used the days between our first two sessions to weigh these
concerns and alternatives. In just one week, she returned to announce that
she had decided to have the surgery. Having a renewed sense of her
decision-making prerogative enabled her to think more clearly about her
own needs. She realized that above all, she wanted to see this grandchild.
If this were impossible, then her legacy to her grandchild would be the
image of her, not as a "coward" but as someone who chose life.*

*MCC emphasized for Frances how she lived, not how long. She re-
gained her sense of integrity, which enabled her and her family to face
with composure the high probability of her death. Despite the danger of
the surgery and the possibility that she would not survive, the month prior
to the transplant was peaceful for Frances and her family. Although Frances did not, in fact, survive the operation, she had lived according to her
values and left the legacy she had chosen.*

When death is a close possibility, some patients begin to detach from
loved ones out of a mistaken, and usually unconscious, assumption that
doing so will protect them or lessen others' sense of loss. They may need
help to recognize this assumption and to reinvest in sustaining relationships.

Another facet of the experience of dying that MCC can facilitate is the
desire of many patients to reexamine their deepest beliefs about death and
life in order to bring their experience and beliefs into harmony. The
counselor can encourage them to look at their experience in the light of
their beliefs—and then possibly to modify and clarify their beliefs so they
are more personally valid: Can they use their philosophical or spiritual
resources to ease this passage? Does their experience lead them to revise
any earlier beliefs that now seem less valid or even harmful? What is the
source of lasting meaning for them? Where do they find comfort and
strength?

Some patients want to consolidate their lives and relationships, their
sadness and regret, their accomplishments and joys. Much of the sadness
associated with dying relates to uncompleted activities and the relationships
that will be ended. The patient may find it helpful to talk about these
anticipated losses. With patients for whom death is imminent, supported
grieving can be a vital step in improving life, by offering a form of closure.
This sense of closure was important to Ellen Suzuki (see p. 83). Although
she labored against powerful emotional and physical odds, in her final

weeks she became more reconciled to the foreshortening of her life, and was able to die in a spirit of celebration with her loved ones.

A final word. In order to help patients and their families deal with dying, the medical crisis counselor must be comfortable with the subject and experience of death. A variety of written materials on bereavement are available to aid the counselor in resolving his or her own feelings about death and cultivating a therapeutic approach with patients and families.[8] There is no substitute, however, for direct experience in this area. If the counselor is fortunate enough not to have experienced the death of a loved one, or if such an experience is unresolved, it would be worthwhile to spend time in the presence of people who routinely cope with this mysterious aspect of life. One possibility is working as a volunteer in a hospice.[9] In my case, personal experience had familiarized me with death, but during my clinical training I sought experience in a hospital burn unit to increase my comfort in the presence of pain and disfigurement.

The Final Session and Treatment Summary

Because of the treatment contract and ongoing tracking of goals, the patient comes to the final session knowing it is the last. The termination has positive significance, because it means that therapy has gone well and the patient has achieved his or her short-term goal. The tone of the final session is therefore upbeat and warm. The patient knows that there is always an option to return for further treatment, as needed.

The final session is the occasion for reviewing what has been covered in counseling, taking stock of insights and accomplishments, and consolidating gains. The counselor can refer to the patient's statements in early sessions as a reminder of the progress that has been made. Together, the counselor and patient review the major insights that have emerged in the course of treatment.

The goals set by the patient in the first session are the primary focus of this final review. This reference point reinforces a well-earned sense of having overcome a central problem. The case illustrations offer some good examples. For Bob and Sally Smithson, the central accomplishment was holding on to their life style and values, even while making life-saving changes. For Terry Fernandez, it was strengthening her sense of self sufficiently to build a wholesome partnership with a man. For Sarah Petrovsky, it was establishing a living arrangement that preserved her dignity, while Ben was released from the perception of having abandoned his spouse.

Marian Davies' central achievement was remobilizing her core personality and talents. Ellen Suzuki's was offering a public expression of love, not anger. The Goldmans learned effective communication that permitted healthy interdependence among husband, wife, children, and professional caregivers.

The objective of the final session, then, is for the patient to complete this brief series of sessions with a clear sense of accomplishment, having consolidated what has been learned. Treatment thus ends as it began, with an emphasis on the patient's strengths.

NOTES

1. See, for example, Golman, D. (1992, December 15). New light on how stress erodes health, *New York Times*, p. C1. Two important studies on the effects of psychosocial intervention on cancer patients are:

• Fawzy, F. et al. (1990). A structured psychiatric intervention for cancer patients. *Archives of General Psychiatry, 47*, 720–735.
• Spiegel, D. et al. (1989, October 14). The beneficial effect of psychosocial treatment on survival of metastatic breast cancer patients: A randomized prospective outcome study. *The Lancet*, 888–891.

2. Cerney, M., & Buskirk, S. (1991). Anger: The hidden part of grief. *Bulletin of the Menninger Clinic, 55*, 228–237.

3. Cerney & Buskirk, 232.

4. Tavris, C. (1982). *Anger: The misunderstood emotion*. New York: Simon & Schuster.

5. Tavris also reminds readers that bad things simply happen for no reason. This subject of random adversity is sensitively addressed in *When Bad Things Happen to Good People*, by Harold Kushner (Avon, 1981).

6. Research is being led by Dr. Lisa Berkman of Yale University Medical School (cited by Goleman, D. (1992, December 15). New light on how stress erodes health. *New York Times*, p. C1).

7. Kiecolt-Glaser, J. (1991). Spousal caregivers of dementia victims: Longitudinal changes in immunity and health. *Psychosomatic Medicine, 53*(4), 345–362.

8. See, for example:

• Koocher, G. (1992). Preventive intervention and family coping with a child's life-threatening or terminal illness. In T. J. Akamatsu et al. (Eds.), *Family health psychology* (p. 67). Washington, DC: Hemisphere.
• Osterweis, M., Solomon, F., & Green, M. (Eds). (1984). *Bereavement: Reactions, consequences, and care.* (A report by the Institute of Medicine.) Washington, DC: National Academy Press.
• Worden, J. (1991). *Grief counseling and grief therapy: A handbook for the mental health practitioner* (2nd ed.). New York: Springer.
• Yalom, I., & Lieberman, M. A. (1991). Bereavement and heightened existential awareness. *Psychology, 54*(4), 334–345.

9. The St. Francis Center in Washington, DC, for example, helps prepare its volunteer "friends" for working with people with serious and terminal illnesses by having them spend a day imagining that it is their last.

CHAPTER FIVE

One Patient's Story

My first knowledge of Lisa Sartorius came as the result of a brief telephone call from her oncologist, Dr. Robert Pomelo. I had received other referrals from this physician and was pleased to hear from him again. We had a comfortable relationship, and he made the referral in an informal manner.

Dr. Pomelo's calls always gladdened me because they underscored his sensitivity to his patients' emotional needs. I had worked hard to encourage that awareness, but this time he had difficulty providing some of the details of Lisa's illness. I surmised this was because she was so young (as was he), and her prognosis was so poor.

Lisa had been diagnosed with breast cancer five years earlier. At that time, she had been treated aggressively and the disease had gone into remission. But now, it had recurred and spread to her bones. She was currently undergoing another round of chemotherapy and, in Dr. Pomelo's view, she was deeply depressed. He asked if I could schedule her as soon as possible.

When I saw Lisa a few days later, I understood Dr. Pomelo's difficulties. Here was a well-dressed, beautiful, blue-eyed woman in her midthirties. Her neatly coiffed blond hair, 5'6" well-proportioned body, and careful grooming bespoke an individual who valued calmness and orderliness. She smiled easily, and her gaze was direct. We established an immediate trust, and I sensed that her physician had prepared her well for this meeting.

A patient's personality, coping abilities and their manifestations, economic and domestic situations, and the quality and quantity of caregiving and support can all influence his or her emotional response to illness. The medical crisis counselor's initial task is to discern and help define which issues are most worrisome to the patient, and then to keep the patient focused on those issues.

Thus, I began the interview with the standard consult questions to learn Lisa's age and a few details of her life. This young, married woman and mother of a three-year-old daughter worked as a secretary in government. Moving quickly into her medical diagnosis, I ascertained the date of her initial diagnosis, her past and current physical symptoms, some particulars regarding her medical treatment, and her overall experience with doctors.

I then asked the single most important question in treatment, "Why are you here?"

Quickly and succinctly, as if she had rehearsed it all in her mind before our session, Lisa replied, "I don't have control over my emotions— especially around my husband, Frank. He bugs me, is irritating, won't listen to me and won't open up. I have friends at work who I can talk to, but more than anything else, I want to be able to talk to Frank. He just won't let me. He puts things on the back burner, and I resent it. Life is short, and I want to enjoy it now."

In a few sentences, Lisa had stated her chief concern: her deteriorating relationship with her husband at the recurrence of cancer. I now knew why she came to see me and, by implication, what she had hoped to accomplish. The one person in her life from whom she desired support and validation had distanced himself from her. She felt overwhelmed and deeply frustrated in her failed attempts to communicate with him. Fortunately, however, she was motivated to correct this problem.

As the interview continued, Lisa's ability to state clearly and concisely her difficulties and her goals impressed me. She had given these issues much thought prior to this visit, and my understanding of them from the outset helped me raise relevant questions to elicit new information and to expand on what she had already revealed. Given her level of self-awareness, I felt Lisa would do well in short-term therapy.

And so I probed further, particularly around the eight issues of chronic illness. I hoped to clarify which she had resolved in the five years since her diagnosis, and which were still a problem for her. This would allow me to focus our sessions on the concerns she was unable to reconcile on her own.

For most patients, certain issues hold more meaning and are expressed more straightforwardly than others. Lisa's experience was typical. She stated some concerns directly, as when she said, "I don't have control over my emotions." She communicated others indirectly, as in, "I never used to be like this," reflecting problems in self-image. Lisa also expressed her dependence issues obliquely when she said, "I used to help other people," implying that now she is the one needing help. She subtly revealed her fear of stigma and her concerns about how others viewed her, saying, "I have several wigs but can't get one to look like my hairstyle." This was not a statement about hairdo but rather about feeling different from others and even disfigured.

When we came to the issue of anger, I discovered that Lisa had directed most of hers toward her physicians and medical treatment. As she described her medical history, I asked how these experiences had affected her emotionally. I hit a nerve. Shaking with emotion, she said, "I finally had to say what was on my mind to my doctors." Clearly, this was difficult for her to do. With tears in her eyes, she said, "I've lost so much time. I could have started chemo a year earlier. Now, I've finally found a doctor who listens."

I discerned that this was a weighty issue for Lisa and planned to return to it in future sessions. In my efforts to keep her focused on the emotional rather than the physical aspects of her illness, I asked if she understood the relationship between stress (from unresolved anger) and physical symptoms. Clearly she did. She had gotten a good start from her experiences in two cancer support groups sponsored by the American Cancer Society — one that she attended soon after the initial diagnosis and one just prior to coming to see me. In fact, Lisa understood that link quite well. She described how her daughter Sylvie's temper tantrums were worsening and becoming increasingly difficult for her to tolerate. As a consequence, she found herself distancing herself from her child, a deep and penetrating loss that she related with a flood of tears.

This was obviously a concern, but I believed it secondary to Lisa's current distress with husband Frank. I planned to discuss Lisa's relationship with Sylvie in future sessions, gently suggesting that we talk more about her daughter at a later date. With Lisa's permission, we returned to our discussion of her marriage. "When did things get so bad at home that you felt you simply couldn't stand it anymore?" I asked.

"The breaking point was last month at a Christmas party with Frank's family," Lisa replied without hesitation. Pursuing the specifics of the current status I asked, "What's happening right now? Last night?"

With a deep sadness in her voice, she replied, "We're drifting apart." And then, revealing some clues to her husband's style of coping she added, "I think he is still denying it" — "it" being the illness and all of its ramifications.

Wishing to keep Lisa in the present I continued, "Why is it so bad at this very moment?"

Her list of complaints was long — Christmas seemed to have been the catalyst. Most of her unhappiness had to do with the lack of emotional support. Her warm and supportive family lived in New Hampshire, and though she was in frequent phone contact with them it did not give her the daily emotional sustenance she required. In contrast, Frank's family, which she described as "cold and unaffectionate," lived nearby but was of little comfort. She also deeply resented the time and attention Frank gave to his widowed mother; he called her daily and spent Sundays performing household chores for her, such as gardening and carpentry. It hurt her to see Frank shower so much loving attention on his mother while being "mean" and hurtful to her. Her longing for this kind of support was obvious.

I wondered what other sources of nurture she had available to her. Friends? Coworkers? I asked Lisa to describe those relationships, and, as I had anticipated, she said, "My boss has been terrific. I can talk to people in my office." She also had many women friends and neighbors in whom she confided. She had been quite wise in reaching out to community resources and attending the cancer support groups.

Remembering these other avenues of support helped lift Lisa's spirits momentarily. She was not as alone as she felt. She also acknowledged how the groups had helped alleviate the sense of isolation that overcame her soon after the diagnosis. Confirming their value, she said, "I felt lost for a year, until I joined an Awareness program." And, indeed, they did help her get through a very difficult period. But now that her disease had progressed, and she was undergoing a second course of chemotherapy and feeling even more physically and emotionally vulnerable with a less optimistic prognosis, she needed more. Besides, all of these outside sources were not the one she longed for with every fiber of her body—the person who shared her life, her husband.

I required several other pieces of information to fully map out the problem. I wanted to establish how Lisa perceived herself prior to her illness, and how Frank had perceived her, so I asked, "How would you describe yourself before your diagnosis?"

In her typically forthright manner, she responded, "I'm one of those amiable people. Also, I keep hanging in there."

I was pleased with this opinion. Being sociable and perseverant ("a survivor") are assets in short-term treatment. Taking advantage of this positive moment, I returned to the subject of stress and cancer; I wanted to hear more about her understanding of the issue. Through her participation in the Cancer Awareness group, Lisa had identified the stressors in her life, including those that had existed prior to her cancer and those that arose as a result of it. She learned that "stress can cause chemical changes in the body," but, unfortunately, she used this information as incriminating evidence against her husband, indicting him for the exacerbation in her illness. "I feel that emotions are the cause of my problem, and I blame him." She concluded that his behavior caused most of her stress. Yet, paradoxically, even as she blamed him, she expressed her fear of his abandonment in statements such as, "He says such mean things to me. We're drifting apart."

Wanting to return to a more positive theme, I asked Lisa to tell me more about her girlfriends and colleagues. I wanted to know how they had been helpful to her.

Now a warm smile crossed her face. She described how wonderful it was to have them available, but still they didn't replace Frank. And interestingly, she added that she received such warm support from others because she was "not the kind of person who goes around feeling sorry for myself."

Lisa was oblivious to the importance of these words. Her coworkers' and friends' lives were not intertwined with hers, their futures were only to a small degree, if at all, determined by her illness. They could be supportive and loving without a deep personal commitment. She expected and demanded less from them and was more appreciative of any thoughtfulness they showed her. By contrast, she required unconditional love and complete attention from her husband. She felt that he "owed" her. She was unaware of how demanding she had become when, prior to her illness, she had been more easygoing.

In this session, Lisa had revealed much information that would be useful for the future. But before we moved on, I wanted her to begin thinking about the changes in her and her husband's behavior since the diagnosis. I asked, "When did you notice a change in Frank's behavior?"

"After the recurrence, he began treating me mean," she said. There was a contradiction here. Earlier, Lisa attributed the return of her illness to Frank's meanness, but now she asserted that the cancer gave rise to his negative attitude. This is an example of some of the irrational thinking that can occur when a patient is extremely anxious. However, since we were just establishing trust, I believed it would have been unwise for me to confront her on this point just yet; we would deal with it later.

As Lisa continued, she unwittingly described her own demanding behavior. "I make him pick me up at the doctor's and other places," she admitted, "but he says he has better things to do with his time." During this portion of the interview, Lisa displayed a deep sadness and some gentle crying. These were difficult issues for her to talk about, yet she continued, and so did I.

After describing the changes in Frank, she began revealing how she had changed. She heard herself saying how she had "made" him do certain things, and she reflected on how she had become more demanding. To confirm what she was already alluding to, I asked, "Are you doing anything differently now than you did before you got sick?"

Lisa now became defensive, protecting her rights as a "sick" person. "He used to control me with a look, but not any more," she said. "I have to put my health first." The changes in Lisa's behavior were becoming clearer to her, but she was still unaware that her husband had noted and responded to them. This was an important piece of information. Ultimately, Lisa would have to recognize the changes (and their causes) that she and her husband had made as a result of the illness. When she fully understood the altered dynamics of their relationship, she would have met the goal of treatment.

"How do you think all this happened?" I wondered out loud.

With renewed energy, she responded, "We created a monster. Before my illness, I did what the 'good little wife' should do."

I was glad that Lisa was finally taking some responsibility for her behavior in this volatile dynamic. Certainly, the blame did not rest completely with her husband. Wishing now to sharpen the treatment goals, I returned to the subject of Frank. "If you could have your wish come true," I asked, "how would you like Frank to act toward you now?"

And without a moment's hesitation, she replied, "Not to say mean things to me!"

This statement revealed Lisa's profound vulnerability and her dependence on Frank's love and approval. His angry response to her demands caused her deep emotional pain. As she reflected inwardly on how hard she had tried to improve this situation, outwardly she wondered, "Is it really worth a fight?" But then, in the next breath, she answered herself, "But I want to get it out!" She needed to vent her feelings about the breakdown of their communication.

Lisa's determination to invest in living was clearly part of what had brought her into treatment. Her desire to make the most of her life was her way of dealing with her fear of dying. "I want to live now, enjoy now!" she repeated in an almost mantra-like fashion. For Lisa, living meant having a loving and close relationship with her husband and daughter again, in whatever time she had left.

Grieving for her past life, she added, "We had such a beautiful life." This statement confirmed her determination to once again find joy in her life and to "have fun."

Continuing in this vein, she explained that she was trying to educate Frank in case something happened to her. This stemmed from her need to share with him her anxiety about their daughter's fate upon her death, her urge to control the future as much as possible, her desire to recognize and confirm that she was, indeed, dying, and her wish to elicit her husband's attention and sympathy.

By now, our interview was coming to an end. It was time to attain closure. Having listened for the eight issues, in the course of the hour, I had identified Lisa's primary concerns. She had resolved the issues of dependence and isolation by returning to work and joining support groups. She had overcome her fear of stigma by surrounding herself with supportive colleagues and friends and by taking care of how she presented herself to the world. In seeking treatment, she had already begun to face her fear of dying. Her major unresolved issues were control, self-image, abandonment, and anger. That's where our work would concentrate if she agreed to come into treatment.

I told Lisa that, based on what we had discussed, I felt she would do well in short-term counseling. I noted that she had clearly expressed her goal — improving her relationship with her husband — and that was a major factor in successful treatment.

Lisa understood this premise and made a commitment to medical crisis counseling. She then declared, "I am going to lay off my husband. I'm going to have fun!" Lisa had already begun to regain hope, and with that, a sense of control over her life.

Lisa was comfortable in treatment from the very outset. Talking came naturally to her, and she began our second session describing a pleasant, lighthearted lunch with a friend the previous day. This gave her the opportunity to relate her friend's reassuring remarks about Frank's feelings. So, even though we were yet to embark on solving Lisa's marital problems, she was beginning on a positive and hopeful note.

Using this opening to go directly into the heart of the problem, I asked, "Do you think, in any way, that anything you say or do could cause Frank to react so strongly and so negatively?"

"Maybe I was trying to force him," Lisa admitted, as though she had already considered this possibility. "I was afraid he would leave me. I know I felt like leaving." But then, considering why she had acted in this destructive manner, she continued, "I can only do this so many times." She began to understand that some of her behavior had provoked a strong reaction from her husband, and that caused her deep pain.

Wishing to continue this line of thought and expression of feelings, I asked, "How bad does it get between you and Frank. Give me some examples."

Choking with strong emotions and fighting back her tears and embarrassment, she described what she called "one of my worst experiences." She and Frank were in bed, and he couldn't make love to her.

Gently, I probed further. "Do you have any idea why this happened?"

With her hands visibly shaking, she replied, "Because of my bald head." This was her perception. "He jumped out of bed," she continued, "and screamed, 'To hell with you! I shouldn't have to pretend.'" Soon after that, he began sleeping in their daughter's room.

But Lisa had not given up hope. She still wanted Frank to talk to her. She persisted in believing that if they could communicate, everything would be alright again between them. She reiterated her desire to know "what he really thinks. . . . If only we could. . . . If he would just open up to me," she said wistfully.

Once she had admitted that Frank was consciously avoiding her, I asked, "Do you have any idea why?"

Retreating a bit, Lisa answered, "No." She felt that she "looked good."

I had to agree. Observing this very attractive woman sitting across from me, I felt her appearance was not the problem. But perhaps attractiveness had a special meaning to Lisa. I asked, "What did you think of the way you looked before your diagnosis?"

Lisa admitted that physical appearance had always been especially important to her. In fact, she had always had a "fat self-image." It had made her feel inferior, "but not stupid," she added. She switched from describing what had been a negative in her life to her positive attributes, and in particular, to her skills at her job. She was proud that she had worked for one man for five years. She liked her boss very much and had learned a great deal from him.

Picking up on this theme, I asked Lisa to tell me what she considered to be her best skill, and without hesitation she responded, "Being organized, but in the government they don't want you to think!" She obviously enjoyed telling me about this satisfying part of her life. Unfortunately, she learned too late that she was bright. Her high school education had limited her opportunities for advancement.

Lisa's revelation of her competence as an organizer proved useful later in treatment. But for now, I wished to keep the focus on her physical self-image as well as give her an opportunity to vent her feelings about the changes that the cancer had caused. And so I said, "Tell me how you felt after the recurrence."

With deep sadness, she began to relate some of her intense feelings. "I felt terrible. I put on weight, and my hair came out right away. Even my scalp hurt. I didn't want to take a shower. I was shedding like a dog." She described her feelings in terms of her drastically altered physical appearance. Having seen how meticulously Lisa dressed and groomed herself for her sessions, I understood how important and painful these changes were to her. "I thought I lost my personality," she added.

And in a way, she had. It became increasingly clear that appearance was not only an important factor in Lisa's relationship with Frank—it was also the very basis for it. She explained how difficult it was for both of them when she started to wear a wig. "I have several," she said, "but I can't get one to look like my hairstyle. . . . When I started wearing a wig, Frank couldn't look at me."

Lisa then explained that she had once pressed Frank to tell her his true feelings about her appearance. He complied, saying, "Lisa, I can't handle your bald head."

Lisa had finally gotten a straight answer from her husband—the truth, which she had so wanted—but it was painful for her. Indeed, she was deeply hurt, having understood him to say that he was repulsed by her physical unattractiveness. In truth, however, as I learned in a very important single session with Frank the following week, he hated seeing his beloved and beautiful wife looking so bad.

Nevertheless, Lisa showed her resourcefulness and resilience by attending a self-image class. She had been unable to do this when she was first diagnosed and struggling with the idea of having cancer.

Because of what Lisa had described as Frank's impotence in their bedroom, I wished to gain more detail regarding their past and current sexual relations. And so I asked Lisa to describe their sex life before and after the illness.

I was surprised when she answered, "We never had a great one." Given the importance of appearance to this couple, I had assumed that their relationship included a strong sexual element. What, then, was the meaning of their diminished physical contact? I suggested the possibility that increased psychological stress for both of them had reduced their sexual interest. That only brought a tentative "no" from Lisa. She needed to think about this possibility some more.

Lisa groped for the source of her stress. "First I blamed the pill, and then the fact that I took shots to stop the flow of breast milk." But as she continued on this vein, I knew these questions would never be answered. I also felt Lisa had never disclosed these thoughts to anyone. Despite her need to discuss the truth with her husband, she now revealed, "I keep everything in."

As a result of this admission, I was able to read Lisa's "need to talk" statements differently. This desire stemmed from her wish to allay and reduce her own anxiety. She was hoping to change a part of her behavior that she thought might be harmful to her. Lisa felt that she had learned a lot about handling stress and that much was "self-created." But now, rather than just blaming her husband, she took responsibility for creating her own stress. She could not give up the idea of the pills and the lactation shots, but this was an exercise in futility. She could not undo these decisions, she could not feel resolved about them, and she was left with the resultant stress.

Wishing to shift Lisa's focus to an area in which she could effect some change, I asked her about her relationship with her daughter, Sylvie. "Tell me what's happening now," I said.

It was difficult for Lisa to discuss this painful situation. She adored her little girl. They had been extremely close but, as Lisa related it, it was she who had moved away. And now she regretted it. "I don't know what to do about it," she said.

She spoke bleakly as she reflected on their old relationship. "Until the recurrence, I loved taking care of Sylvie, teaching her, taking her shopping. It's not the same anymore. And when she acts out, I can't even seem to discipline her. The other day, she kicked her grandmother in the leg!"

Rather than being a source of joy and comfort, one of Lisa's most precious relationships was causing her intense emotional pain. I knew that we could correct this problem and began immediately to do so.

"What do you think has happened between you and Sylvie?" I asked.

Fighting back tears, Lisa said, "I've turned a lot of Sylvie's care over to Frank. Now he's the one who undresses her at night and reads to her in bed. And he's the one who makes her breakfast in the morning and drops her off at nursery school." Her voice dropped to a whisper. "I thought she might as well get closer to the parent who's going to be around."

Selfless Lisa was unwittingly giving up her precious, limited time with her daughter to make sure that a close relationship developed between father and daughter after her death. But, in an attempt to avoid the grief associated with this anticipated loss, Lisa had also decathected from the person she loved most. In the hopes of assuaging some of her family's pain, she was sacrificing her need for this warm, loving, satisfying relationship.

Lisa needed reassurance that her behavior was perfectly normal. "It's quite common to pull back under such painful circumstances," I explained. "But, you're also giving up precious, satisfying time with your daughter—moments that are the source of joy and sustenance for you. You need to reclaim your role with Sylvie not only for yourself but also for your daughter. In that way, she will always remember you as wonderful, rather than cold and distant. In fact, she may feel hurt and angry that you're staying away from her."

As Lisa listened, her eyes filled with tears. But I offered her hope and practical suggestions. "There's no reason you can't go back to doing what you used to," I said. "And you can begin as soon as you get home." This inspired a litany of activities that Lisa and Sylvie could immediately pursue.

Wishing to use the last minutes of the session to bring the self-image issue into sharper focus, I then asked, "How is this bout with cancer different from the first one?"

Lisa knew that I was referring to her and Frank's emotional responses. Yet, again, she answered in terms of physical appearance. "Frank hates my bald head." This constant reference to her hair seemed a shallow response, but I viewed it as a symbol for the basis for their marriage. Since she and Frank both believed their relationship was about appearance, and, given her reconstructed breast her appearance could never be what it once was, their union was almost completely shattered.

Grieving these losses, Lisa reflected, "We were the perfect couple. I was so proud of the way we looked together. We have the same coloring. He dresses well, and his voice sounds like a radio announcer's. And Frank always liked the way I looked. He knew that I worked to keep up my appearance to please him. I always watched my weight and had my hair done. When we got married, Frank told me never to wear rollers to bed, and if I ever got fat, he would divorce me." Then she added that Frank once told her, "'The guys notice you, and I feel proud of that.'"

Now, all of the values they both shared were threatened. She was helpless to change her baldness or her scarred, misshapen breast. She could hide these flaws in public, but not from Frank. His earlier remarks resounded clearly in her head. Except for his admission that he couldn't handle her baldness, he had never discussed with her his feelings about her physical changes, and he responded with real anger when she pressed him. Given this volatile situation, she feared he would leave her—and in a sense he already had, by sleeping in their daughter's room.

At this very low point in our session, though, Lisa remembered an incident from the previous week. She had again pressured him to speak about his feelings, and this time he did answer, however briefly. Responding to her less threatening tone this time, he said calmly and directly. "But Lisa, I never talked *before*."

I could see that counseling was beginning to work. Lisa could ask the old, angry question in a new, more relaxed way. In the coming weeks, I hoped to help Lisa see more clearly that, like her, Frank was also under extreme stress. He was trying to cope in his own way; when she continually prodded him to "talk," she was asking him to behave in a manner that was totally new and foreign to him.

We ended the session reviewing briefly what we had discussed and what Lisa planned to do during the following week, particularly with her daughter, Sylvie.

Based on the consult and this session, I sent brief case notes to Dr. Pomelo, the referring oncologist. In three paragraphs, I described how our patient appeared during the consult, referring to the issues we covered in the session and Lisa's decision to enter MCC. I wrote that she had left the consult feeling "vastly relieved," and in the second appointment she had reported "sleeping better and feeling somewhat better." I told him which issues we would expand on and thanked him for this excellent referral. I promised to keep him apprised of Lisa's progress.

The following week I met with Frank. Lisa had wanted him to see me, and he had resisted. But, finally, he agreed to one session, which proved to be invaluable for our work.

Frank's resistance was rather typical of many spouses who fear that they will be attacked by the therapist, or that the therapist will try to change them. But I was able to convince Frank that I understood his pain and frustration. These feelings were normal. I gave him support for his difficult situation, and he was grateful.

I learned much from this single session. Most importantly, I learned that Frank loved Lisa deeply. He avoided her because he couldn't bear to see her suffer. He didn't consider her ugly or unattractive—he just couldn't look at the scars on her body or the loss of her beautiful hair. He had a hard time "talking" because he couldn't bear the prospect of losing Lisa and the possibility of raising their child without her. Lisa's pressure to know his intimate thoughts and fears only compounded his need for avoidance.

And even though he refrained from expressing his feelings, he was as distraught as she was.

Frank was uninterested in counseling for himself, but I explained to him that his coming in was quite valuable in helping the situation. Without violating confidentiality, I was able to use the insights gleaned from this meeting to help Lisa understand his point of view.

At the next session with Lisa, she greeted me with the satisfying news that her relationship with Sylvie was back on track. She had resumed some of their former activities, and was enjoying their relationship more than ever.

But as she gave me this positive news, she also confided that she believed her medical treatment was having minimal effect. Although she didn't state it directly, she feared the possibility of dying. She expressed this fear by telling me that she and her family—particularly her mother—had been discussing alternative methods of treatment, including visiting faith healers.

When I asked her how she felt about this, she replied that she didn't believe in healers but was trying other methods such as acupuncture and nutrition.

But, even though Lisa dismissed faith healers, she did have some religious concerns. In particular, she feared not being "saved." Indeed, when I asked her to write out for me her worst fears, "Not being saved" topped the list. "If I don't believe that I will be saved," she said, "I won't make it." (Her other fears involved physical symptoms and what they might mean: the pain in her neck and leg, the specter of being crippled, doubts about the efficacy of chemotherapy.)

Listing these fears allowed Lisa to express her darkest thoughts as well as give them some distance and perspective. Still, her basic fear of not being saved arose from her fundamentalist upbringing. And whereas her mother and sister were urging her to come back into the fold, her husband's Catholic family was pushing her in another direction. Caught between these conflicting religious viewpoints, Lisa, when questioned, stated, "I don't believe in either one."

I asked her to tell me what she did believe in, and she explained that she had a strong belief in God, but not in the rituals of either religion. And, since she seemed on the edge of discovering where she stood, I suggested the name of a young Catholic priest for further discussion. (In fact, Lisa did meet with him, and resolved her beliefs, much to her relief.)

Once again, Lisa returned to the theme of the lost "beautiful life" that she and Frank had enjoyed prior to her illness, and we closed the session with a much clearer sense of how she would deal with the pressures from both families, and how she would come to an understanding of God on her own terms. From this confrontation with dying, Lisa achieved a sense of peace that lasted till her death. She knew how she would cope with her final hours.

I continued to see Lisa weekly over the next two months, and eventually, we moved to monthly sessions. Throughout our time together, we continued to examine the eight issues, concentrating on those that were still unresolved.

As the weeks went by, dependency became a non-issue for Lisa, although she still would have wanted someone—particularly her husband—to give her unconditional love and attention. But, with therapy, she came to realize that Frank was doing the best he could. Lisa resolved her feelings of isolation through her own resourcefulness. Relatively early in her treatment, she took more control over her life—she had only to decide how she wanted to handle her strained relationships. Her fear of abandonment persisted, but to a lesser degree, and she came to terms with her fear of death as I described above. What remained were self-image and anger, and eventually even the self-image issues diminished in the face of her anger and the imminence of death.

Lisa's anger constantly resurfaced and was almost solely directed toward the one person whom she needed the most to be kind, gentle, and compassionate toward her. Her anger was becoming ever more self-destructive as she became increasingly emotionally vulnerable. She vented much of it during our sessions, but she still had to recognize what was provoking it, and who was suffering most from it.

The home situation had deteriorated. "We're constantly fighting, and I'm getting fed up," she explained. Frank even met her simple requests, such as turning on the air conditioning, with negativity, saying he was unwilling to pay the $300 it would cost to run it. He continued to tune her out and had not returned to their bedroom. Feeling desperate, she said, "I'm tired of it. I'm not going to live this way. I'm not going to live an unhappy life." The stress had become unbearable for her.

We needed a breakthrough. The current behavior patterns were causing Lisa deep distress. In hope of alleviating her suffering, I felt it might be wise for her to change the relationship or shift her need for support to someone else. And so I asked, "Why is Frank the one person you want to talk to?"

Her reasoning was simple. "Because I'm living with him. I'll never give up trying to reach him. Still, he's there but he's not there" – physically but certainly not emotionally. And again she cried for their old relationship. "We used to have a charmed life. We had goals and hopes and dreams. We have nothing now. Once we were close but now we're like strangers."

Now I was feeling frustrated. Lisa had a much clearer understanding of her problems and had, in fact, resolved a number of them. But, the conflict within her relationship with her husband – the primary goal of her treatment – seemed intractable.

Part of the problem stemmed from Lisa's limited perspective on the marriage. Even though she had related what had been important to them prior to her illness, she could not fully recognize that what had brought them together – their attractive physical appearance – could no longer bind them. In fact, this priority was now an obstacle.

Lisa continued to fear that Frank could not adjust to her diminished attractiveness, and she knew that no matter how hard she tried, she could never make it right again. Lisa had devoted her life to pleasing Frank. By her own account, she had "blindly" idolized him. But now, when she needed support from him other than his approval of her appearance, she felt he was not forthcoming. Her curtain of admiration had come crashing down, making all of his weaknesses glaringly evident. He was not the man she thought he was. Lisa was filled with disappointment and frustrated needs. Things seemed to have reached "rock bottom."

Yet, as so often happens in the therapeutic process, when the patient touches the nadir, great progress – the result of all the hard work that came before – can occur. And that event, acting like a catalyst, can bring about change.

Lisa was able to use what she had learned to achieve just such a breakthrough. One day, she strode into my office with a copy of a letter she had written to Frank and right away reported that the situation at home had improved.

Lisa's letter was remarkable, particularly in its clear, direct, and non-threatening tone. She opened by telling Frank what she had learned about herself in therapy – that there were things worse than death, like not seeing their three-year-old grow up. She was determined to "live and enjoy life" now.

Most importantly, she took responsibility for her own provocative behavior. "I know I am more sensitive than usual," she wrote. She then explained that this extra sensitivity came as the result of her having to cope with cancer.

She described specifically what it was like to live with the disease—the pain and diminished energy. She pointed out how difficult all of it has been for her, how depressing were the obstacles that the illness presented. She explained how she helped herself by returning to work and gave herself credit for handling the challenge as well as she did.

She then wrote about what she needed from him. She wanted to be close to him again, to set goals as they once had, to act once more like a team. And praising, rather than blaming him, she told him how much she appreciated his help around the house and with Sylvie.

Then, with great clarity, Lisa pinpointed what was stressful for her in their relationship. She could not control the fact that her reduced vigor had limited her activities and she did not wish to feel guilty about having cancer. It was taking all of her energy just to survive. Frank's complaints about her limitations were distressing to her. These statements were a result of the reflection she had engaged in during her sessions.

The letter closed with Lisa's explanation of why she went into counseling. It was "to help us, not just me." She continued, "I needed to understand what we're going through, and now I understand that you are angry about the cancer and that's why you lose your temper."

Finally, she asked that they discuss their feelings with a new awareness. "My life is too short to be spent under stress," she wrote. "A person's outlook on life changes drastically with cancer. You learn to live each day, to find beauty and enjoy it. You learn not to live too far in the future. Each day I have to deal with the reality of my life and with what cancer has done to me and my family. It hurts me deeply when I think how it has driven us apart." Lisa clearly laid the blame where it belonged, on her cancer.

Then she expressed her hope that she and Frank could "be happy, communicate, and work together. In this way, we can still have a fantastic life, the charmed life we once thought we had."

Lisa was investing the resources at her disposal into making her life as positive as possible. She enlisted Frank's participation, but did not allow her sense of well-being to depend on it. This was a major step forward.

August 11 marked Lisa's last visit to my office; I planned to summarize her treatment. We reviewed Lisa's accomplishments and used some of her new insights to prepare for an unpleasant course of chemotherapy that would take place in two weeks. I particularly wanted her to be clear on what she had achieved. She offered an apt summary: "I'm learning to tune into myself more"—rather than into Frank or his family.

I reviewed the link between mind and body, her new insights, as well as techniques she had developed to reduce stress. She had learned to identify her problems and what to do about them. I reinforced the idea that without that insight, it is difficult to sustain the techniques for addressing them. (For example, if she felt depressed, she needed to know why in order to take action.)

Offering an example of her progress, Lisa told me that she no longer waited for Frank to help her with household tasks. Having recognized the frustration and anger that his inaction aroused in her, she began avoiding these reactions by doing more for herself. With this simple decision, she had taken more control of her life and had thereby reduced her anxiety and depression. She had also begun avoiding stressful arguments and hurtful words. "Frank is beginning to be very good to me," she added. That pleased us both greatly.

I continued to drive home the point that Lisa deserved credit for these changes in behavior. "You are making the plans," I told her. "You are in control of your life once more. You need never again feel that 'this is out of my hands and there's nothing I can do about it.' There *is* something you can do, and, in fact, you're doing it." In anticipating stressful events, she was planning alternative solutions. This "planning" derived from her competence as an "organizer" and fit her coping style perfectly. Indeed, she did not have to learn a new coping style—she was doing what came naturally to her.

Eagerly, she added, "I now recognize how I deal with things. Before, I didn't even know what I was depressed about."

As Lisa shared this valuable insight, I decided she was ready to move to a specific application. I wanted to help her plan for the upcoming treatment. And so I asked, "What are you going to be depressed about in two weeks?"

Her response was right on target: "I have to take my chemotherapy, and I hate it. I'm sick of it, but I've decided that I've got to do something to handle it. That's why I've come up with this plan." Her strategy was to come home after the treatment and sleep for the afternoon. The following day, instead of staying home, she would work in the morning and rest at home in the afternoon. "That will make me feel better," she said.

Wishing her to understand and remember the process she had just utilized, I reiterated it in my own words: "You know that you're going to feel better when you take the steps that you plan, and you also know why you're doing it. You are," and Lisa chimed in at that point, "in control." Continuing, I reemphasized, "there may be a lot that you can't do anything about, but as much as possible, within your power, you will control this."

To further emphasize this point, I pressed Lisa to consider more aspects of the upcoming treatment from the point of view of a worst case scenario. "What if you don't feel well enough to go to work in the morning?" I asked. "Can you anticipate how you would feel about that?"

"I would be depressed," Lisa replied, "but I've made up my mind that I won't let it happen. I usually feel better when I dress up and put on my makeup."

I continued to press her. "But what if that morning comes around and you find that you're weaker than you expected? You even get partially dressed, but then you say, 'I just can't make it.' What then?"

Lisa was unhappy about my pushing her on this extremely unpleasant point. But then she responded, "I could try going to the office in the afternoon."

I explained why I took her though this painful exercise and I congratulated her. Rather than falling apart in a highly stressful situation, she had thought of other options. Indeed, I called her attention to her positive response: "Instead of saying, 'Oh well, I'm going to sit down and cry,' you came up with an alternative plan."

Picking up on my point, she continued, "I'm giving myself more time to get myself together. I sort of push myself." Again I applauded her on how she took charge of difficult situations and came up with workable solutions, rather than feel frustrated and depressed.

And finally, I heard what all therapists hope to hear at some point in the treatment process. "I think it's going to work out," Lisa said. "I feel positive about it. I feel good that I decided this." Her hard work had paid off.

Continuing our discussion of control, I said, "When someone has cancer and is going through chemotherapy like you are, he or she usually feels out of control. You can't anticipate how you will feel. The doctor has a plan, but the patient doesn't know it. The patient is left feeling suspended . . . "

"Like you're fighting in a paper bag filled with air," she interjected.

"But anticipating this dreaded event gives you some control over the situation. You're able to control whatever is in your power to control. You're not fighting the treatment (because it's so scary), but rather going with it. You're not running from the unknown but facing it with a plan that can make it better."

"And easier," she added.

Wanting her to see the broader implications of this behavior, and in response to her earlier assertion that she hated chemotherapy and dreaded going through with it, I continued, "You're not resisting the doctor's protocol or the medication. Mentally and physically, you are flowing with the procedures. You are riding on the wave, rather than pushing against it with a build-up of negative feelings."

Continuing on this high note, Lisa conveyed how different weekends had become for her and Frank. "Sitting around at home isn't relaxing for me," she said. "So I decided to take matters into my own hands, and arrange activities for us."

"Why haven't you been doing anything till now?" I asked.

"I realized just last week that before I got sick, I had always planned our recreational activities," Lisa explained. "If I didn't plan, we didn't go. So, Saturday night, I took charge again and we went to a movie. Sunday morning, we enjoyed a relaxed brunch. I hadn't recognized that I had been waiting for Frank to take over. And, when he didn't, I felt angry and frustrated. Now that I'm doing this again, life is better for me, and really for both of us. And that's exactly what I wanted to get out of therapy—a better life."

I wanted Lisa to understand how these new insights came about; I wanted to show her her accomplishments. "You become very relaxed when you have a plan," I pointed out. "That's your way of coping. A plan not only gives you something to look forward to, but also relieves your anxiety. Waiting for Frank to make decisions just frustrates you."

Confirming my statement, Lisa added, "He bugs me when he won't make a decision, and I just sit around and wait. That gets on my nerves."

Repeating her statement to imprint it in her memory, I said, "You not only relieve your frustration, anxiety, stress, and anger when you make plans, but you also derive a great deal of pleasure from it. And so, it seems, does Frank."

I wanted to increase the likelihood that Lisa would use this technique to reduce some of the stress related to her upcoming chemotherapy protocol, so I asked, "How long will the treatments last?"

"The doctor hasn't told me," Lisa admitted, "and I haven't asked."

I knew why she had avoided the issue, but I felt it best to confront it directly with her, so I asked, "Why?"

"I think about it," she replied, "but when you're stuck with it anyway, why ask? I hate dates. I find that I get very uptight and stressed when I think about it."

I was encouraging Lisa to consider in advance how badly she would feel, and to plan for it, while she was hoping to avoid thinking about this issue altogether. My questions gave her the opportunity to talk in greater detail about her feelings related to chemotherapy, and how much harder this course would be than the first one.

Wishing her to continue expressing her feelings about the impending therapy, I asked, "How often do you have to go for the treatments?"

Now that she was considering a real event rather than a fantasized one, she observed, "Well, maybe depression is playing a part in my feeling sick. Having a plan should help."

I believed that her newfound ability to separate the mental aspects of her illness from the physical would help her adjustment. We reviewed her ability to distinguish medicated from nonmedicated states. I rehearsed with her the plan: the duration and disabling nature of her tiredness and her strategies for staying home or going to work.

When she finished with this seemingly endless exercise, she said aloud to herself, "Okay Lisa, this time you know what's bugging you. You're going to have to change things." Then, still continuing to herself, "So I went in and found myself so much better. I came home rested, and it made the evening easier for me, too. Maybe the next time, I'll find out I'll do even better."

Several months elapsed before I saw Lisa again. This time I visited her in her suburban home because she was too weak to come to my office. I met her mother-in-law, who greeted me with a grunt, but I was glad to see Lisa cheerful on the phone, talking with her many friends and neighbors.

About a month later, Frank called, informing me that Lisa had died. A few weeks after that, he came to my office, asking for a referral to Parents Without Partners. He felt the group would help him during this transition period. Lisa had taught him something about coping.

In summary, Lisa obtained from MCC what she had sought: better and less stressful relationships with her husband and daughter during the final moments of her life. She had struggled with all eight issues, and was able to resolve a number of them on her own. Treatment focused on those she could not ameliorate alone: control, self-image, abandonment, and anger.

At the completion of treatment, Lisa had regained a sense of control over her life. She had learned to recognize and respect the great differences between her coping style and her husband's. She had reduced her stress considerably by returning to her former style of managing – planning for herself rather than feeling furious at Frank for constantly disappointing her. Her self-image was restored when she learned that he still thought her beautiful and that his avoidance was linked to his pain at seeing her suffering and anticipating his eventual loss—not to an aversion to her.

She also learned not to press her husband for more intimate self-expression than he was capable of, and that the calmer and more accepting she was of Frank, the calmer and more accepting he was of her. She knew who she was and what she believed in.

As her anxiety lessened, she was able to develop her own strategies. The letter she wrote to Frank—an excellent example of these self-generated strategies—became the catalyst to the treatment process. She undertook this letter entirely on her own initiative. What she had processed in therapy now emerged as clear, nonthreatening statements that her husband could accept about her needs and feelings. Their relationship improved markedly after that turning point. We had reached our goal.

CHAPTER SIX

The Family

It is not unusual for the question of definitions to arise in contemporary discussions of the family. Families today are often self-defined, and that is a useful approach for this book. The reader or clinician, and ultimately the patient, should use his or her own notion of family in applying the concepts presented here. A broad definition of family involves some combination of kinship, shared living arrangements, intimacy, continuity, mutual support, and/or a commitment to caregiving. In the context of medical crisis counseling, caregiving and ongoing mutual support are key elements.

The family's ability to support and care for the medical patient, balance conflicting demands, and integrate the illness into family life is one of the major determinants of the medical patient's quality of life, and quite possibly even a factor in his or her survival. Family members sustain life-affirming family activities and provide companionship and support. They may have to devise special housing and transportation arrangements. They may be responsible for carrying out or enforcing treatment regimens, possibly ones with life-or-death ramifications.

THE FAMILY AND MEDICAL CRISIS COUNSELING

For these reasons, the family is almost always a player in MCC, whether or not it ever comes "on stage." Family relationships are a central concern for people with chronic illness, and many of the issues they must address arise and are played out in the arena of family life. Medical patients may worry about causing hardship for the family and struggle with a welter of other emotions such as anger, resentment, and guilt. A key aspect of MCC is helping the patient sustain or improve crucial family relationships. The counselor plays a strategic role in cultivating empathy, enhancing communication, and reinforcing coping capacities in the family. This is true regardless of how many members of the chronically ill person's family, if any, are seen in treatment.

A good deal of family work is accomplished through the medical patient. The family orientation begins in the consultation. The initial interview includes several questions regarding the family (see Table 3.2, page 43). Information-gathering and problem-solving on family matters continue throughout treatment. Role-playing is often used, a significant objective of which is to prepare the patient for encounters with family members. Typical scenarios are initiating a difficult conversation topic, explaining feelings, and asking for a particular change in attitude or behavior. Whenever possible, MCC encourages patients to take the lead in helping their families adapt to the illness, modeling for others by being as honest and direct as possible. Because the reality of the illness seldom, if ever, leaves the medical patient, he or she may reach a state of acceptance before others do.

The issues of dependency and abandonment that arise for virtually all medical patients explicitly concern their relationship with the informal caregiver, who is probably a family member. The medical crisis counselor teaches patients to watch for the warning signs of burnout in their caregivers, and to give them "permission" to seek respite. (Warning signs of burnout include being more irritable or emotional, falling ill more frequently, or having more trouble communicating with the medical patient than previously.)

Primary caregiving responsibility usually falls to one member of the family, and most people in this position are initially eager to provide needed care. As time passes, however, they may find themselves exhausted and even resentful of the demands on their time and energy. Family caregivers receive little attention and sympathy from professionals and friends, and regrettably few guides exist to help family members develop their caregiving capacities and accept their limitations.[1] Eventually, family members may find themselves feeling resentful of the intrusion on their lives, guilty for having such feelings, and fearful that the medical patient will sense their resentment. The physical and emotional stress to which caregivers are subjected puts them at greater risk of disease.[2] A caregiver's downward cycle of exhaustion and despair can actually bring about the very specters most feared by the medical patient, such as emotional or physical abandonment.

For all of these reasons, targeted professional intervention can make a crucial difference in a family's adjustment to serious illness. My experience suggests that the medical crisis counselor can expect one-third to one-half of his or her patients to be family members, usually the principal caregiver.

SOCIAL FACTORS

The social trends affecting the modern family take an especially heavy toll on families with a chronically ill member. Few people in this country have the benefit of an extended family that shares caregiving responsibilities. Family size is shrinking, as is the number of families living near relatives, thereby depriving medical patients and caregivers of traditional sources of support. Roughly half of all marriages end in divorce, removing a potential caregiver from many households. In a majority of two-parent families, both adults work outside the home so there is no one at home to provide care during the day. Having one breadwinner remain at home as either a patient or a caregiver places a severe additional financial burden on the other. One thing that has not changed, however, is that women continue to carry the major caregiving burden, even if they also work outside the home; men are twice as likely as women to have a spouse as a caregiver.[3]

At the same time that the family's caregiving capabilities are diminishing, the demands on it by the health care system are increasing. The life-saving advances in medical technology that are lengthening people's lives are also placing the burden of care ever more heavily on the family. The American Medical Association reports that for every patient in a nursing home, three severely impaired patients are being cared for at home.[4] As has already been mentioned, 70 to 95 percent of caregiving takes place in the informal sector—generally, of course, by family members.[5] The burden on the family may increase even further as cost containment efforts further reduce hospitalization. Patients are being discharged sooner after procedures—some call it "quicker and sicker"—and many policy makers and families regard home care as a desirable alternative to nursing homes. "Who cares for the caregiver?" is one of the large unanswered questions to be faced by future policymakers.

ADJUSTMENT ISSUES

Chronic illness affects the entire family. Family members contend with the same eight issues that the patient does: control, self image, dependency, stigma, abandonment, anger, isolation, and death. As they address these issues, families carry out tasks in four interacting dimensions: interpersonal relations, practical problem-solving and managing, emotional processing, and cognitive work. Families vary as to which of these tasks is most challenging.

Interpersonal relations are probably the most obvious dimension of family life; family members continuously struggle to maintain intimacy and mutual support. Besides strengthening their communication and coping skills for new challenges, they must reconcile members' differing coping styles and developmental needs and levels. There is a complex and sensitive balancing act among the needs of each member, those of the family as a whole, and those of the ill person. Each person's aspirations and developmental tasks do not disappear simply because a member of the family is ill.

In addition, families with serious illness or disability face a host of difficult *practical tasks*, including the reallocation of roles and careful time and resource management and planning for the future. To sustain themselves over the long haul, family members must assess their needs and if necessary find additional support and resources. They may be responsible for such aspects of health care as gathering information, working with medical professionals and participating in decisions, as well as performing direct caregiving tasks. (In doing so, the medical patient and family can gain enough knowledge to become "experts" on the medical condition. This can lead to, or even necessitate, a shift in their relationship with professional caregivers.)

In the *emotional* arena, the family must process grief and loss, and understand the powerful negative emotions, such as anger and guilt, that the illness arouses. Members must somehow remain flexible in the face of change and unpredictability, often while coping with severe physical exhaustion and mental stress. It is natural for families to avoid meaningful communication when some topics are emotionally charged. But yielding to this tendency usually leads to feelings of isolation. Above all, the family's challenge is to sustain hope and stay emotionally involved with one another, including the ill member.

Cognitive work is closely related to these emotional tasks. The pressures of the situation force the family—individually and collectively, directly or indirectly—to clarify their values and reexamine priorities. In order to maximize the adjustment to the medical condition, it may be necessary to cultivate more informed and adaptive attitudes—attitudes about role allocations or social stigma, for example.

In all, having an ill member creates recurring stresses on the family's equilibrium. To maintain stability, extra effort is needed to foster a sense of continuity with the past and to thoughtfully and realistically prepare for the future. Setting priorities is a crucial means of maintaining equilibrium. As it does so, the family must take into consideration its beliefs, values, and objectives as well as the constraints caused by its changing circumstances—constraints such as reduced mobility, the shortened life span of one member, or increased demands on financial resources. Uniting around a shared sense of priorities can be extremely difficult for a family under severe, long-term stress; it also can instill a renewed awareness of the preciousness of family life.

TIMING OF INTERVENTION

The family is particularly vulnerable at the three crisis points already identified as optimal times for an MCC intervention: diagnosis, release from hospitalization, and exacerbation. The family is also vulnerable when facing major life transitions, such as a child's leaving for college, a marriage, a move, or the loss of a job.

Families face the greatest stress when a medical crisis coincides with other developmental and life cycle events. At these moments, members will have to handle extraordinary demands on their time and other resources. For example, family members may find it necessary to give up leisure activities with friends, to sell assets, or to cut back on sleep. For many families, even more difficult choices are called for when crises occur: A child may have to forego college in order to care for a parent; a spouse may have to relinquish a job that requires travel; or a parent may have to spend less time with a new baby in order to care for a sick older child. Each situation of this kind forces the family to reconcile anew the conflicting demands upon it, and to make painful decisions and choices. The insight of crisis intervention theory is that these times of intensified vulnerability also afford special occasions for growth.

VARIATIONS FOR FAMILY PARTICIPATION IN TREATMENT

As mentioned in Chapter 1, the family therapy and family practice fields have generated a rich clinical specialization and literature on the interactions of family systems and psychosocial medicine. Two recent books are especially notable. One, by Susan McDaniel, Jeri Hepworth, and William Doherty,[6] uses the phrase "medical family therapy" for psychosocial work with families around medical issues. The other book, by John Rolland,[7] presents the family systems illness model. Books such as these can be valuable resources for the medical crisis counselor.[8]

MCC contrasts with medical family therapy and the family systems illness model in that family dynamics do not have the centrality in MCC that they do in the other two. Although this difference is in part due to MCC's brief time frame, it is primarily a function of its tight focus on the medical condition and its effects. The focal unit of MCC is typically an individual, either the medical patient or a single family member. Both the nature and the salience of family issues vary with each patient. This in turn is a function of the patient's age and living arrangements, the strength of primary relationships prior to the illness, and many other factors. Family issues enter the picture insofar as they relate to the eight issues around which MCC is structured.

In MCC, there can be as many arrangements for family treatment as there are cases. Some family members seek MCC treatment for themselves as the primary patient. In other cases, they are brought in as adjunct patients to participate in a few sessions with the primary patient, the ill relative. This may be their own idea, or it may occur at the request of the physician or the medical patient. The counselor should be mindful that the caregiver who most needs counseling may have the greatest difficulty getting away from his or her duties to take advantage of it. This calls for flexibility and ingenuity on the counselor's part to find a workable time and venue. Whether the family member is the primary or adjunct patient, treatment may involve individual sessions, joint sessions with the medically ill person, or a combination of the two.

All of these variations, however, fall into two basic scenarios of MCC family treatment. In the first, *the family member (usually the major caregiver) is the primary patient.* In this case the standard MCC clinical model is used, beginning with goal setting and proceeding through the eight issues to the final review and stock-taking session. The treatment goal is the basis on which the counselor and patient organize, move forward, and measure progress. The counselor may suggest bringing in the medically ill relative as an adjunct patient for one or more sessions.

In the alternate scenario, *the family member is an adjunct patient,* and here there are many variations. For example, he or she may participate in anywhere from one to ten sessions. Sessions may be held jointly with the primary patient or separately. The family member may have asked to see the counselor, or may have been referred by the physician or invited by the ill relative. He or she may or may not be receptive to counseling. The focus of concern may be the sick family member or personal matters resulting from the illness.

Whatever the circumstances, this time with the adjunct patient, the family member, provides the counselor with invaluable information about the primary patient and also provides the family member with new insights and support. Often, just a single session can be extremely fruitful in yielding information and validating the patient's feelings. Although the counselor still uses the eight MCC issues as a framework to guide the discussion and assess the patient's needs, sessions with adjunct patients are generally less structured than in the standard MCC model. As always, however, the medical focus is carefully maintained to maximize effectiveness.

Some Brief Examples

The varied arrangements for MCC family work can be seen in several of the cases discussed in Chapter 4. The differences among patients in this regard stemmed from the fact that family issues had a varying impact on their adjustment to the illness. Conversely, they also stemmed from differences in the impact of the illness on family relationships.

Larry and Marian Davies (page 66) initially came to treatment together, then at my suggestion had several separate sessions, after which they completed treatment together. The Davies' relationship proved to be a major cause of Marian's depression and her difficulty integrating her condition. Besides working with Marian individually, MCC helped the couple become aware of the subtly destructive dynamics between them.

In sharp contrast, Bob and Sally Smithson (page 53) were a united front whose relationship was never part of the problem in the adjustment to Bob's lupus. Indeed, it was a major resource for dealing with it. They were devoted to each other and able to accommodate the changes required in their relationship. Finding a source of support to replace that which was lacking in their extended family was a focal issue for the Smithsons. Sally made the initial contact with me, but from the outset Bob was the primary patient. She withdrew after two sessions, in which they had addressed joint concerns.

I saw both Sarah and Ben Petrovsky (pages 76, 80) separately on a regular basis, although Sarah was my primary patient. The animosity between them had reached such extreme proportions by the time they entered treatment that expectations for improving their relationship were modest. Nevertheless, keeping open the lines of communication, however strained, was a vital therapeutic goal.

Ellen Suzuki's husband (page 83) came in for two MCC sessions in the four years in which she received episodic treatment. He needed help, above all, to understand the source of Ellen's fierce expressions of hostility, and to avoid internalizing them. This couple's relationship, like that of the Petrovskys, had deteriorated so much that the goal of therapy as far as the marriage was concerned was simply to minimize the damage they inflicted on each other.

I worked with Todd's wife, Kelly, (page 73) for one very fruitful session, which helped to permanently reverse the couple's drift toward estrangement. They had the resources to handle the challenges of Todd's MS once he resolved his fears and misconceptions about stigma.

MCC often involves at least one session with nonspouse family members, such as parents or children. For example, toward the end of Ellen's life her parents asked for a session to exchange information and get acquainted with me. Ben Petrovsky reluctantly agreed to a session with his mother-in-law, who desperately wanted a reconciliation in order to see her only grandchildren. I worked individually with each of Jack and Marilyn Goldman's four children (page 79); the older Goldman children also participated in group treatment with their parents.

PRINCIPLES AND STRUCTURE OF FAMILY TREATMENT

Consultation

Treatment with all primary MCC patients begins with a consultation. The structure and objectives of this session are the same whether the patient is the medically ill individual or a family member. The interview questions included in Table 3.2 (p. 43) can be easily adapted to take a family member's history, with emphasis on his or her role and relationship to the medical patient. If the family member is the principal caregiver, information should also be gathered on the support system that can be called upon.

The family characteristics affecting the experience of chronic illness include socioeconomic status, role allocation, and belief systems. Other critical factors are the family's access to and ability to use outside resources, its communication and coping styles, and the developmental stages of each member. In addition to these preexisting characteristics, a major determinant of the illness's impact on the family is the position of the ill member. While some adjustment issues are unaffected by this factor, others can be expected to vary greatly depending on (for example) whether the ill or disabled person is the sole breadwinner, the live-in grandmother, the new baby, or the college-age eldest child.

Another set of important variables derives from the illness itself: how and when it began, how much functional impairment it causes, the intensiveness of care needed at home, and its short- and long-term prognosis. Obviously, the needs and capacities of someone with a progressive condition such as MS or Parkinson's disease are different from those of a person suddenly incapacitated by a stroke or spinal injury. The amount of medical care needed by the individual also varies greatly. For example, a late-stage AIDS or kidney disease patient may depend on considerable medical technology at home, while the needs of a person in the later stages of MS may largely be a result of declining mobility.

Because they are critical to everyone's adjustment, family-related factors such as these must be assessed by the medical crisis counselor whether or not family members are seen in treatment. Whoever is the MCC patient, general information about the family provides the context for addressing his or her specific needs. The family as a system has distinctive characteristics. In addition, each member of the family has a unique relationship to the medical patient and singular priorities, coping strengths and weaknesses, and attitudes toward illness. These individual aspects also must be assessed, especially in regard to the principal caregiver.

One-Time-Only Patients

The medical crisis counselor should bear in mind that for family members, as for medically ill individuals, the consultation may provide enough information and support to make immediate subsequent visits unnecessary. If the caregiver is seen for only one session, several important messages should be conveyed; the counselor should

- stress that more counseling is always available in the future, if needed;
- caution against burnout, pointing out its negative consequences for all concerned;
- encourage realistic expectations, and urge the caregiver to consider his or her own needs as well as those of the medical patient; and
- present the need for respite and support in altruistic terms, if necessary; explaining that failure to meet personal needs will eventually harm the person being cared for.

The counselor is in effect "giving them permission" to care for themselves.

The Eight Issues of Chronic Illness

The eight issues of chronic illness arise for family members in the same way that they do for their ill relatives (sometimes mirroring those of the ill person) and are always contextualized by factors such as personality and position in the family.

1. Challenges to a sense of *control* and security are usually the first to arise.
2. These are generally followed by a crisis in the *self-image* or identity of family members.
3. *Dependency* issues directly concern the relationship between the family caregiver and the ill person.
4. Families face social *stigma* together, and in addition individual members may feel particularly embarrassed by their ill relative as well as guilty for feeling that way.
5. As we have seen, the medical patient fears *abandonment* while family members may vacillate between escape fantasies and a tendency to be over-responsible.
6. As for *anger*, a natural byproduct of chronic illness, family relations can be seriously undermined by its suppression or misdirection. At the same time, the family is an ideal environment in which to promote its constructive release.
7. *Isolation* is a problem for the family as a whole, and may be especially difficult for some members.
8. The unpredictability that pervades chronic illness is nowhere more troubling than it is for the family as it deals with the possibility of *death*. With some chronic illnesses, family members undergo a long process of preparing for the eventual death of their sick loved one. In some cases, family members may be unable to satisfy the medical patient's need to talk about the end of their lives.

Medical Crisis Counseling Principles

The MCC principles outlined at the beginning of Chapter 2 apply to family members as fully they do to medical patients. The first and most important is that the medical focus be strictly maintained. The family issues addressed in treatment are those that relate to the medical condition: factors that affect adjustment to the illness and the effect of the illness on the family as a whole as well as on individual members.

Counseling focuses on the problems and needs that are interfering with the family's adjustment—with a clear understanding that they are problems *because* of the medical condition. Neither therapist nor client expects to remedy preexisting family problems in a few weeks of focused counseling.

The medical crisis counselor's emphasis is on helping the family identify and reinforce its strengths. Because of the corrosive effects of guilt and the sometimes overwhelming needs of medical patients, family members may be acutely aware of their failings and perceived inadequacy. Counseling can make a strategic difference in helping them develop realistic expectations and accept that they are doing the best they can. This emphasis on capacities also provides a context in which the family can encourage the medical patient to be as self-reliant as possible.

Closely related to this is another MCC principle: tolerance for a wide range of problem-solving approaches. Families vary enormously in the ways they face hard realities, express and respond to emotion, allocate roles, gather information, and make decisions. Within these unique patterns are strengths that can be the foundation on which greater adaptive capacity and empathy are built. MCC always stresses the self-conceived solution with family members, as it does with medical patients. It supports them in reaching their own solution rather than pushing them to accept one based on someone else's notion of "normal" or "correct" outcomes. Authentic solutions and coping mechanisms such as these are the ones that can be sustained. The therapist assumes that MCC patients want to do the right thing and will do their utmost to do so once they understand their situation and receive support.

THE THERAPEUTIC RELATIONSHIP

Often, the most urgent need of family members in MCC is simply to vent emotion—grief, anger, fear, despair—in a safe place. They may have few other opportunities to express these emotions. It is not unusual for them to redirect their anger at the therapist, who can use such occasions to help family members gain perspective on their emotions and their source. Family members benefit enormously from having their feelings validated as understandable and normal.

Beyond these initial emotional needs, family members come to MCC with specific problems they wish to address. These must be elicited and translated into goals. The family member may be having difficulty communicating about sensitive subjects, confused about balancing caregiving and other priorities, or simply wondering how to be more positive and helpful. Such concerns become the focus of treatment, whether it lasts one session or ten. The objectives for family members are no different than they are for chronically ill persons: to adjust flexibly to the medical condition and to develop capacities, make contributions, and enjoy life to the fullest extent possible.

Providing support for the principal caregiver and helping to prevent burnout is a major objective of MCC. The counselor has a critical role in assessing how well the family is functioning and, if needed, in supporting a search for additional resources and supports. Counseling can help family caregivers detach from a sense of exclusive responsibility so they can assess their personal needs and take appropriate actions to meet them. A mother of a paraplegic teen-age girl sought counseling to deal with her severe depression and her recurrent battles with her daughter. MCC helped her come to terms with her anger, and facilitated cathartic exchanges between her and her daughter over their differing role expectations and perceptions of dependence and independence.

An important task for the therapist is to ensure that each family member's priorities are honored to the fullest extent possible. The counselor often serves as an informal advocate, helping clear the way for them to meet personal needs. Marilyn Goldman, for example (page 79), needed to give herself "permission" to take a break from caring for Jack to visit her ailing father. The Goldmans' eldest son was able to voice his concerns about his family's financial prospects—he had been so worried that he was finding it impossible to concentrate on his studies. Ben Petrovsky (page 80) received support for fully accepting his decision to institutionalize Sarah in order to invest in his professional and parenting responsibilities. Marta Simmons (page 45) gained perspective on her daughter's other commitments by recovering her sense of autonomy. The husband of a highly passive MS patient entered MCC treatment after his wife terminated hers. Because of her dependence on him, he had made a commitment to himself, one with which he was struggling, to stay in a loveless and enervating marriage until their son left home. As a result of MCC counseling, he reached the difficult conclusion that he could only honor this commitment at the expense of his integrity and health.

The counselor also heightens family members' awareness of their differing ways of thinking, feeling, and coping. This awareness is the foundation for understanding and accepting differences. Many people under the duress of caring for a sick or disabled loved one have unrealistic expectations about what they should do, and are thus unreasonably hard on themselves or others for their weariness or impatience. Part of the counselor's role is to help family members gain perspective and develop a more accepting attitude about each one's needs and limitations—particularly their own. The counselor can actually reach out to the entire family through the primary MCC patient to encourage greater tolerance and self-acceptance.

This awareness and validation of individual differences can greatly reduce the potential for resentment and misunderstanding. It might be said that the medical crisis counselor cultivates a kind of "system consciousness" in family members, increasing their awareness of the dynamics of family life and each person's role in them. Family life is so elemental that individuals may not be conscious of it until it is subjected to increased pressure—much as one becomes aware of the air one breathes only when it carries allergens or toxins. It is an MCC principle not to call for basic changes when people are in crisis. But this constraint heightens the need for awareness and understanding.

Much can be done through simple measures to improve communication and mutual support without disturbing the family's fragile equilibrium. One such measure, for example, was arranging to see Larry and Marian Davies in separate sessions (page 66). This not only enabled, but also forced, Marian to speak for herself. Another simple measure was persuading Jack Goldman to show more overt and frequent appreciation for his wife's loving care. Merely pointing out to Marta Simmons and to Frances that they had made their own decisions to consult with me fortified their sense of control and reduced their resentment of family members. Encouraging Eric, the young man with serious epilepsy (page 70), to take the bus to treatment rather than rely on his exhausted mother increased his self-esteem and gave her a brief respite. A one-time-only patient, the sister of a young man with Down syndrome, realized in an MCC consultation that her greatest need was not for counseling but for more information on her brother's condition. I referred her to the local Association for Retarded Citizens. Indeed, seemingly superficial changes can have a large impact on family relations and the individual's sense of well-being.

As we saw in Chapter 4, the central issue in Marilyn and Jack Goldman's case was their way of handling anger. My role was to help Jack understand the effect of his outbursts on Marilyn, and to increase his sensitivity to her need for appreciation and support. Marilyn and the Goldman children learned that Jack needed to vent the anger that boiled up inside him and that they should not take it personally, regardless of the way he expressed it.

Although Jack was diagnosed with MS when he was in his twenties, he only began to have serious impairments at age 42. When he and his family entered treatment soon thereafter, he was constantly projecting his anger onto Marilyn, and his verbal abuse was causing her great distress. As a result of these practical and emotional pressures, she was severely depressed and each of their four children was having difficulty in school. Nevertheless, there was strong love and mutual regard in the family. They recognized the strains and warning signs and worried that the family was falling apart.

My first task was to learn how the Goldman family typically expressed their feelings, positive and negative, to one another. I learned that Jack had always vented his emotions loudly and aggressively, without regard for the effect this had on others. Marilyn typically internalized her feelings for fear of hurting someone. This contrast had existed from the beginning of their relationship, but with the added strain of the illness (which brought with it more to get angry about), it had become pronounced and destructive.

My work with the Goldmans stretched from the few months we initially agreed upon to episodic treatment over several years. They needed periodic support as Jack's condition worsened. In the first series of sessions, we worked through the eight issues; but new problems, such as the eldest son's academic troubles and difficult decisions about Jack's housing, subsequently brought them back into treatment. I not only counseled the eldest son about his fears about the future, but intervened with his school to explain the stress he was under.

Each time the Goldmans returned to treatment, it was necessary to reestablish their awareness that the medical condition, rather than Jack, was the problem. As they were released from the emotional grip of the immediate problem, they would again be able to find solutions and the energy to implement them. When Jack became severely incapacitated, the family not only avoided moving him to a nursing home but acquired a special van so he could continue attending his beloved sports events. Despite severe stresses, they were able to stay together as a family and provide loving and flexible care for Jack until his death. At that point, they knew that they had done everything possible for him.

MCC thus provided an interpreter between two very different emotive styles. It helped the family work through the practical and emotional issues involved in caring for Jack as he progressively lost his mobility and required more care. In addition, MCC treatment provided a setting in which family members' individual needs and developmental issues could receive attention. As we will see in the next chapter, the Goldmans gained further support and perspective by participating in MCC family groups, where they were able to discuss common issues with families in similar situations, and to gain insight into their own style by observing others.

NOTES

1. A recent exception is *Helping yourself help others: A guide for caregivers*, by Rosalynn Carter with Susan K. Golant (Times Books/Random House, 1994). This book includes an extensive list of resources for caregivers.

2. Kiecolt-Glaser, J. (1991). Spousal caregivers of dementia victims: Longitudinal changes in immunity and health. *Psychosomatic Medicine, 53*(4), 345–362.

3. Costello, S. (1994). *The American woman, 1994–1995*. Washington, DC: Women's Research and Education Institute.

4. Staff. (1993, January 12). The expanding need for home health care. *Washington Post*, p. 5. The same article reports that a 1992 survey by the National Association of Medical Equipment Suppliers found the following reasons for needing home health care: serious disease/illness, 49%; recovery from severe accident, 33%; ailments of old age, 25%; and birth defects, 4%.

5. Edwards, R. (1990). Professional and family caregivers: A social work perspective. In *The professional and family caregiver: Dilemmas, rewards and new directions*. Inaugural Conference Papers, Rosalynn Carter Institute for Human Development, Georgia Southwestern College. This article includes a useful discussion of social and other forces affecting family caregivers.

6. McDaniel, S., Hepworth, J., & Doherty, W. (1992). *Medical family therapy: A biopsychosocial approach to families with health problems*. New York: Basic.

7. Rolland, J. (1994). *Families, illness and disability: An integrative treatment model*. New York: Basic.

8. Also see the quarterly journal *Family Systems Medicine*, edited by Donald A. Bloch, which contains useful articles on "the confluence of family therapy, systems theory and modern medicine."

CHAPTER SEVEN

Group Treatment

Medical crisis counseling groups are an excellent setting in which to work with patients, either as a follow-up to individual treatment or in lieu of it. MCC groups afford patients the combined advantages of exploring shared experience in the company of peers—a powerful form of social support from which the benefits have been clearly demonstrated—and having the guidance of a skilled clinician who helps maintain focus and movement toward goals. The MCC clinical model is a highly effective conceptual framework for short-term group treatment.

The MCC model was developed in a group context in the late 1970s. Because of my affiliation with several large medical institutions, I was able to create and lead targeted MCC groups for people with a broad range of medical problems, including kidney transplant candidates; families in which a parent had MS; middle-aged couples in which a spouse had MS; people with epilepsy; women in wheelchairs; men with disabilities caused by stroke, MS, or Parkinson's disease; recently-diagnosed young female MS patients; and family members of people with cancer. Three of these groups will be profiled below.

It was in the group setting, through my work over several years with hundreds of patients and families, that a consistent and predictable pattern of issues revealed itself again and again as group members shared their concerns and experiences. I gathered enough evidence to become convinced that these issues are a meaningful basis for a psychosocial intervention with groups and individuals. The evidence extended beyond my own clinical work to that of other therapists, offering further confirmation of the finding that the principal psychosocial issues of chronic illness are the same, whatever the condition that precipitates them. I supervised several medical crisis counselors who led their own groups for people with cancer, AIDS, muscular dystrophy, lupus, and heart disease. At our regular clinical conferences, we had no difficulty discussing the key issues and themes of our work despite the wide variety of our patients' physical problems.

MCC patients have been enthusiastic about the benefits of MCC groups. One group member said she appreciated the "feelings of friendliness, rapport, and lack of competition" in her group. Another spoke of the kinship she found. The husband of an MS patient said he valued his group's "exchange of views and information," which he contrasted with "sitting alone in a library." One member said, "I'm not a marked person any more. I have learned to think better of myself." One group identified a sense of perspective, reduced feelings of isolation, and greater comfort about their situations as major benefits. Members also appreciate the characteristics that are distinctive of MCC groups: the maintenance of a medical focus, the professional leader's understanding of the eight issues of chronic illness, and the emphasis on goals.

In such a supportive setting, some topics actually can be addressed more easily and fruitfully than in individual treatment. In family groups, for example, family dynamics are apparent and easily objectified because participants observe them in other families. Members become more aware of the normalcy of certain problems and of the unique ways they have found to deal with them. Troubling symptoms become less burdensome when they are discussed with others who are also experiencing them. Often, members learn useful solutions and coping techniques they had not found on their own.

In addition, simply talking about a shared problem—or hearing others talk about it—helps normalize it. Patients may enter a group having had trouble even saying that they had a particular condition. Talking about it with others in the security of the group increases their comfort level and their ability to integrate the difficult reality. Groups counteract the isolation that can be acute for people with serious chronic conditions.

STEPS TO FORMING A GROUP

In the ideal MCC group, members not only have the same medical condition but are also at similar stages in its course. From the outset, this commonality affords a level of trust and empathy based on shared experience that is much more difficult to attain when members have different physical problems; the unspoken sense of rapport and mutual support can be very powerful. It also increases their ability to draw support and hope from each other, and reduces the chance that members will become alarmed by encountering someone at a more symptomatic or impaired stage of their illness.

Obviously, the clinician's flexibility in creating groups and the degree to which the ideal of homogeneity is attainable depend on the size of the available patient population. Those working with a large hospital, specialized clinic, or voluntary health association, for example, may be able to create highly specific groups, while those working in other settings may need to consider an alternative arrangement, such as a heterogeneous group (discussed below).

Fortunately, there are many workable arrangements short of the ideal. For example, there are a variety of bases for group formation in addition to medical variables. Primary and adjunct patients can be combined — for example, a group of spouses — and other organizing principles can be used, such as age, gender, and family makeup. Good judgment about a group's feasibility and careful screening of members are the critical preconditions for successful groups. Although the group modality is widely applicable, some patient populations are not as suitable for groups, and some individuals are not appropriate candidates for membership (the reasons for this are discussed below). Making these judgments usually requires consultation between the medical crisis counselor and medical staff.

Consultation with health care providers about group formation gives the medical crisis counselor an excellent chance to learn about the specific issues, medical and otherwise, associated with a given condition. Health care staff are often eager for patients to have access to counseling groups. Doctors, nurses, and other staff, such as technicians and receptionists, can help determine the feasibility of a group and assess patients' candidacy. Office staff can play a key role because they have continuing informal contacts with patients as they come and go, and thus many chances to observe them. Both medical and administrative staff members should be sensitized as to what characteristics to watch for in patients. (See, for example, the risk factors listed in Table 3.1, on page 39.)

Establish Feasibility

The first thing that must be determined in considering group formation is the likelihood that enough patients will be interested in group membership and capable of sustaining a several-week commitment. This is the "threshold question" for MCC group formation. The counselor begins by identifying a medical condition (or combination thereof) for a possible group. The organizing principle is chosen most often at the urging of medical caregivers, and sometimes (but not often) at the request of MCC patients. If the counselor is affiliated with a medical practice, the records of eligible patients can be reviewed to identify possible candidates for group participation. Ideally, the individual's appropriateness for group membership is assessed in an interview with the therapist.

As I have indicated, I have found that group formation is more feasible with some health conditions than with others. A major determinant is the relationship between the patient and the medical provider, because the frequency and regularity of the contact between these two varies widely in different practices. For example, a cardiology practice is likely to draw patients from a wide geographic area for its surgical interventions. Patients may have little sustained contact with the cardiologist either prior to or following hospitalization. In contrast, patients of nephrology, oncology, neurology, and dermatology practices, among others, tend to have long-standing and frequent contact with physicians and nurses and are thus relatively easy to combine into a group.

In addition to the nature of the doctor-patient relationship, other important determinants of the feasibility of a particular group are the condition itself and the demographic characteristics of the patient population. The condition must permit enough mobility to get to meetings for several weeks. Obviously, the target population also must have enough individuals for the group to reach "critical mass." In addition, they must have enough in common (be it age, marital status, medical condition, type of disability, or other characteristics) to feel some affinity and comfort.

Assess Potential Members

Once the decision is made to form a group, the next step is to develop a list of possible members who fit its specifications. This is a lengthy process. The selected individuals are contacted, either by the prospective group leader or another trained professional, to discuss possible group participation. In a telephone or in-person interview, the counselor can assess both the patient's interest in group participation and his or her suitability for the group.

Counselors should screen group members carefully to minimize the chances of including someone whose experience, appearance, or attitude would be discouraging to other members. Apart from these disqualifying characteristics, the crucial factors to look at are the patient's willingness to participate and readiness to interact with others with the same condition. The principles of screening for group formation often boil down to one characteristic that is the *sine qua non* for group membership, over and above interest: the ability to make and keep a commitment to group sessions. As anyone who has worked with groups knows, continuity is critical to their success; in groups, more than in individual sessions, content is often based on what happened in the previous session. Whatever their motivation, however, people with a serious medical condition often face obstacles to sustained group participation. Obviously, some of these cannot be predicted or avoided, but an effort must be made to minimize their likelihood: The counselor first makes a judgment in the screening process, then talks with the prospective member about commitment and the ability to get to sessions. Having prepared as thoroughly as possible, the counselor must then be flexible.

The following illustration emphasizes these points. Two members of a kidney transplant group I was leading had to miss one session. I taped the session and provided them with a transcript so they would know of the group's discussion the week before and continue as full participants. This gesture had the desired effect of stressing the importance of each member to the group, and allowed the group to move forward without having to bring the absentees up to date.

Another incident illustrates a counterbalancing principle: the importance of flexibility to accommodate the physical constraints faced by MCC patients. A member of kidney disease group arrived at a group session nearly an hour late, after riding public transportation for two hours to get there. My co-leader reacted punitively, scolding her for her tardiness. I intervened immediately in the presence of the group to praise her for her obvious commitment. Despite feeling weak and ill from her previous day's dialysis treatment, she had continued her almost endless bus trip. She was to be admired and complimented rather than upbraided.

Prepare Members for Participation

Even after careful screening, preparing members is critical. Stressing commitment and explaining the code of confidentiality are two key aspects of preparation for group participation. Another vital step is shaping their expectations and readying them for encountering others with their condition or a similar one.

Consider a Heterogeneous Group

As mentioned above, many medical crisis counselors will not have the luxury of creating targeted groups because they do not work with a large enough patient population. However, as long as they insist on careful screening, preparation, and guidance, they should not hesitate to form more diverse groups if this is the only way to give patients a chance for group participation. Given the number of possible combinations short of the ideal, all that can be said here by way of advice is that the greater the specificity, the greater the group's chance of being effective. In general, the counselor should avoid combining people who are in very early stages of a condition with those in very advanced stages of the same condition; confronting the manifestations of an illness at an advanced stage can be very disheartening for people in its early stage.

As already discussed, screening members is always important, and this is especially the case with diverse groups. In forming such a group, the counselor must talk with possible members to ensure that they are amenable to interacting with people with other conditions and/or at other stages. For example, the counselor can ask patients to imagine how they might feel interacting with people with more serious functional limitations. Once such a group is formed, the leader must be highly attentive to the dynamics among group members and play an active role in maintaining the focus on shared issues. It is even possible to point out how these issues manifest themselves at different stages. For example, at the outset the therapist can address the apparent lack of commonality among patients, and explain that what they have in common is more important than their differences. Although a generic chronic illness group cannot discuss physical symptoms the way medically homogeneous groups can, their psychosocial problems are the same.

Know the Limits of Homogeneous Groups

Early in my professional life, I learned that there are limits to the benefits of homogeneity in MCC groups. I had gone to considerable lengths to bring together a group of wheelchair-bound women who shared the unusual combination of being young (in their twenties) and at an advanced stage of MS. Two of my patients with these characteristics had expressed great interest in meeting with others who shared their life situation. They waited for nearly a year until another woman with similar characteristics entered my practice.

Knowing the importance of preparing group participants, I talked at length with each prospective member about meeting with others who were facing similar challenges. Each of us approached the first session with high expectations that the group would be extremely supportive and helpful. Contrary to all expectations, however, the experience proved to be highly traumatic for the patients. Encountering women who were mirror images of themselves had the overwhelming effect of forcing them to confront the harsh reality of being young, female, and severely impaired. The implications were so painful that they eclipsed anything positive the members might have given each other. Their only impulse was to retreat. By mutual agreement, these women never met again.

This distressing experience taught me to be careful not to create groups in which the identification among members is too complete or too intense. Differences as well as similarities can be instructive. Just as important, they afford some relief from constantly engaging one's pain.

APPLYING THE MCC CLINICAL MODEL AND PRINCIPLES

The clinician familiar with group work should have no difficulty adapting the MCC treatment model to a group setting. The principles, content, and course of treatment are essentially the same as in individual MCC sessions. Perhaps the only difference in process between the two modalities occurs in the initial session. With groups, the elements of the consult outlined in Chapter 3 (patient history, treatment description, and commitment to treatment) are addressed prior to convening the group. The counselor usually meets one-on-one with the individual, taking a history and explaining the group process. At that stage (rather than in the first group session) the patient makes a commitment to group treatment and establishes personal goals.

The first group session is used by the members to get acquainted and share their respective treatment goals, and for the counselor to describe how the treatment will take place. It is stressed that the group will stay focused on the medical problem and its effects on members and their families. Members are given the standard reminders about confidentiality and not monopolizing group time.

For the same reasons that apply to individual treatment, MCC groups are always time-limited, focused, and goal-oriented. If members have already been in individual MCC, group treatment can be condensed into fewer than 10 sessions. The shortest program advisable is 6 sessions, with those at the beginning and end reserved for getting acquainted and wrapping up.

As in individual treatment, at the outset members set goals that they hope to accomplish during the treatment period. (In subsequent sessions, they will report periodically on their progress toward them, possibly with a reminder from the counselor.) In addition, the counselor knows that the salient issues for members are control, self-image, dependency, stigma, abandonment, anger, isolation, and death. These provide the focus and underlying structure for discussions.

The counselor plays much the same role in MCC groups as in individual therapy—helping members stay focused, asking clarifying questions, making sure that all eight issues are addressed, and retaining members' goal orientation. In addition, of course, the counselor is responsible for group process factors such as ensuring that everyone participates and that no one dominates.

Groups are a productive setting for accomplishing a number of objectives that members may not recognize at the outset. They include gaining the latest knowledge about the medical condition, understanding stress and techniques for dealing with it, grappling with changes in self and body image, learning new strategies for coping and communicating, and confirming one's innate ability to cope. Out of the stimulus of group interaction, insights emerge about common concerns such as troubling symptoms, anger over the disease, frustration with physicians, and coping techniques.

I want to emphasize that MCC groups are therapy groups and not social or support groups. Under the guidance of a professional, members work toward the overarching goal of normalizing and integrating their illness. Participants confront issues, express powerful emotions, and set and pursue goals, all within the framework of the MCC treatment model.

PROFILES OF THREE MEDICAL CRISIS COUNSELING GROUPS

Young Women with MS

All seven members of this group were under the age of 40 and had been diagnosed recently. They came to the group with personal goals that in each case represented a desire to feel better physically and mentally and to maximize control of their lives.

The first subject to arise, as is usually the case, was physical symptoms. Even as the members introduced themselves at the beginning of the first session, they mentioned the impact of the illness on their energy, sexuality, and mobility. I encouraged them to compare notes, and as they did so they discovered both similarities and differences in the way MS manifests itself in different people. One similarity among the women was the fact that stress aggravated their symptoms. I asked them to give examples of the effects of stress, and to describe how they dealt with it. As they told their stories, members shared their techniques for managing common symptoms and husbanding their limited energy. These techniques—for example, diet, yoga, resting—were clearly helping them maintain a sense of control. The group also discovered humor to be another, possibly less familiar, coping technique; members found much to laugh about in every session.

The impact of the disease on their sexuality was a recurring theme for these young women, whether they were single or married. They worried about whether they would remain attractive, be full sexual partners, and have children. Unmarried members had especially strong concerns in this area, wondering if they would ever marry. One remarked in response to another's story, "It's good to know someone with MS is still attractive to guys."

MS was imposing many physical and emotional changes: loss of mobility, reduced physical activity, inability to work, feelings of unattractiveness. To draw the members out about such changes, I asked them to describe their reactions to their diagnoses. Sharing their stories evoked comments on what they felt they had lost, and how they were changing. In response to my query about how they viewed themselves now, they discussed the impact of these deep changes on their self-images and their efforts to adjust. One member said, "I feel brokenhearted . . . as if someone I love deeply has been taken away from me." Members found they attached differing degrees of importance to physical strength and agility. One said mockingly, "I finally have an excuse for being a klutz!" In general, simply talking in this way about MS and its effects promoted its integration in the members' self-images.

Because of the debilitating effects of the illness, dependency was a strong theme. Although serious impairment was a long way off, the specter still raised troubling questions about career, marriage, and children. Wanting the members to articulate their needs and receive validation from the group, I asked about the kind of help they wanted from their spouses, families, and friends. Despite the similarities in their symptoms and psychosocial problems, they found they had quite different attitudes toward wanting sympathy, as well as varying abilities to ask for and receive help. This pointed to underlying differences in their personalities and coping styles that were a source of interest throughout the sessions. I encouraged the women to compare notes about how they talked with family, friends, and coworkers about their limitations. Some were able to candidly communicate their needs, while others tended to express them in indirect and sometimes inappropriate ways. (One outcome of this group was that three members continued in individual therapy with me or a psychiatrist.)

Because they were in the early stages of MS, members had many questions about revealing their condition to others. They were unsure about whom to tell, when, and how. I asked them to describe some of their experiences with revealing the illness. They had many stories—some of support, some of rejection. One member told of her husband's deep resentment that she and her family had concealed her condition until after their marriage. Members discussed people's reactions to their sometimes clumsy movements, and talked about how to handle embarrassing situations. I helped them distinguish their views of themselves from their perception of others' reactions. The strong kinship among these women and the safety established in the group allowed them to express emotion freely, laughing and crying together. They shared how they had experienced and dealt with depression—with one member saying that "many times" she had "just wanted to end it all."

Members spent a great deal of time comparing their adjustments. I reminded them that many forms of adaptation are appropriate, pointing out the variations in this small group. The women attached great importance to their primary relationships, and found that they afforded differing amounts of support. I drew them out on this subject by asking them how others could help them. For the married members, relationships with their husbands were of vital importance. The resiliency of these relationships was a critical factor, and was largely determined by the quality of the relationships prior to diagnosis. Even in strong marriages, however, abandonment was a common fear, and a subject to which the women returned again and again. Some members handled their vulnerability by constantly testing their spouses and coercing reassurance that they would not be abandoned. As is common with groups, the members often had sensible advice for each other. One wisely observed that another member's constant suggestions to her husband that he should leave her were a way of trying to maintain control over his departure.

The women found it helpful to discuss their anger—at medical professionals, family members, and themselves. My role in this regard was to help them focus their anger on the MS, and away from inappropriate targets. I drew the members out about their frustrations, and asked how they expressed them: "What helps when you're upset?" Many members were deeply frustrated at what they saw as their failure to handle the MS satisfactorily. Some diverted their anger onto other people, usually those on whom they were most dependent. One member admitted, "I'm just trying to find someone to blame it on." Group membership was therapeutic in providing a place for members to vent their frustration and disappointment. The net result of discussions such as this was that members recognized that they were, in fact, making an adjustment.

The issues of isolation and death were still remote for these recently-diagnosed young women. Fears of isolation were implicit when they talked about changes in their social lives and explored ways of staying active and involved with others. I made sure that they talked about what activities they had been forced to stop, such as sports, and what they could still do, such as going out with friends. One declared, "Without my job, I'd go crazy." As with most people facing chronic illness, the prospect of death was far less troubling than that of living with diminished capacities. In general, they found that they were coping with the present realities of their lives and expecting to face new challenges as they arose.

I was pleased to be able to carry helpful messages to these women from a more mature couples group (described below) about what to expect later in life. Because of the stability and wisdom of the couples in the older group, their messages were quite helpful and hopeful. The older group also passed on tips about specific coping techniques. This was one of the many benefits of having a large enough patient population to create targeted groups.

In our final session, I asked the members what they had gotten out of the group. They agreed that seeing how others were accepting and adapting to the MS had been very supportive. We discussed the variations among the members, and I pointed out that one implication is that not all changes or problems should be attributed to MS. Members enumerated some of what they had learned about taking care of themselves, both physically and emotionally. I observed that simply recognizing and accepting the need for care was an accomplishment in itself. Members remarked on feeling less isolated and more comfortable since joining the group. It had given them "a place to talk," and helped them feel less anxious and more in control. Like the final session of most MCC groups, this one was largely devoted to members' expressions of their sadness about leaving the group.

Mature Couples

One spouse in each couple in this group of six couples had MS. Those who had not already had individual treatment came somewhat reluctantly. Despite their doctor's encouragement, they were uneasy about facing the issues surrounding their illness. But while one couple withdrew from the group after the first session, the other members continued and became enthusiastic and appreciative participants. Three couples then went on to

form a new two-part group to which they brought their teenaged children
(see below).

These couples, all of whom were in their forties and fifties, had dealt
with MS as a part of married life for many years. In contrast with the
young women's group described above, they had achieved perspective on
their situation and integrated the MS into a broader view of life that did
not focus on the illness. They had also developed a battery of coping skills
and sustained stable marriages.

My first questions to the group explored why they were there, and
what they hoped to get out of the group. The reasons cited for joining a
group at this stage of life included achieving a higher level of coping,
gaining new information, and interacting with others who shared their life
situation. Their general goals for the group included: to acquire new
information about MS; to broaden their social involvements and use of
community resources; to focus on the ill spouse's abilities, increase his or
her self-esteem and self-sufficiency, and preserve his or her role in the
family; and to improve family communication.

As usual, physical symptoms proved to be a recurring theme and source
of interest. I encouraged members to exchange ideas about their ways of
minimizing stress and its physical effects. They discovered they had quite
differing views about whether to suppress "negative" feelings, but all agreed
on the importance of staying calm.

Communication was a central theme in this group. Members voiced
many concerns about the impact of the illness on their children, agreeing
that "MS is a family problem." I encouraged members to compare notes
about the ways their families communicated about the illness.

Even though they had stable marriages, many members seemed to gain
new insights about themselves by listening to others. For example, the
Goldmans (whom we met in Chapters 4 and 6) had segregated family
roles to the extent that Marilyn was completely excluded from financial
decision-making; after the group discussed role reallocation, Jack decided it
was time to let her in on these decisions. This was a significant change for
him, because it represented a further diminishment of his role as the
family's breadwinner. It reflected his growing understanding and acceptance of the inevitable changes in their lives.

Adjustments to role changes were in fact an important theme, one with
traditional gender overtones. The men with MS had more trouble adjusting to diminished capacities and needing help—one lamented, "I can't find
a place for myself!"—while the women with MS showed more variety in
their degree of self-reliance. This contrast was in itself illuminating to

group members. I reinforced members' objectivity about gender factors by asking them to imagine a reversed situation in which the other spouse had MS.

Issues of independence and dependence were also important. As their conditions worsened, those with MS had been forced to learn new skills and adaptations. One man said he didn't feel "dependent"; he felt "useless." But he added that he loved finding new things to do, and then described some of them. Most group members considered it very important to stay busy and be as independent as possible. They "pounced" supportively on the one withdrawn and passive member. In response to a query from me, the members with MS shared how they filled the time and found ways to be useful.

I opened a sensitive subject by asking caregivers how they handled burnout. Their list of practical responses gave evidence of the fact that burnout is indeed a problem. The group's discussion of this issue affirmed the importance of supporting a caregiver's need for respite. It also gave MS patients a chance to voice their feelings about occasional overprotectiveness on the part of their caregivers. The couples compared notes on their ways of handling joint and separate activities, and talked about the guilt that accompanied carrying on activities without the ill spouse. It was clear that the ill spouses in these seasoned relationships had weathered changing conditions for decades, and generally had less fear of abandonment than people whose marriages are newly subjected to the stress of a chronic illness.

I asked members about their techniques for expressing anger and frustration. They identified a common desire to avoid exacerbating the ill patient's symptoms or placing undue stress on the caregiver; beyond this, as might be expected, their solutions varied. The preferred ways of dealing with anger and frustration ranged from reading (by an MS patient) to going away and "yelling like hell" (by a spouse).

The degree to which group members were attuned to each others' needs and capabilities was impressive. They were able within just a few weeks to discuss intimate subjects such as sexual desire and incontinence. They gently prodded each other in the directions they considered most constructive, while honoring each other's vulnerabilities. Partly to reinforce their sense of coping, I asked these couples what words of wisdom they had for the group of younger MS patients. The thrust of their response was, "It gets easier over the years."

At their last session, members expressed great appreciation for the warmth and rapport they had found in the group, and real regret at the prospect of breaking up. One member described his realization that "a lot of our problems aren't peculiar to us," which he said "takes a load off." Both the commonalities and the variations they discovered had afforded a broader perspective on their experience with the illness, and brought to light new possibilities for coping with it. One member with MS reported being able to go back to work and "not feel like a bump on a log any more." Someone else described the group as "a safety valve" for talking about difficult issues; another member said the group helped him "learn to live with myself." Several couples remarked on the benefits of participating in the group together, notably improved communication. One member summed up her feelings with some regret—"I'm just sorry we didn't have this sort of group 10 years ago."

Concurrent Family and Adolescent Groups

Several members of the mature couples group identified a shared concern: their relationships with their teenaged children and the effect of the MS on their family lives. As a result, we decided to create a setting in which they could explore these subjects with their children. Although the parents were concerned about getting their children to participate, three families joined. The members were the Goldmans and their two teenaged children, a son and a daughter, and two other couples, each with a teenaged daughter.

This group had a distinctive format. The young people and parents met separately for half the time (45 minutes), followed by a joint session for 45 minutes. The group's composition certainly lent itself to enormous flexibility, because the adult members had already explored the core MCC issues in other treatment contexts. The goals for the group were clear: to explore the effects of MS on members' lives and relationships.

Initially, there were motivation issues to address. I asked everyone to state what they expected to get out of the group. While the parents wanted their children to express their feelings and any problems they were having coping with the illness, the adolescents had come primarily to please their parents. Meeting separately gave the young people a chance to express their resentment and ambivalence, and then move beyond it. Once they had aired their initial feelings, the teenagers invested in exchanging with and learning from each other, and showed great interest in discussing their experiences.

I helped focus their discussions with questions about how they had felt when they learned of their parents' MS, and how MS had changed their lives. The young people explored a host of adaptive issues such as living with the erratic ways of the disease, a parent's marginal health, body image, anger, and guilt. They shared their concerns about money and their frustration about missing out on social activities with their friends. I talked with them about having sources of support in whom they could confide.

A question about what they did to help around the house brought to light the fact that dependency was a major issue for these teens. They were intrigued to discover wide variations among their parents' attitudes toward needing and accepting help. This turned out to be an important issue for their parents as well; but the decisions they would all face in the near future about leaving home made the issue especially acute for the younger generation.

Both parents and teenagers shared a desire to learn more about MS and its progression, and at their request the entire group met with a physician in the second week. The young people questioned him about genetic factors, treatment, drug reactions, and death. Among other things, the information they gathered made it easier for them to comfortably explain their parents' condition to peers. The Goldmans' daughter even reported having captured her friends' interest in the subject.

One outcome of this dispassionate medical discussion of MS and its symptoms was what Marilyn Goldman described as a communication breakthrough for their family: Their son and daughter kidded Jack about his leg tremors, a subject they had never openly discussed.

One of the parents' major goals was to increase communication between them and their children, and in some areas this was accomplished. Early on, the adults identified a desire to discuss such awkward subjects as shifting family roles, financial difficulties, and possible changes in children's college and career plans. Both groups discovered that they shared a desire to know certain things about each other, and acknowledged their reluctance to ask direct questions about sensitive topics. I encouraged members to experiment with asking questions in the safety of the group.

The group provided a safe environment for exploring the physical effects of the disease and the ways various members felt about and dealt with them. My query to members about what embarassed them helped open the topic of wheelchairs, the many pros and cons of which became a recurrent topic. Members also responded openly to my suggestion that they describe what they did when they felt "down."

Although I always performed the role of focusing discussion and pursuing topics in greater depth when needed, the members themselves often supplied penetrating and constructive questions. For example, a teenager asked one of the adults with MS, "Has MS altered your personality?" And an MS patient asked a teenager from another family, "Does it bother you when your mother uses a cane?" This function of members is not unusual in groups. The counselor's role is to make sure that key topics are raised; if the members themselves do the raising, so much the better.

Throughout these sessions, I made sure to call attention to the variations among families, as well as the similarities. Members found it useful to observe the dynamics within other families and to see their own patterns as a version of "normal." Parents were able to recognize the normalcy of the teens' preoccupation with their own lives, their need for privacy, and even the somewhat strained nature of intergenerational communication around sensitive topics. Gaining these insights in the company of other parents was enormously helpful. One member said with some relief, "I realize that I am so absorbed in my illness that I think they are too. I learned that my daughter was never as concerned as I was."

Similarly, the adolescents were supported in their extraresponsible family roles by observing others in similar positions. I reinforced this by praising them for their maturity and generosity. Both they and their parents gained awareness of the sensitivity, empathy, and independence that they had developed in response to their parents' needs. I also told the adults that as a counselor, I found it reassuring that the teenagers put their parents' needs in a developmentally appropriate perspective. Once they had expressed their fears regarding MS, they showed a healthy desire to return to the primacy of their own teenage problems.

Typical of groups, the family group members—especially the adults—showed strong feelings of loss as they approached the termination of their sessions. They had much to say in response to my standard question about what they had gotten out of the group. One member said she now felt more comfortable and relaxed. All three families said they were more comfortable talking about the MS. A teenager said she learned that her mother should be more active. Another said she had a better idea of what her father wanted and didn't want. A parent with MS said she felt less guilty about her limitations. Another said he realized he needed more support, and should seek it from his friends. All of the parents reported feeling reassured about their relationships with their children.

PART II

Administrative Issues

CHAPTER EIGHT

Establishing a Medical Crisis Counseling Program

In addition to being a clinical philosophy and methodology, medical crisis counseling is a practical program designed for adaptation to varied health care environments. It has evolved in close interaction with medical treatment and with the needs and constraints of health care institutions in mind. In the following pages, we will look at several health-oriented psychosocial programs. They illustrate the range of settings in which MCC can be offered, and the various ways that the relationship between medical care and counseling can be structured. The profiled programs are examples of the MCC model as well as others that provide brief therapy and focus on the medical condition.

In my experience, an excellent arrangement for an MCC program is affiliation with either a hospital or a specialized medical clinic. While it is certainly possible to offer MCC in an independent practice, this arrangement is more difficult because of the links that must be created and maintained with the medical community, both to generate referrals and to communicate about patients. In contrast, a relationship with a health care setting permits institutional support in such areas as start-up financing, office space, referrals, medical and other consultations, informal contact, quality assurance, billing and third-party payment, records, follow-up treatment, and links to community resources. While the foregoing list may seem daunting, provisions for the program within the institution can actually begin quite simply—for example, using office space within the medical facility, minimizing administrative staff, and hiring counselors on a contract basis.

Let us begin by looking at the three counseling programs that I founded and directed in the 1970s and 1980s. Two of them were based in health care settings.

THE NEUROLOGY CENTER, WASHINGTON, DC

When I wished to begin an MCC practice in 1976, I sent announcements to a large mailing list of local specialists. I received a response from Dr. Marvin Korengold, the senior partner with eight other neurologists in a large neurology practice that was providing comprehensive care. They already had a physical therapist and a biofeedback specialist in-house, and he expressed strong interest in bringing my expertise into their practice. We subsequently agreed that I would work in their office suite three days a week for three months, on a salaried basis, with a mandate to set up a program. At the end of that period, we would assess the feasibility of offering that kind of service in his practice.

To determine what services the professionals in this practice would like to offer, I began talking with the medical and support staff about their patients. One medical assistant had been particularly active in "counseling" patients, and had even started a group that she co-led with one of the doctors. When I arrived, she was already beginning to recognize that the group was not as effective as it might be in helping patients address their concerns. She was an eager, naturally supportive person, and wished to offer more to these very needy people. In response to my queries about what group of patients they believed to be most in need of psychosocial intervention, staff members identified young adults with MS. These young people had their adult lives ahead of them, with no meaningful treatment prospects and much uncertainty as to the quality of their lives.

I decided to form a group of young, recently-diagnosed females who were still relatively symptom-free, and who were amenable to treatment because it was brief and called for a limited commitment of time and money. Fortunately, these young women benefitted greatly from their brief group treatment. They expressed confidence in the counselors, and reported a greater sense of well-being and even a reduction of their symptoms and stress.

In addition to these benefits to the patients, the MCC program was benefitting the practice in terms of new revenue and recognition, as other medical practices in the community heard about this program and wanted to do something similar. One of the notable benefits to staff members was a reduction in the number of phone calls to the doctors and nurses. Recognizing these benefits, the partners invited me to join their staff on a full-time basis. I hired another social worker within three months, and within a year had hired another.

The Neurology Center treated patients with all neurologic conditions, including MS, epilepsy, and stroke aftereffects. Initially, most referrals came from two neurologists with the greatest interest in the counseling program. Over time, a combination of their enthusiasm and the demonstrated effectiveness of the program led to more referrals from their colleagues. It was advantageous to the MCC program that I was salaried, because this increased the partners' motivation to make the counseling service an integral part of the clinic.

I learned the necessity of maintaining visibility, as the doctors tended to stay focused on the physical. My staff and I carried on a steady campaign to remind the medical staff of our counseling service. We walked through the office hallways daily, leaving notes on the desks of referring physicians about their patients and informally discussing cases with those we encountered. Referring physicians received brief written reports after the initial consultation with each patient, and an easily identifiable MCC "Case Notes" Report on a colored sheet of paper was placed in the medical record. In addition, I kept in close touch with the medical staff, asking them what they found especially useful. To stimulate their involvement, we even circulated charts with weekly totals of the number of patients referred by each doctor.

On a more formal basis, I met once a week for an hour with each of the two senior physicians. With one of them, discussions focused on program planning and business matters. We evaluated the cost-effectiveness of various programs and explored areas in which others might be offered. One result of these discussions was a request that I design a headache clinic, incorporating counseling and biofeedback.

My weekly meetings with the other neurologist centered on case reviews. This was mutually beneficial: I gained insight into the attitudes of his colleagues, learned more about the medical dimension of patients' conditions, and was able to influence him and, through him, his colleagues; he pursued and deepened his understanding of the psychological dimension of his patients' experience, and learned to work with them more sensitively and effectively. For example, at his request I coached him on how to talk to patients about a referral to counseling.

I took time at the outset to compile a useful list of community resources, including information on insurance, transportation, assistive medical equipment and self-help groups, among other things that were relevant to our services, with current information on contact people at each location. In this manner, I not only helped the Center make its services more helpful to patients, but also helped patients use all of the community resources available to them. (In Chapter 10 we will return to the subject of links to the community.)

The Neurology Center was a good setting for an MCC clinic. The doctors were committed to early intervention for psychosocial issues. The Center offered the support and accessibility of referring physicians and a large patient population from which to create groups. A salaried status gave me time for patient screening, recruitment, consultations, and program planning.

THE LINDA POLLIN INSTITUTE,
CHEVY CHASE, MARYLAND

Paradoxically, it was the success of the Neurology Center program that led me to leave that host setting to create the Linda Pollin Institute, a community-based outpatient clinic. The brief, structured intervention I had developed had proven effective, and I was eager to offer it to people with all kinds of long-term medical conditions. I was acutely aware of the widespread need for such services.

This necessitated the creation of a nonprofit organization. I began by recruiting outstanding people for the Institute's community governing board and medical board. Staffing was another necessity. Based on my investigations of the organization and staffing of other community clinics, I decided to hire counselors on a contract basis, splitting the fees for each patient encounter. Within three months, there were twelve part-time counselors. Patients were charged on a sliding scale based on their ability to pay. In addition, there were two salaried positions: a half-time administrator and a half-time medical director. I served as Executive Director, and also saw some 25 patients a week.

I used letters and flyers to notify my large referral network in the Washington, DC area of this new center, and my current and former patients also spread the word. While referrals from physicians who already knew of my work formed the core of the practice, we also received referrals from several other hospitals and health plans, including Group Health and the Johns Hopkins Medical Center. Our patients represented a wide range of conditions, and we worked with family members and groups as well as with individuals.

The Linda Pollin Institute was successful in the sense that we had a large patient load. But a new clinic requires time to become financially viable, and the fundraising required to sustain our operations demanded more and more of my time. After two years, I decided that I preferred working on improving my clinical model, and regretfully closed the clinic, maintaining a private practice.

It should be noted that it probably would have been difficult to launch this community-based program had I not already established a broad referral base and reputation in the community. For this reason as well as the difficulty of sustaining community financial support, I would not recommend this organizational model. It may be viable in some communities, provided that a nonclinical staff member can be responsible for fundraising and organizational development, and if it has the active support of its governing board and other volunteers, but it is a difficult way to begin.

THE WASHINGTON HOSPITAL CENTER OUTPATIENT MEDICAL CRISIS COUNSELING CENTER, WASHINGTON, DC

My relationship with the Washington Hospital Center, a large general hospital in inner-city Washington, DC, began in the mid-1980s with my creation of the Humanizing Health Care Task Force. I worked as a volunteer for more than a year with top hospital administrators and the department heads of clergy, social work, and nursing as Chair of this Task Force, and in this manner learned the hospital system. These activities and relationships helped to lay the groundwork for the later development of the Outpatient Medical Crisis Counseling Center (OMCCC) in the hospital.

As I came to know the hospital and its services, I began to envision a counseling program for the hospital's ambulatory patients. I went to the Chief Executive Officer of the parent company, Medlantic Health Care Corporation, and proposed the idea. I pointed out that an outpatient medical crisis counseling center could give them another service, "humanize" current care, and also provide the hospital with a new revenue source. Like other community hospitals, this one was eager for good public relations. The result of this discussion was a go-ahead to design a counseling program.

Armed with this mandate, my next task—and one that proved far more difficult—was to gain the cooperation of clinical staff. Unlike the cooperation I had enjoyed from some of the doctors at the Neurology Center, I encountered resistance from medical and psychiatric staff. To clarify boundaries and address their other concerns, I promised (and then developed) a tight quality assurance system for the proposed clinic. We also agreed that the OMCCC would provide short-term therapy with medical patients around their medical problems. Patients with mental illnesses would be referred for psychiatric treatment.

The OMCCC was structured as a separate department, an adjunct to the Washington Hospital Center's other programs. As in the Linda Pollin Institute, the counselors—licensed clinical social workers and psychiatrists—worked on a contractual basis and were required to attend monthly case conferences, keep appropriate case notes, and consult regularly with a psychiatric consultant.

The hospital's Director of Social Work was a strategic ally and an enthusiastic participant in the development of the OMCCC. His knowledge of the institution was invaluable. In addition, with his encouragement the hospital's social workers became a major referral source as well as contract staff for the Center.

The OMCCC began with a start-up commitment from the hospital of $250,000, spread over two years. We spent this on office space, computers, telephones, a receptionist and publicity. We kept overhead expenses to a minimum. The only full-time salaried person was the receptionist, who became a strategic staff member with a strong personal commitment to cultivating relationships with hospital staff and patients. She maintained useful records of referrals and patient load to chart our progress.

Both the OMCCC's Medical Director and I (as its Executive Director) worked part-time and were paid on a contractual, fee-for-service basis. All counselors were independent contractors, responsible for their own malpractice insurance and benefits. For therapy sessions, we shared space with the hospital's social work department. We kept computerized data on referrals, encounters, and patient and family histories and demographics. We continued the MCC practice of providing regular written reports to referring physicians.

To build receptivity to the counseling center in the hospital, it was necessary to have a "success story." Rather than spending time "pounding the pavement" where there was little interest, experience told me to concentrate on developing relationships with and designing programs for the physicians who expressed interest. It was important to find a department head who recognized the need for a medical counseling service.

The MCC program tapped into an urgent need in the Nephrology Department. This program was losing patients who were not observing proper self-care and maintenance procedures following kidney transplant surgery. The problem with these nominal "treatment failures" was not their medical care, but their attitudes and behavior following discharge. These, in turn, were largely the result of a failure to help them deal with the psychological issues of having kidney disease. Once our program was established, the Nephrology Department made counseling a precondition of receiving a transplant, and we set up a group for prospective kidney transplant patients. Despite economic deprivation, low educational levels, and (for many) drug addiction, most of the patients in this group were able to make the necessary changes in their attitudes and behavior to qualify for a transplant. Those with drug addiction problems were identified for follow-up treatment in a drug rehab program.

With the success of this program, the word about the OMCCC spread around the Washington Hospital Center. The head of the Nephrology Department sponsored Grand Rounds to showcase our program to colleagues. This led to more patient referrals and requests for special programs. During my tenure, the OMCCC designed four distinct programs for the Hospital Center, tailored to the needs of patients and providers in the cardiology, dermatology, oncology, and nephrology departments. We also saw individual patients with a wider range of conditions.

As the program gained recognition, the volume of patients rose steadily—a trend that has continued to this day. Having opened its doors in 1987 with three regular patients per week, by February 1989 the OMCCC was handling more than 80 patient encounters a month, and by May 1991 that number had risen to 200. By 1991, the Center was contracting the services of 14 licensed counselors, with medical specialties in several areas. The fact that the program is still thriving eight years later is testimony to both the need for it and its viability from clinical and management standpoints.

THE MEDICAL COUNSELING CENTER, WASHINGTON HOSPITAL CENTER

Since my departure, the OMCCC's name has been changed to the Medical Counseling Center. The Center continues to provide focused, brief counseling for inpatients and outpatients with serious illnesses. Its 22 contract therapists (all licensed social workers) have an average of 320 patient encounters per month, representing a caseload of 40 to 50 patients. Patients are referred by physicians affiliated with the Washington Hospital Center, as well as by social work staff, nurses, and nurse practitioners; or they are self-referred. With a few exceptions, services are provided on an individual basis. (The Center continues to run groups for renal patients, and also facilitates a group for cerebral palsy patients on contract with the Cerebral Palsy Society.)

The Medical Counseling Center remains a separate program in the hospital, managed by the Department of Social Work. Part of its budget is drawn from the Department of Social Work, and it is under the administrative umbrella of Resource Management, headed by the Associate Medical Director of the hospital. The Director and Assistant Director of the hospital's Social Work Department administer the program, and are paid separately, on a contract basis, for their clinical services. The counselors also work on a contract basis. Patients or third-party payers are billed on a fee-for-service basis. In addition to the social work staff, the Center has a full-time, salaried Staff Assistant to handle scheduling and billing. A hospital psychiatrist serves as the Medical Director, consulting with counselors as needed and participating in monthly case conferences.

This hospital program is unusual in that it is based in the social work department rather than the department of psychiatry. Its use of staff social workers as counselors helps keep seasoned social workers on the hospital staff by giving them the opportunity to do intensive counseling work on a consultant basis. Patients benefit by having access to experienced therapists who are familiar with problems such as theirs and understand them as normal to the adjustment process. Counselors do a thorough diagnostic screening of every patient, and, as originally agreed, those who manifest a major psychiatric illness are referred for psychiatric treatment.

Virtually all of the conditions treated at the Washington Hospital Center are represented in the Medical Counseling Center's patient population. The Center has developed several specialized programs in addition to the one for kidney transplant candidates. A presurgical behavioral conditioning service uses hypnosis and other means to prepare patients for lengthy gastrointestinal cancer surgery. Another oncology-related service offers relaxation hypnosis and visualization for anxiety-related conditions associated with chemotherapy. The Center's staff are currently developing a counseling program for asthma patients, as well as a stress management clinic for cardiac patients.

The directors of the counseling program stress that physicians and other medical colleagues (e.g., nurses and physical therapists) must be able to identify those patients who need intervention for psychosocial issues, and have devised a variety of ways to educate them about the psychological risk factors in chronic and acute illness. They distribute literature and hold information sessions for new medical staff. They also stay in touch with referring physicians about their patients' status.

The Center's directors describe a growth process whereby the Counseling Center has become fully "acculturated" as a viable referral source within the hospital. Partnerships continue to form with various medical staff members and administrators, to create new services to meet patients' needs. Unlike newer medical counseling programs, the major issues for the Washington Hospital Center's Medical Counseling Center are those associated with longevity and size. The challenges now, say its directors, are to fully integrate psychosocial services into the medical care environment, to ensure that the Center's operations (documentation, quality control, and so on) are consistent with those of the hospital, and to demonstrate its cost-effectiveness. The underlying theme of all of these activities, they note, is accountability.

Currently, considerable attention is being focused on gearing up for health care reform. As the host institution positions itself for contracts in the anticipated managed care environment, staff are positioning the Medical Counseling Center to be the hospital's provider of mental health services. As with other medical counseling programs, this one has reason to look forward to improved conditions under health care reform. In the best of the scenarios being considered, at least, payment sources would be simplified and stabilized; the program's emphasis on prevention and comprehensive services would be consonant with national health policy; and an explicit mandate would exist for providing psychosocial services along with medical treatment.

The next three programs described were created and are directed by mental health professionals currently or previously affiliated with the Linda Pollin Foundation.

MARYLAND CENTER FOR MULTIPLE SCLEROSIS, UNIVERSITY OF MARYLAND HOSPITAL

The Maryland Center for Multiple Sclerosis is part of the Department of Neurology of the University of Maryland Hospital in Baltimore. Its Director of Counseling began her relationship to the hospital as a Fellow of the Linda Pollin Institute. The idea for a multidisciplinary center for evaluating and managing MS patients originated with the head of the Department of Neurology and one of his colleagues. He asked the MCC Fellow to design and implement the clinic, an activity made possible in part by her fellowship. She has served as its Director of Counseling since 1989.

Although there has been a close collaboration between physicians and counseling staff from the inception of the Center, forming alliances with other hospital staff was the first priority when it was established. At the outset, meetings were held over a period of several months between counseling and hospital staff, with the goals of establishing a consensus that Center for Multiple Sclerosis was needed and emphasizing that all staff had a "stake" in it—that is, the need to provide the best patient care.

MS patients of the Department of Neurology are assessed by a neurologist, a nurse, and a social worker. Those who are judged to need counseling are referred to the Center. Most patients are seen individually or with family members for brief treatment. Most are seen on an outpatient basis, referred either by physicians in the Department of Neurology or by hospital social workers. Counseling services include psychosocial evaluations, individual, marital, and family treatment, and group programs.

The Center has an ongoing relationship with the Maryland Chapter of the National Multiple Sclerosis Society. The two collaborate on cross-referrals and jointly lead marital groups, and the MS Society provides an annual grant to the counseling program.

The fact that the counseling program is housed in the hospital affords regular contact between the counseling and hospital staffs. Like others in this field, she stresses the importance of actively nurturing the multidisciplinary perspective of the institution, and of educating medical colleagues about the psychological risk factors associated with the medical conditions they treat.

THE CENTER FOR LIVING, DUKE UNIVERSITY MEDICAL CENTER

The Center for Living at Duke University Medical Center was begun in 1978 as a cardiac rehabilitation facility. New residential programs were established in 1993 to meet the need for an integrated rehabilitation program that complements and consolidates the effects of medical treatment. The behavioral medicine component began in 1993 under the direction of a former Linda Pollin Fellow.

The Center for Living integrates four services: fitness, nutrition, medical treatment, and behavioral services. The coordinator of the behavioral component is an employee of the Medical Center and a member of its Psychiatry Department. The behavioral program is expected to have a staff of six within three years, including psychologists, psychiatrists, social workers, nurse practitioners, and physician assistants. All staff will either have prior experience in health counseling or be trained at the Center for Living.

Roughly half of the Center's patients make use of the Center's facilities and classes on an outpatient basis. The other half participate in 2- to

4-week intensive residential programs that combine the four components listed above. While the cardiology department continues to be the major referral base, the Center has developed widespread referrals for diabetes, pulmonary illness, and cancer, as well as disease prevention. Patients at all stages of disease use the services. Ten to twenty patients, all adults, are seen during each of the intensive residential programs.

The behavioral medicine component of the Center for Living program begins with an intake evaluation of all patients. Thereafter, they are introduced to the concepts of behavioral medicine and participate in stress management classes and a therapeutic support group for their medical condition. Individual therapy, focusing on the issues of coping with the medical crisis, is also available, as are classes in yoga, tai chi, and meditation. Psychological counseling combines cognitive, affective, and behavioral approaches. Patients pay a flat rate for the programmatic services in the rehabilitation program, and extra for additional consultation. Many third party payers reimburse for a portion of these services — a reflection of the fact that insurance companies are beginning to reimburse more fully for such lifestyle improvement rehabilitation programs.

The Center for Living also assigns a health counselor to each patient. These staff members, trained at the Center, see patients at the beginning, in the course of, and at the end of their stay and then contact them monthly to reinforce the behavioral and psychological changes made during the program. The Center also provides continuing professional education in conjunction with its intensive treatment program.

The Duke University Medical Center has exercised leadership in the health care field by creating this broad-based, integrated program. The university's vision is to demonstrate a model of care and prevention that will be widely emulated. Randomized, controlled prospective studies are being conducted to evaluate the impact of this program, looking at survival rates, economic factors, and objective and subjective health improvement measures.

PSYCHOSOCIAL SERVICES AT CHILDREN'S HOSPITAL/ JUDGE BAKER CHILDREN'S CENTER, BOSTON

Children's Hospital/Judge Baker Children's Center, a teaching hospital of Harvard Medical School, provides advanced training in psychosocial counseling and consultation-liaison work for psychiatric residents, psychology interns, and social work fellows. The hospital provides psychological assessment and counseling services, as needed, for all of its inpatients, including those who are indigent. Psychosocial services are provided by the hospital's Department of Psychiatry, in close cooperation with the hospital's medical staff.

One population served by the hospital's psychosocial services is cystic fibrosis (CF) patients. The Department of Psychiatry's Chief Psychologist supervises two to three psychology fellows a year as consultants to the CF service and to the inpatient wards where CF patients are admitted. Most of the psychological intervention takes place when persons with CF are inpatients. Some patients continue counseling on an outpatient basis after discharge. They gain additional continuity by returning periodically (normally two to three times a year) for inpatient treatment, whenever possible seeing the same counselor. The staff maintains a file of status reports and records to facilitate tracking patients' status and to maximize continuity.

Medical and mental health specialists collaborate closely on patient assessments, which are pivotal to the services at Children's Hospital. In the CF program, as with those for other conditions, the mental health consultants meet weekly with medical and adjunct staff (physicians, nurses, dietitians, continuing care nurses, and physical therapists) to review the psychosocial status of each CF inpatient and to identify those who are at risk for psychological complications. These individuals are then offered brief, intermittent counseling. The clinical intervention focuses on the clinical issues at hand, such as reactive depression in response to loss of function and disease progression, medical noncompliance, and family conflicts.

The counselors use regular reporting mechanisms to keep their program visible and to maximize its benefits to patients. A note is entered in the medical record for every patient contact, and mental health staff members maintain regular informal communication with their patients' primary physicians. Graduate students and postgraduate fellows also take part in other services at Children's Hospital, such as the Renal and Solid Organ Service and the Pain Service. In the first setting, some young patients are anticipating transplants that will radically change the course of their long-term disease and thus in their lives, whether or not they are successful. This is a prime intervention point for MCC. For children and adolescents undergoing dialysis, helping them talk about the issues around their illness and treatment reduces the chance that they will act out inappropriately, perhaps by resisting treatment. The many hours a week they spend undergoing dialysis are used for talking with counselors. (A dialysis support group's choice of a name—DREAM, or Dialysis Rules Every Aspect of Me—is a vivid example of the centrality of control issues.)

The Pain Service is a multidisciplinary program in which psychologists work with other specialists to strengthen patients' ability to manage and reduce chronic pain. Biofeedback and other methods allow patients to experience a sense of control over their bodies. The program instills in patients a sense of themselves as active participants in managing their conditions.

The programs described above show considerable institutional and even programmatic variety. The Neurology Center MCC program was affiliated with a specialized ambulatory medical practice. The Linda Pollin Institute was autonomous and had a broad referral base as well as financial support in the community. The programs at the Washington Hospital Center are an integral part of its services, although the extent of collaboration varies from department to department. Both the University of Maryland Hospital's and Children's Hospital's programs serve a segment of their patients, the former primarily for outpatients and the latter, for inpatients. Duke's Center for Living integrates four complementary emphases from screening through follow-up, in close partnership with medical providers.

Some of these programs were the idea of the mental health professionals who created them, and others came about because the host medical institution recognized their patients' need for psychosocial services and sought out specialists who could provide them. It is worth noting that for virtually all of these programs, developing a referral base has meant cultivating trust and a track record within a single medical institution and often within a single department.

To broaden the picture of possible settings and relationships for MCC programs, we now turn to two other models that are not housed in a medical institution.

HOME HEALTH CARE

Alternate site treatment is the fastest growing segment of health care today, and within that, home health care is the dominant sector. It is a mode of delivery that will probably continue to expand as national health care policy is reconfigured to realize more of the potential advantages, both financial and qualitative, of providing care at home.

While a large portion of the home care patient population receives treatment (such as infusion therapy) for acute illness, a growing number have chronic conditions. For these individuals, home care normally continues for life, often lasting many years, and usually involving strong family participation.

If the provider agency has a stable staff, these long-term relationships with nurses, drivers, physical therapists, case managers and physicians can afford an ideal opportunity for providers to assess the psychological status of patients, discern changes over time, and recommend counseling as needed.

Obviously, home health care suggests a unique version of the interface between medical and psychosocial treatment, as well as a unique site for providing treatment. In this context, the medical crisis counselor is likely to have a contractual relationship with the home health care organization to provide the psychosocial facet of its services. In addition to providing MCC, the counselor might consult in assessment conferences, helping caregivers identify the patients who need counseling. Alternatively, the counselor might provide consultations for some or all patients, at least those in high-risk groups. The medical crisis counselor would also be available to support staff and help them with burnout issues.

INDEPENDENT PRACTICE

The challenges of sustaining an MCC practice without a formal affiliation with a medical care institution have been amply noted. These challenges may become prohibitive if health care reforms restrict third party reimbursement to mental health professionals who are affiliated with an institution. Assuming that the payment issues can be resolved, there may be two conditions under which an independent MCC practice is viable. The first is when the counselor has already developed a strong reputation in the community, along with a good referral network. The other condition is when patients with health-related issues are part of a broader patient population in a mental health practice with a diversified referral base.

When I was an independent practitioner, beginning in 1983, I attempted to create another set of conditions that would both stimulate referrals and provide a mechanism for mutual support among professionals. I organized a group called "REFNET" (Referral Network), composed of independent health professionals—including nurses, speech therapists, psychologists, and social workers—who were working with the chronically ill. To my knowledge, it was the first organization of its kind in the country. We met once a month for discussion and educational events, and jointly publicized our network to local hospitals and clinics. At its most active, the network had 10 members, but it proved impossible to sustain because of the lack of a paid staff person to handle referrals.

This is an appropriate context for noting the many benefits of relationships with voluntary organizations concerned with specific illnesses (a subject discussed in more detail in Chapter 10). National organizations exist for all of the most prevalent chronic illnesses (cancer, diabetes, heart disease, etc.) as well as for many others (epilepsy, CF, MS, etc.). While their emphases and ranges of services vary, most publish informative materials and many have networks of local self-help/support groups. Links to such organizations are important to the independent practitioner, for they provide a vehicle for publicity and referrals. But their benefits far exceed this one function. Just as the medical crisis counselor augments the services of medical caregivers, peer organizations afford natural access to social support and psychoeducation, which are critical resources in the adjustment process.

BUILDING A MEDICAL CRISIS COUNSELING PROGRAM

The programs described above illustrate the range of designs and institutional settings that are possible for medical crisis counseling programs. The beginning medical crisis counselor faces two critical tasks:

- Choosing the optimal setting
- Building the alliances and structures on which a viable program depends

Choosing A Setting

Outpatient. In most communities, there are a number of theoretical options for a setting (although in fact few or none of them may be receptive). Relevant outpatient medical providers include dialysis centers, neurology clinics, cancer clinics, and orthopedics/physical rehabilitation programs, as well as general ambulatory care centers. Outpatient services are offered in a variety of other sites and under a variety of auspices, including independent physicians' offices, HMOs, community health clinics, and hospitals.

Hospital-based. A hospital-based MCC clinic may work with inpatients, outpatients, or both—with the treatment tailored accordingly. The nature and extent of the counselor's interaction with inpatients depends on many factors, including hospital policy and staffing, the relationship of the counselor to the facility, the length of hospitalization, various medical considerations, and the urgency of the patient's psychosocial issues. In some cases, contact with inpatients focuses on laying the groundwork for postdischarge treatment. Even if contact with inpatients is limited, however, it can help maximize the effectiveness of counseling by facilitating assessment and early intervention.

Most hospitals provide some form of psychosocial care through consultation-liaison psychiatrists and psychologists, social workers, and/or nurses. Respecting the boundaries between MCC and the work of these other professionals is important for optimizing the hospital's services to patients.

Inpatient. The inpatient setting can afford the medical crisis counselor easy access to both the patient and the medical providers. The hospital is often the ideal place to begin MCC treatment, assessing the patient and establishing communication and trust at a time when he or she is open to new resources. The disadvantage of this setting is that interaction is constrained by treatment regimens, and the patient is generally under physical duress because of surgery or other difficult procedures.

Whether patients are counseled on an outpatient or inpatient basis, a hospital affiliation offers the beginning medical crisis counselor an excellent chance to become familiar with a wide range of medical conditions. It also permits first-hand knowledge of the operations of the medical facility and an opportunity to develop relationships with medical colleagues. This experience will be invaluable, both as preparation for work within such institutions and as groundwork for private practice at a later time.

Private practice. The medical crisis counselor in private practice usually does not have the links to referral sources enjoyed by those affiliated with a hospital or other medical practice. For this reason, as has been noted, it is a difficult way to practice—but it can also be the most rewarding. The hallmark of MCC is adaptability to the patient's needs, and the independent practitioner has more freedom to add patients, vary schedules, and be flexible on payment than would be possible in most institutions. One drawback is that because the patient pool is smaller and more diverse, there are fewer opportunities to form groups. The independent practitioner will probably have to take the initiative in maintaining contact with medical colleagues in order to stimulate referrals and report and consult on patients.

Other. One option for the independent medical crisis counselor is to see clients through *home visits*, possibly on contract to a home health care service. Although this mode of delivery is time-consuming and takes counselors away from their offices, it also makes it possible to observe patients and families in their own environment, where they may be more at ease. Seeing patients in a *nursing home* or *hospice* is much like home visits, in that the patient, although institutionalized, is not undergoing acute care.

Building Alliances

The "threshold" condition for an MCC program is that those with medical concerns, including families, know about its services. To promote the integration of medical care and counseling, it is preferable for patients to be referred by a health care provider, rather than to be self-referred. It is also important that the counselor communicate with the referring physician. Although there are a number of means to these ends, we will concentrate here on the most common and feasible one, which is affiliating with a medical institution.

A medical institution may affiliate with or support an MCC program for a number of reasons. A likely one is a desire to maximize the effectiveness of medical treatment through early intervention and/or follow-up. In the best instance, the host institution underwrites the MCC program's start-up and gives it time to become self-sustaining. A commitment by the institution to the program's creation is a sine qua non, made manifest through cooperation by the institution's staff. Cooperation can be operationalized in such ways as designing integrated services, making referrals, facilitating communication, and giving visibility to the MCC program.

Steps To Building A Medical Crisis Counseling Program

The following is a simplified outline of steps involved in establishing an MCC clinic.

1. *Study its feasibility and the market*
   - Learn about the health care system in your community, including its private and public agencies, institutions, professional networks, and community resources.
2. *Build visibility, relationships, confidence*
   - Build relationships and alliances with local health care institutions and professional circles, and with consumer groups and community services.
3. *Commit to a context and structure*
   - Choose the most viable treatment setting with which to affiliate.
   - Secure an agreement from the institution to offer counseling services. (This can be either a mandate from the top administration or an alliance with someone in the system, such as a department head).
   - Work out details of employment or contractual relationship.

4. *Organize the internal set-up and management*
   - Arrange for an administrative coordinator (who must be trained regarding the program's philosophy and procedures).
   - If the program is to have more than one counselor, engage counselors to complement your expertise and plan their training.
   - Establish mechanisms for training, supervision, clinical conferences, and quality assurance.
   - Establish criteria and procedures for assessment, referral, and treatment.
   - Set up a referral network, minimally with one assured referral source. (The program may be custom designed if there is only one referral source.)
   - Design special protocols and services as needed (such as preop and postop assessments or routine consultations).
   - Plan any services for special patients (deaf, non-English-speaking, indigent, etc.).
   - Develop patient education materials and procedures.
   - Establish a community resource file and links to community services.
   - Develop patient files and report mechanisms, compatible with the host institution's practices.
   - Set up billing and reimbursement (or other financing) arrangements, including provisions for indigent patients.
5. *Invest in maintenance and growth*
   - Initiate and maintain public relations activities and outreach to health care colleagues, to give your program visibility and support.
   - Continue to build relationships in the wider community, for the same purpose.
   - Review and evaluate outcomes on an ongoing basis, and develop new programs and services as needed.

Barriers

It is not unusual for innovation to be met with resistance and obstacles — some stemming from people's attitudes, and some that are a function of institutional structures and procedures. These obstacles can be part of the reality in which the medical crisis counselor must operate. In my experience, the attitudes that create barriers include mistrust, apathy, ignorance about psychosocial processes, competitiveness, and interdepartmental tensions; structural factors include rigid payment schemes, limited operating funds, lack of communication mechanisms, and the inertia that is the path of least resistance in any organization.

What can be done about such obstacles? Anyone who has set up an MCC-type program will have experience-based answers to that question. Here are a few.

- Organize the program as a pilot, entailing a limited financial risk and an end date by which it must either meet stated goals or be terminated.
- Set realistic goals.
- Analyze the interests of each constituency, and tailor outreach and problem-solving accordingly.
- Communicate clearly about the distinct benefits and accomplishments of the program.
- Educate medical colleagues about psychosocial factors in the illness process, and how they should be addressed.
- Be sensitive to the constraints and needs of the institution, and realistic about the slow pace of institutional change.

A Few Suggestions for Starting A Medical Crisis Counseling Program

Start modestly and keep it simple — but think big. Part of understanding the medical setting is knowing the scale of its operations and its flexibility and tolerance for risk. As you contemplate a particular setting, it is important not to underestimate the institution's capacities. Taking financial and other risks is part of every business, including health care.

Nevertheless, change happens slowly, and even in propitious times most managers are cautious. Hence the injunction to start modestly and to keep things simple. In my experience, the important thing has been to get one's foot in the door. In the early days of my two "affiliated" clinics, I requested modest working conditions. My purpose was not only to show good will and keep costs down but, equally important, to maximize the likelihood that the program would be given a chance. When these programs stabilized and demonstrated their value, both host institutions insisted on providing more adequate office space and staff support.

Take seriously the needs of the host institution. The clinic or hospital that is being cultivated as the host institution is most likely to be receptive to an MCC program that is sensitive to the realities and constraints under which it operates. This subject is discussed more fully in the next chapter.

Expect and prepare for resistance. It is in the nature of institutions to resist change, and it is in the nature of innovations to stimulate resistance. Analyze your environment to know in advance about possible sources of resistance and how you will handle it. The flexibility that is so important in MCC begins with finding new ways to accomplish goals when the original plans do not work out.

Build a cohesive, broad-based counseling staff. Patients benefit when the MCC staff comprises a range of expertise. Depending on the patient population, desirable areas of experience and specialization can include AIDS, cardiology, neurology, diabetes, genetics, gastroenterology, hemophilia, nephrology, oncology, ophthalmology, and orthopedics. Other forms of specialization and differentiation can include group work, family therapy, and various clinical techniques such as hypnosis, visualization, and behavior therapy.

Whatever their similarities and individual strengths, however, the staff must agree about its treatment philosophy. Such consistency comes from clear initial training and orientation, followed by regular staff conferences. These conferences, which can be daily, weekly, or monthly, afford the chance to review and consult on cases, as well as to increase the internal consistency and strength of treatment.

The ability of the clinical director to articulate the philosophy, objectives, and content of MCC can be tested with mental health colleagues as well as with patients and medical professionals. It is important to be able to say what is distinctive about this approach, and why it unfolds in a particular way. In my mind, there is no contradiction between this statement and the principle that counseling is an art in which the professional uses considerable individual judgment and a unique set of skills and instincts.

Keep services affordable. One certainty with patients with chronic illness is the ongoing financial burden they bear for such expenses as medication, different kinds of therapy, hospitalization, medical equipment, and home care. In addition, the illness may have caused a reduction in their income. Although therapy is sometimes viewed as a dispensable luxury, the small and fixed number of MCC sessions make this intervention feasible when others may not be. If at all possible, fees should be set on a sliding scale so that low-income patients can use it. Many hospitals, of course, subsidize whatever psychosocial support they offer patients, especially those on public assistance.

Be flexible. Much of the administrative shape of an MCC program is determined by the needs of the specific patient population it is serving. The underlying principle is simple: Do the utmost to accommodate patients' needs. Every illness has its own set of exigencies that must be taken into consideration.

It must be understood that as a group MCC patients are different from those of a typical psychotherapy practice. A simple example is missed appointments. While last-minute cancellations or tardiness may be assumed to indicate resistance in another treatment context, in this one there can be a host of practical, physical reasons for the delay.

Flexibility with patients is needed across the gamut of operations: in appointment scheduling, payment issues, involvement of family members, the site of care, and the number of sessions. Special efforts may be needed to ensure access, given the functional limitations associated with many chronic conditions. The energy level of patients will also vary, both from patient to patient and from time to time.

Reach out to patients. In all three of my MCC programs, I always stayed alert for common concerns among patients in order to develop new groups. Whenever I started a group, I called patients who I thought might find it useful. Some therapists (as was the case for some of my staff) have difficulty recruiting patients in this way. But in my experience, it is an entirely appropriate way to inform people of services. The tone of the contact is simply to encourage them to pursue the opportunity *if they are interested*. Staying visible with potential referring physicians is another way of reaching out (indirectly) to patients.

Make services visible to medical colleagues and to the wider community. Patients will benefit most when the community at large, health and self-help organizations, and medical professionals are aware of MCC services. Creating and maintaining visibility is a challenge, and requires a consistent effort. From the sponsoring institution's point of view, publicizing valuable services is both good community relations and good business. There is thus a shared interest in maintaining visibility for the MCC program. In addition, informing referring physicians of outcomes is not only good marketing, it is good patient care. Sharing success stories has the added benefit of bolstering the morale of patients and staff.

CHAPTER NINE

The Alliance With Medical Care

It should be clear from the program descriptions in the previous chapter that a multitude of ways exist for operationalizing the relationship between medical crisis counseling and medical care. In all cases, however, these structures should meet two objectives: They should be compatible with the needs of the medical and counseling programs, and they should promote cooperation between them. The atmosphere should involve mutual respect, consultation, and collaboration, based on the belief that a comprehensive approach benefits the largest number of patients and affords them the best care.

However this relationship is operationalized, it is always based on the same principles:

- The patient is a multifaceted person and not simply a diseased physical system.
- Both medical and counseling skills are important in promoting healing.
- The medical/MCC alliance is itself embedded in a broad therapeutic alliance that involves not just professional caregivers but also the patient and family members; each of these participants has something of unique value to contribute to the healing and adjustment process.

THE COUNSELOR'S CONTRIBUTIONS

To this therapeutic alliance, the medical crisis counselor brings skills and insights to significantly help people for whom medical science can do little more than treat symptoms and limit damage. The counselor also helps patients address psychological and emotional issues that otherwise might prompt inappropriate visits to physicians, thus freeing the physician to spend time on medical problems.

Medical crisis counselors can increase medical treatment efficacy by mobilizing and supporting positive attitudes and behaviors in patients. They can also help patients identify problems in their relationships with health care providers and develop ways to improve them. Most people find comfort and support in simply knowing that their health care providers and counselors are in contact. This knowledge also reinforces for everyone the awareness that the process is a holistic one.

The counselor is constantly assessing and tracking the patient's emotional status, and is therefore in a position to call the physician's attention to special concerns, as well as to factors that could affect the patient's health, such as family and work stresses. If given the mandate, the counselor can instruct and coordinate the health care team around psychosocial issues, and advise medical colleagues on their approach to patients' concerns. Promoting understanding and effectiveness in this manner can help medical workers avoid the extreme frustration, discouragement, and burnout that can come from working with patients with severe, protracted conditions.

Some counselors coach health care providers on such matters as how to convey a difficult diagnosis, and when and how to refer patients for counseling. A successful referral is made in a reassuring, nonthreatening manner, and stresses that the physician is concerned about the patient's personal life and regards counseling as a potentially helpful resource in the adjustment process.

In sum, the medical crisis counselor helps optimize the patient's participation in medical care and health promotion by enhancing the ability to communicate, acquire information, and take responsibility for behavior that has an effect on health. A related role is stimulating active information-sharing among caregivers, to track the status of patients and to support the best decisions about treatment. Equally important, the counselor supports professional colleagues and also educates them, raising their awareness of the psychosocial aspects of long-term illness and the value of prevention and early intervention.

The counselor also may have occasion to serve as an advocate for recommended treatment and self-care procedures to which the patient is resistant, and/or to identify areas of confusion. (Medical questions are always referred back to the physician.) Conversely, he or she may be called upon to represent the patient to the physician in regard to specific concerns. Critical information can be exchanged with the physician, for the benefit of the patient.

THE MEDICAL PROFESSIONAL'S CONTRIBUTION

For their part, medical professionals bring to this relationship a knowledge of medical factors, the individual patient and the broader patient population, and the health care system. They also, of course, are a major referral source, and they bear primary responsibility for patients' care and well-being.

Medical professionals can contribute to the longitudinal, comprehensive perspective on patients by communicating their observations of changes in physical and mental status. In addition, they are likely to have some contact with family members and can be alert to their need for counseling. They have an overview of the patient population that is potentially served by the medical crisis counselor, and thus are important consultants in group formation. They also know and control links to the health care institution and its staff and, if so inclined, can advise the counselor on working effectively in the system.

Of course, physicians are not the only health care professionals with whom the medical crisis counselor develops relationships. Others to whom much of the discussion in this chapter applies include nurses, physician's assistants, physicial therapists, occupational therapists, social workers, and consultation-liaison specialists, as well as hospital clergy and administrative staff.

Social workers and administrative staff such as receptionists are especially important sources of referrals to MCC. They often have repeated contact with patients, and of an informal, non-task-oriented nature that inspires trust, a key precondition of a successful referral. These professionals also develop considerable knowledge of patients, and are able to observe changes that may signal a need for counseling. In some cases, patients learn about MCC through these relationships and may seek it on their own, or ask their physicians about it.

THE BENEFITS AND GOALS OF A VISIBLE RELATIONSHIP

One advantage of a close and visible working relationship, especially when it begins early in the patient's illness, is that it mitigates the stigma often associated with psychotherapy and "mental problems" and reinforces the notion that counseling is a natural component of health care. Visible links and overlaps between medical and mental health elements of treatment transform "integrated, comprehensive care" from a theoretical construct to a practical reality.

The institutional structures set up between the host institution and the medical crisis counselor exist to promote referrals, communication, and constructive information exchange between counselors and medical professionals. Within these structures, much of the substance of the relationship takes place between individual practitioners, and largely in regard to specific patients.

At a minimum, the relationship between the medical provider and the medical crisis counselor consists of referrals by the former and reports by the latter. These two elements form the essential core. In the most dynamic and complex, and arguably the most fruitful, form of partnership, the MCC program is housed in the medical institution (hospital or clinic) and the consultation and joint activity between them have many facets.

In a 1979 paper, James Rosen and Arthur Wiens proposed such an arrangement, urging that psychologists be included in medical teams and regarded as "physical" health professionals. With such an arrangement, they argue,

> Physician and psychologist are viewed by the patient as part of one health care team, and it is not necessary for the physician to refer the patient elsewhere for psychological consultation. This obviates the sense of rejection or self-perception of failure in treatment that all too often characterizes the patient who is referred elsewhere, perhaps even more so when the referral is to a mental health professional.[1]

The authors base their argument on the fact that many visits to physicians are prompted by psychological causes, making it cost-effective to facilitate access to the proper specialist. Many related arguments for such a team approach could be put forward.

Despite the existence of such arguments for well over a decade, in many places it is still a struggle to gain a foothold for psychosocial care in medical settings. It is only natural, therefore, to view the relationship with medical providers in terms of "selling" the MCC program and simply getting it "in the door." While these may, indeed, be the conditions under which the program begins, its viability will be directly related to the extent to which it is truly integrated into the health care system, both structurally and attitudinally. This does not necessarily imply a multifaceted relationship; interaction may involve no more than the two core elements mentioned above—referrals and reports. However, even these minimal conditions will be achieved only when the MCC program is accepted within the institution and not perceived as imposed; when the value of its services is recognized, at least by some practitioners; and when its operations are compatible with the host institution's values and modes of operation.

Ultimately, the goal is for the relationship between the MCC program and the host institution to be mutually beneficial and organic—in other words, to allow the specifics to change and evolve along with circumstances. To achieve this integration, the medical crisis counselor must first understand the environment and its needs, and then be prepared to adapt the MCC program accordingly. It must be remembered that MCC plays a supporting role in a medical treatment setting and is there to enhance medical care. Every system has its culture, operating requirements, and short- and long-run goals. To create the conditions for an effective working relationship, the counselor must be knowledgeable about the system, attentive, and willing to be flexible.

The practical areas in which the alliance can take place reflect the types and degrees of integration between counseling and medical treatment. In addition to referrals and reporting, there can be collaboration in such areas as program development and coordination, patient assessment, case consultations, quality assurance and program evaluation. The programs described in Chapter 8 illustrate each of these types of collaboration. Generally, the more of these elements that are involved, the better it is for the MCC program and the patient. Of course, the counselor plays the major role in designing the counseling program; the collaboration focuses on integrating those services into the overall operations of the institution.

ESTABLISHING TRUST

Even if both medical and counseling professionals bring to their working relationship a commitment to integrated treatment, they still must develop trust as individuals. And before this can happen, the medical crisis counselor must "know and be known." Usually, although not always, the counselor takes the initiative in establishing a relationship with health care providers.

It is important for the counselor to have achieved a reputation as a credible and competent professional among medical providers in the community. The programs described in Chapter 8 offer several good examples of ways to establish trust, beginning with gaining visibility. This can come, for example, through doing volunteer work in the community or for a health care institution, publicizing professional activities and their results, and showing expertise by offering educational services on the psychosocial dimension of illness. As was observed in Chapter 8, the medical crisis counselor must be able to compellingly articulate what MCC is and why it is needed.

The more the medical crisis counselor knows about the structures, interests, and modes of operation of the institution and its major players, the better. The counselor acquires such information at the outset, when considering alternative settings and then establishes an affiliation with a health care institution. Thereafter, information-gathering is focused on identifying changes that might be necessary or beneficial, such as opportunities for new programs. This is part of the maintenance and growth effort listed as the "last step" in building an MCC program (page 170).

Being attuned to the needs and interests of the health care institution will enable the counselor to identify ways to be useful — that is, for example, which hospital department might be most receptive. Here, a sensitivity to economic and business factors as well as to medical factors is crucial. Often, business rather than clinical considerations create the initial openness to offering MCC in a medical setting.

In general, the idea is to find the institution's incentives for having an MCC program. Perhaps offering additional services gives the institution a competitive edge; perhaps too many patients are seeking medical treatment for nonphysical concerns; perhaps the institution is seeking ways to operationalize its commitment to prevention and early intervention. Whatever it is, this incentive provides the first opening for building a relationship and suggests the specific ways in which it will function.

COMMUNICATION

Once the relationship is established, communication is the thread that runs through all facets of the medical crisis counselor's activity with physicians and other health care colleagues. The process normally begins with the referral, although there is a prior step when counselors assist in screening potential patients. In the initial consultation, the counselor discusses with the patient the benefits of having ongoing communication with the referring physician, and ideally secures permission to establish or maintain this contact. The counselor communicates with the referring physician only if the patient gives permission.

If this is granted, the physician is kept informed of the patient's progress in counseling. Most communication is in written form, through case notes that are brief, clear, up-to-date, and free of psychological jargon. The purpose of these notes is to keep the physician informed of the patient's mental state, and, if needed, to call attention to specific problems. The counselor also may occasionally contact the physician for special consultations.

PUBLICITY/VISIBILITY

As every health professional knows, visibility is one of the keys to getting referrals. No matter how effective a program is clinically, there still must be ways to get the word out so that new patients can benefit from its services. For an institution- affiliated program, visibility can be maintained through contact with individual physicians, appropriate hospital department heads, nonphysician hospital/clinic staff, other health care institutions, consumer groups, and the community at large. Letters, personal visits, brochures and flyers, television and radio appearances, newspaper and newsletter articles, speeches, receptions, and provision of free services for the community are vehicles for gaining visibility.

A hospital or clinic public relations department can be a useful resource for publicizing the MCC program. The public relations department's contacts with the media can lead to print and electronic coverage that would be difficult or impossible for the counselor to arrange personally. Institutional public relations staff also have control of important vehicles such as newsletters, bulletin boards, and advertising budgets.

These "broadcasting" activities supplement and undergird the patient-focused, one-to-one communication that is the medical crisis counselor's chief priority and which is at the heart of contact with medical professionals. The purpose of these broader efforts is to publicize the program more widely to health professionals and the community at large. The balance among different approaches to communication and publicity must be carefully worked out in the light of local conditions and attitudes.

WHAT THE COUNSELOR MUST KNOW

What must the medical crisis counselor know to build and contribute to a good working relationship with health care professionals? The knowledge falls into three areas:

1. The health care setting itself (discussed above)
2. The patient's medical condition: symptoms, major impacts, typical course, treatment, and self-care regimens
3. Details of the patient's pathway through the medical system

Most counselors will acquire general knowledge about relevant medical conditions early in their practice. Often, the specifics of these conditions influence the way counseling is structured and integrated into the medical setting. To this general knowledge is added whatever specific information the clinician needs in order to counsel individual patients, some acquired through the patient interview and some from other sources.

It is critically important for the counselor to be familiar with the details of the patient's pathway through the medical system because they have a significant impact on MCC. Here is the kind of information that the counselor must acquire from the patient, or other sources, about his or her past, present, and anticipated medical experiences:

- What is the medical diagnosis and prognosis?
- What are the patient's treatment and self-care regimens?
- When was the patient diagnosed?
- What has transpired medically since the diagnosis?
- When was the patient referred to MCC?
- Who referred the patient?
- Is referral routine for that provider or institution?
- What were the conditions of that referral?
- Is there resistance on the part of the medical patient or family?
- What kind of communication does the referring physician want to have with the medical crisis counselor (written, telephone, meetings)?
- What is the patient's relationship to medical caregivers at present? (On-going treatment? Periodic consultation?)
- What is the relationship between the family and the medical care providers? What role has the family caregiver had in treatment?
- What are the functions in the health care institution of consultation-liaison psychiatrists, social workers, and other psychosocial staff? What are their attitudes to MCC?
- What relationships does the institution/provider have with community organizations and agencies?

INVOLVING THE FAMILY IN THE THERAPEUTIC ALLIANCE

As we have seen throughout this book, family members play a central role in the care of people with long-term illnesses: They are often heavily involved in relating to medical professionals and carrying out instructions for home care; they are an important conduit of information on the medical condition; and they monitor the patient's welfare on a daily basis.

Yet despite their critical role, they often have frustrating, or at least ambiguous, relationships with health care professionals in which they struggle to define and protect a caregiving role.

The medical crisis counselor can play a strategic role in promoting communication and cooperation between these vital caregivers. If given the opportunity to coach family members in their relationship to the physician, for example, the counselor can help them articulate their unique caregiving role as well as its boundaries. Family members may need help to identify problems they wish to discuss with the physician. For their part, medical professionals may be receptive to advice about how to communicate more effectively with family members about caregiving.

MS patient Jack Goldman and his wife Marilyn were introduced in Chapter 4 (see page 79). Their story illustrates the way that the medical crisis counselor, the patient, family members, family physician and specialists can all cooperate in managing a patient's illness and maximizing the quality of life.

The Goldmans took the lead in establishing links among the various parties in this alliance. I began working with them while on the staff of the Neurology Center, so it was easy and natural for me to communicate with Jack's neurologist about his condition. I learned, for example, that emotional volatility is a typical side-effect of Prednisone, which is used to treat MS symptoms, and I was able to alert the neurologist when Jack was having an adverse reaction to the medication.

The Goldmans saw to it that I was also in contact with their primary physician, and that he and their neurologist conversed. These links afforded easy communication among us, but equally important, they reinforced in each member of this therapeutic alliance, including Jack and Marilyn, the sense of being engaged in comprehensive care for a person, not just in a fight against a disease. Indeed, the care was for the entire family, not just an individual. All this was accomplished with very little expenditure of time by any of the professional caregivers involved.

TRAINING HEALTH CARE PROFESSIONALS
FOR EFFECTIVE RELATIONSHIPS

As I said in the first chapter, most medical professionals cannot be expected to have the time or skill to meet all of their chronically ill patients' psychosocial needs. I believe that physicians who, for whatever reason, are unable to meet these needs should not be perceived as poor doctors. However, they do have a responsiblity to recognize those needs and to refer their patients to specialized counselors.

Looking beyond individual practitioners to the health care system as a whole, I believe that health care institutions are responsible for cultivating the alliance between medical professionals who assess and refer and mental health professionals who provide psychosocial support.

The process begins with professional education, including training for screening, assessment, referral, counseling, and professional consultation, among others. Health professionals should be sensitized at the earliest possible stage—that is, in school—to both the psychosocial aspects of illness and their normalcy. They need to understand, as we saw in Chapter 1,

- that the balance has shifted from acute to long-term medical problems;
- that "chronic" and "terminal" are not synonymous;
- that there is a growing "population of survivors" with special physical and emotional needs;
- and that these shifts represent diminishing opportunities to cure patients and growing opportunities to care for them.

In addition to improving their own ability to communicate with and support patients—such as when they have the painful task of giving an unwelcome diagnosis—health professionals need to identify patients who need professional help to adjust to their illnesses, and know how to recommend counseling in an unthreatening way. These are just some of the subjects that should be a routine and integral part of medical professional training.

Recognizing these needs and opportunities, Harvard Medical School launched a program in 1994 to develop MCC as a facet of its curriculum. It will also offer programs whereby health professionals already in the field can earn continuing professional education credits for strengthening their skills and knowledge in this area.

The other side of the medical/mental health alliance, of course, is specialized counseling. As I have noted, the health field has made significant progress in this regard over the last decade; but much more is needed. A workshop on MCC held in Bethesda, Maryland, in 1989 articulated a vision of the kind of education and training needed to equip mental health professionals to fill the service gap. After that meeting, a training committee released a report entitled "The Need for Multidisciplinary Training in Counseling the Medically Ill,"[2] which stated,

> [G]ood counselors will need training in the essentials of coping, communi-
> cation, and support, in addition to the proper credentials of their specialty,
> whether in medicine, psychiatry, psychology, social work, or nursing. Such
> training will require 1) a sound appreciation and respect for the patient as
> an autonomous individual, 2) firsthand knowledge of disease in all its
> manifestations, and 3) experience and guidance in assessing psychosocial
> problems and in adapting and applying major modes of appropriate inter-
> vention.
>   Training for medical counselors requires that medicine and psychiatry
> give up the position that counseling is only a negligible offshoot that almost
> any professional can readily do. [3]

Many of these principles are now being implemented in training efforts
around the country, including those supported since 1988 by the Linda
Pollin Foundation. After four years of providing MCC training in several
outstanding institutions, the foundation consolidated its postgraduate Fellows program in Boston in 1993. The current MCC training program
reflects the rich diversity of the health field: Postgraduate Fellows are
placed in a number of Harvard-affiliated health care institutions (including
Children's Hospital/Judge Baker Children's Center, where the program is
housed); they work with a variety of illness populations and age groups;
they have been trained in several disciplines (e.g., psychology, social work,
nursing); and they come from and will return to diverse health care settings
around the country.

The experience of one Linda Pollin Foundation Fellow illustrates the
multidisciplinary nature of MCC, as well as the practical experience in
teamwork that young professionals are getting through the training. This
individual worked in three programs in 1993–94: the Renal and Solid
Organ Service and the Pain Service, both at Children's Hospital, and the
Children's Oncology Service at the neighboring Dana Farber Institute.
In all three settings, assessment and treatment activities regularly enlist
contributions from a range of professionals, including physicians in many
specializations, physical therapists, psychologists, social workers, nurses in
several categories, and child life specialists. Thus, this clinical psychologist's
postgraduate training—like that of many others—is familiarizing him not
only with the medical and psychosocial issues of his patients and their
families, but also with the dynamics of working in a multidisciplinary team
to promote patients' wellbeing.

We can hope for more training of this kind around the country, to
produce skilled and sensitive counselors for the millions of Americans who
need their assistance.

NOTES

1. Rosen, J., & Wiens, A. (1979, May). Changes in medical problems and use of medical services following psychological intervention. *American Psychologist.* 420–431.

2. Reports from this meeting are published in *General Hospital Psychiatry* (1992, November), *14*(6)(Suppl.).

3. *General Hospital Psychiatry,* p. 4S.

CHAPTER TEN

Community Resources

In recent years, a number of forces have converged to place the biomedical model of health care in a broader framework, conceptually and practically. This new framework is called by a variety of names, reflecting different sources of the impetus to broaden the focus of health care. To a greater or lesser degree, each of these models looks beyond the organ-level pathology to the person, and beyond the person to the relationships and the broader environment of which he or she is a part—including the family, socioeconomic status, and other community and environmental factors. The practical result of these conceptualizations, both individually and collectively, is to broaden the focus of health care.

Medical crisis counseling is a natural part of this broad-minded approach. The medical crisis counselor can only be effective by being familiar not just with clinical techniques and medical conditions, but also with the systems in which patients live—the systems that affect them and upon whose resources they can draw.

The fact that MCC is a brief intervention makes it especially important to maintain this sense of context. Its focus on capacity-building involves identifying and drawing on external as well as internal resources. Even if patients return for periodic counseling, the thrust of MCC is to enable people to live full lives in their communities. The integration that is sought extends beyond personal emotions and attitudes to the person's place in the family and the community.

The counselor can promote this goal by ensuring that patients are familiar with the resources available to them when they complete counseling. Being linked into the community through a neighborhood activity, a service project, a self-help group, a health association, or other venue will enable them to continue to affirm and build their capacities. Organizations that focus on their condition will afford access to information, vital social support, and channels for advocacy in that area.

One way to illustrate the connections between MCC and community resources is to look at the eight issues framing MCC treatment in terms of relevant community resources (see Table 10.1). Obviously, there is considerable overlap among the categories, and there could be many versions of the list that appears in the table. The purpose of this version is merely to suggest the range of resources that lie outside the counseling office, to consolidate and extend what takes place inside it. To avoid repetition, self-help groups are indicated as a resource in respect to only one issue. Anger was chosen for this illustration because of self-help groups' unique value as a place to express emotions. In fact, they could have been listed opposite every issue because of the scope of benefits they offer, which include information, support, advocacy, and volunteer opportunities.

BENEFITS FOR COUNSELORS

Of course, community resources exist for counselors as well as their patients. They can help counselors indirectly by strengthening patients, thereby making counseling more effective and sustaining its results. There are many more direct benefits as well. Health-focused organizations like Cansurvive, the American Diabetes Association, and Heart to Heart can provide a means of communication and visibility between counselors and the patient populations they serve. The counselor may be able to serve as

Table 10.1
CONNECTIONS BETWEEN MCC AND
COMMUNITY RESOURCES

Issue	Community Resources and Services
Control	Health information; financial aid and advice
Self-image	Employment advice; volunteer opportunities
Dependency	Recreation and entertainment
Stigma	Advocacy
Abandonment	Caregiver support
Anger	Self-help groups
Isolation	Friends programs; Meals on Wheels
Death	Home nursing; hospices; bereavement support

an expert resource for a consumer group or to collaborate on programs, and this service in turn may lead to referrals.

Some examples of counselor-community alliances of this kind were mentioned in Chapter 8. The Director of Counseling at the Maryland Center for Multiple Sclerosis is in regular contact with the local MS Society, which provides some financial support for her program and publicizes its services. The Medical Counseling Center at the Washington Hospital Center runs a group for people with cerebral palsy under contract to the Cerebral Palsy Society. Some home care companies support patient advocacy efforts to gain full use of entitlements for themselves and others.

In the information area, many community resources exist for counselors. Libraries, databases, and health organizations are useful sources of information on medical conditions. These sources can supplement the information available from professional networks and academic and professional journals, and usually provide it in nontechnical language that can be shared with and easily understood by laypersons. Many counselors also have access to electronic communities of interest, through on-line databases. Like the other information sources, these electronic resources are also available to patients, provided they have the financial and technical capacity to take advantage of them.

Counselors who are called upon to help patients deal with practical issues or to support their self-advocacy can increase their effectiveness by knowing the policies and practices of local social service agencies. Depending on patients' needs, services can include home nursing, nursing homes, schools, entitlements, transportation, employment, workman's compensation, and housing. The possible arenas are too numerous for the counselor to be knowledgeable about all of them. At a minimum, however, counselors should know how to begin the problem-solving and advocacy process. If some issues are likely to arise frequently because of the nature of the patient population, the counselor is advised to become familiar with that arena at the outset. It may also be useful to establish relationships with relevant agencies.

ASSESSING RESOURCES AND BUILDING INFORMATION FILES

Program and Service Information

The following lists can be used to identify and assess the resources that exist in the local community. Information on programs and services such as these can be maintained in manual files and/or on a computer, for use by the counselor and patients and family members.

Community services can include:

- Day care
- Recreation and entertainment
- Meals on Wheels
- Home nursing
- Health information
- Respite support
- Companionship
- Financial aid or advice
- Advocacy
- Special transportation
- Peer support
- Hotlines

Local organizations that may be sources of such services, or at least sources of information about them, include:

- Volunteer caregiver organizations
- Religious congregations
- Local health organizations (including chapters of national organizations)
- Local caregiver organizations
- Hospices
- Drop-in centers
- Public and private social service agencies
- Information clearinghouses
- Self-help groups
- Self-help clearinghouses
- Hospitals and other healthcare institutions
- Libraries

In addition, the following types of *national or regional organizations* and programs offer services to the public:

- National, state, and regional self-help clearinghouses
- Government health and human services agencies
- Health organizations and other interest-based organizations
- Databases and electronic bulletin boards
- Specialized information services

Several sources of information on regional and national resources are listed in the Appendix.

At the risk of belaboring the obvious, it should be noted that especially with local organizations, but even with national ones, the names, addresses, telephone numbers, contact persons, prices, and all manner of other details can change frequently. An out-of date resource list can be almost as useless and even more frustrating than having none at all; so it is advisable to store the information in a form that permits easy updating, and to create a mechanism for actually doing so periodically.

In addition to gathering information on these local, regional, and national resources, the counselor may wish to develop relationships with some organizations. The extent and nature of these relationships will vary greatly, depending on the counseling practice and the community in which it operates.

Health and Treatment Information

The counselor will also wish to acquire, and to help patients acquire, literature containing patient information on medical factors and related subjects such as recommended treatment and treatment options. Most major health organizations have information of this kind. Additional sources, of course, are journal articles and entries in reference materials such as the *Physician's Desk Reference*.

In general, there are so many written materials available to patients that the term "bibliotherapy" has become standard usage, and its practice routine, for many therapists. Patients with fewer educational advantages may need assistance in learning how to use such resources.

ASSESSING AND SUPPORTING PATIENTS' USE OF RESOURCES

Helping patients make use of local and national resources begins with assessing both what they are already doing in this regard and their personal capacity to use the resources. (It is assumed that the counselor already knows what resources are available.)

Determining what the patient is already doing is relatively simple, and can be addressed through a few questions in the early stages of treatment. Some people enter MCC well-grounded in community life, and active in such groups or organizations as religious communities, cultural groups, neighborhood programs, or self-help groups. In such cases, the counselor need only play a supportive role and look for ways to augment these involvements, as needed. Alternatively, the counselor may help patients reexamine any involvements that seem counterproductive, as in the case of Jennifer in Chapter 4 (page 88).

Assessing a patient's capacity to use community resources is more complex. First, the counselor must be aware of personal biases in order to minimize their influence. For example, people in some ethnic groups are sometimes perceived as infrequent users of community resources because they may be less likely to use public or institutional ones. However, studies show that they are more likely than other groups to have access to support and resources within their ethnic communities.

Second, the factors that influence people's actual and perceived capacities in this area are subtle, and lie beyond the usual purview of psychology. In particular, socioeconomic status and educational level can have an impact both on people's awareness of local resources and on their confidence in using them. In some cases, people may have experienced discrimination or poor treatment, giving them the understandable impression that the services of a particular organization or agency are not for "their kind of people." Such experiences naturally cause reluctance to explore and use public resources. It is also possible that the patient is currently encountering barriers in his or her attempt to use community resources.

And third, even if they are already linked to community resources and activities, newly diagnosed patients may be unaware of the resources for people with their condition. If they are fortunate, these will include both a national organization and one or more local self-help/support groups. Most people are comfortable contacting the former to request information on their condition. They may be less so when it comes to exploring the latter (which are discussed in greater detail below).

CONTRIBUTING TO THE RESOURCE BASE

As members of their communities, patients and counselors can be more than just consumers; they can also contribute to local assets by creating resources. The story below of the National Family Caregivers Association created by a former MCC patient is a stellar example of the self-help process: people doing something for others that is also helpful to themselves.

There are a host of ways in which people with medical conditions can reach outside themselves and discover the benefits of helping and working with others. The possible settings and activities include advocacy to change public policies, person-to-person service programs, entertainment and arts projects, and communication and information services. Although most of these services are offered on a volunteer basis, some have the potential to generate income for the provider because consumers are willing and able to pay for them.

RESOURCES FOR CAREGIVERS

Although they are limited, many communities have some services and self-help programs for family caregivers. These may include special care-giver support groups, or the inclusion of family members in groups that focus on specific medical conditions and disabilities. Some such groups run parallel activities for those with the condition and their caregivers. In addition, some community organizations and social service agencies offer respite services, to enable caregivers to get away from their duties from time to time.

The National Family Caregivers Association

The National Family Caregivers Association (NFCA) is a self-help effort on a large scale. A young organization with some 1100 members at present, it is laying the foundation to be a resource, advocate, and net-worker for the estimated 17 million Americans who care for ill and disabled family members.

NCFA's two founders both care for chronically ill family members— one, a husband with MS; the other, a mother with Parkinson's disease. They launched the organization in 1992, wishing to do something con-structive about the paucity of resources addressing caregivers' issues and concerns. Although age-specific and condition-specific caregivers' organiza-tions existed (such as the Well Spouse Foundation, Children of Aging Parents, and the National Alliance for the Mentally Ill), there was no national membership organization to speak for all caregivers and to con-nect them to resources.

NFCA publishes *Take Care!,* a quarterly newsletter for family caregivers. The newsletter was the founders' first priority, designed as an educational tool to convey "actionable information" that could make a difference in readers' lives. NFCA's leaders have a multiyear plan for developing its resources and programs, recognizing that a newsletter addresses only a small fraction of caregivers' needs. A new speaker's bureau speaks both to and on behalf of caregivers. NFCA is currently developing a resource guide that will list informational materials, groups, services, equipment, and other resources for caregivers on a wide range of conditions.

Because relatively little is known about the nation's family caregivers, NFCA's leaders plan to survey the organization's members, and then to use those findings as a basis for designing and securing funding for a national survey of caregivers. One issue they want to know about, for example, is caregivers' needs for and abilities to take advantage of self-help/ support groups. Other programs under consideration at NFCA are a hot-line and a clearinghouse, to maximize the accessibility of their resources.

The organization is also looking for ways to provide respite for caregivers, as this is known to be a critical need. People are often placed in a nursing home not because of their own deterioration, but because their caregivers have burned out. The Alzheimer's Foundation has estimated that if the 2.5 million most dependent people being cared for at home were placed in a nursing home at public expense, it could cost the nation $54 billion.

SELF-HELP GROUPS

When he was Surgeon General of the United States, Dr. C. Everett Koop stated at a September 1987 national workshop of self-help leaders that he had "long believed that self-help groups can play an extremely useful role in preserving and restoring health, and that the self-help movement ought to be regarded as a valuable partner in the formal health care system."[1]

The participants at that historic meeting agreed on a definition of self-help groups, for which there is wide agreement in the self-help movement: Self-help groups are "self-governing groups whose members share a common health concern and give each other emotional support and material aid, charge either no fee or only a small fee for membership, and place high value on experiential knowledge. . . . In addition to providing mutual support for their members, such groups may also be involved in information, education, material aid, and social advocacy in their communities."[2]

While such groups are often referred to as support groups (and the terms are used interchangeably in this book), activists in the field prefer the term "self-help" because of its emphasis on the mutual aid efforts of people with shared concerns and experience, and on the nonmonetary nature of the interaction. Obviously, recognizing the legitimacy of these endeavors does not in any way negate the need for professionally led therapy groups such as those described in Chapter 7, much less the need for individual counseling.

Some mental health professionals have concerns about self-help groups because of the absence of professional facilitators and members' presumed vulnerability to a variety of harmful, or at least unhelpful, practices. To be sure, some groups engage in activities that are of questionable therapeutic value. But peer groups are also incomparable sources of social support, the therapeutic benefits of which have been extensively documented. In addition, they provide practical information on such things as dealing with symptoms, reaction to drugs, and relating to physicians. Thanks to clearinghouses, meetings such as that convened by Dr. Koop, and other resources, the national self-help movement is increasingly sophisticated and able to help local groups be genuinely helpful.

In view of these considerations, it behooves the counselor to be familiar both with specific local groups and with the general principles of their operation, so as to avoid making judgments on the basis of hearsay or bias. In some cases, this knowledge may lead to caveats about particular groups. More importantly, knowledge will enable the counselor to help patients make judgments for themselves about what they are looking for and whether a given group is helpful. Here, two things come into play: the characteristics and needs of the patient, and the nature of the group. The counselor can assist patients by having information about groups in the community.

Resources that can enhance the medical crisis counselor's knowledge in this area are listed at the end of this chapter. Outside of the codependency/addiction/twelve-step arena (the various "anonymous" groups), few self-help groups have a prescribed format or philosophy—although many have a commitment to being goal-oriented and not simply engaging in "symptom-swapping" or "war stories."

The best way to get a sense of one's compatibility with a specific group is to attend a meeting. The Director of the American Self-Help Clearinghouse advises that groups in which several people have visible roles and responsibilities show more flexibility and vitality, and thus are generally preferable to ones with only one strong leader. Another hallmark of a good self-help group is that it knows its limits, and therefore does not attempt to advise members on medical or psychological matters that require professional judgment.

Counselors wishing to recommend a self-help group may encounter three possible responses from patients. Some need only to be provided with a telephone number and suggestions about evaluating a group's appropriateness. Others need considerable encouragement, and perhaps even coaching or role-playing, before they are ready to reach out to a group of peers. For others, groups are simply not appropriate, for any of a number of possible reasons. Counselors should always follow up with patients after they have visited a group, to find out their reaction and whether they think the group will be helpful.

Counselors may also have patients with the energy, resourcefulness, and skills to form their own groups, as we shall see below. A 1990 article on self-help groups[3] points out that many national and local self-help organizations began with the help of a professional. This help is particularly needed when there is no national self-help organization to provide assistance to local citizens. The author says, "By the very nature of their specialty work, professionals are often in a very favorable position to identify, encourage, and link together persons who have the potential to start a mutual help group. . . ." *The Self-Help Sourcebook*[4] is an invaluable resource in starting a group.

A FINAL COMMENT

MCC is a brief and focused intervention; counselors have at most 10 hours with their patients, at least initially. In this brief period of time, the medical crisis counselor obviously cannot be an employment counselor, volunteer placement coordinator, or resource librarian.

Nevertheless, the goal of counseling is to strengthen the patient's ability to live a full life. By maintaining a sense of the community context and offering a few judicious suggestions and pieces of information, the counselor can strengthen links to a support system that can buttress and nourish the patient and family both during and after the counseling period.

Budman and Gurman point out (Table 2.1, page 35) that much of the work of brief therapy takes place between sessions, and moreover that many of the benefits of therapy will be realized after the counseling process is completed. It is in that spirit that this discussion of community resources is offered.

It seems appropriate to end this chapter and this book with a note of realism—one that returns us to the major point of the first chapter: Many additional resources are needed for people with long-term medical conditions. It is true that community resources exist, and that counselors and patients should know about them and use them. It is also true, however, that although health professionals, family members, citizens, and organizations are laboring valiantly in communities throughout this country to help people with serious health problems, the local and national resources for them are a small fraction of what is needed. This is nowhere more true than in rural areas and inner cities.

In some areas, then, counselors, patients, and families alike will find that the only result of their effort and searching is to identify the woeful gaps in community resources. They will then need to rely on their personal resources and those of their circle of family and friends—just as they must do as they face the incurable medical condition itself. Even under these circumstances, though, those concerned about chronic illness have some options. One is to join forces with others to create new programs and services that meet needs and fill gaps. Another option is to join others in advocating for changes in public policies and budget priorities, so that more resources are allocated to enhancing the lives of Americans with serious long-term health problems.

NOTES

1. Quoted in the introduction to the published proceedings of that meeting (Washington, DC: U.S. Government Printing Office: 1988, Report No. 224–250, p. 4).

2. Ibid., 5.

3. Madara, E. (1990). Maximizing the potential for community self-help through clearinghouse approaches. *Prevention in Human Services, 7*(2), 109–138.

4. White, B. J., & Madara, E. (1992). *The self-help sourcebook: Finding and forming mutual aid self-help groups.* Denville, NJ: St. Clares-Riverside Medical Center.

Resources on Chronic Illness

Health Information Clearinghouses

National Health Information Center
PO Box 1133
Washington, DC 20013–1133
800/336–4797, 202/205–8611

Provides information on a wide range of conditions, run by the U.S. Office of Disease Prevention and Health Promotion. A brochure in the Center's "Healthfinder" series, "Federal Health Information Centers and Clearinghouses," gives the names, addresses and telephone numbers of more than 50 information clearinghouses operated by the federal government, on such subjects as alzheimer's disease, cancer, AIDS, arthritis, diabetes, and kidney disease. Another publication is called "Toll-Free Numbers for Health Information."

National Rehabilitation Information
  Center (NARIC)
8455 Colesville Road, Suite 935
Silver Spring, MD 20910–3319
800/227–0216

NARIC is funded by the National Institute on Disability and Rehabilitation Research. Its *Directory of National Information Sources on Disabilities* lists more than 500 organizations, and can be ordered from NARIC. The organization also maintains the ABLE-DATA database and conducts REHAB-DATA searches, both available for a small fee.

Health Organizations

AIDS

American Foundation for AIDS Research
5900 Wilshire Boulevard
Los Angeles, CA 90036
213/857–5900

Pediatric AIDS Foundation
1311 Colorado Avenue
Santa Monica, CA 90404
310/395–9051

198   *Medical Crisis Counseling*

Allergy and Asthma
American Allergy Association
PO Box 7273
Menlo Park, CA 94026
415/322-1663

Asthma and Allergy Foundation
  of America
1125 15th Street NW, Suite 502
Washington, DC 20005
202/466-7643

Alzheimer's Disease
Alzheimer's Disease & Related Disorders
  Association, Inc.
919 North Michigan Avenue, Suite 1000
Chicago, IL 60611-1676
800/272-3900

Amyotrophic Lateral Sclerosis
ALS and Neuromuscular Research
  Foundation
California Pacific Medical Center
2351 Clay St., Suite 416
San Francisco, CA 94115
415/923-3640

Arthritis
The American Juvenile Arthritis
  Foundation
800/283-7800

The Arthritis Foundation
1314 Spring Street
Atlanta, GA 30309
800/283-7800

Cancer
American Brain Tumor Association
3725 North Talman Avenue
Chicago, IL 60618
312/286-5571

American Cancer Society
1599 Clifton Road, NE
Atlanta, GA 30329
800/227-2345

Breast Cancer Advisory Center
PO Box 224
Kensington, MD 20895

National Children's Cancer Society
1015 Locust Street, Suite 1040
St. Louis, MO 63101-1323
800/532-6459

Cerebral Palsy
United Cerebral Palsy Associations
800/872-5827

Cystic Fibrosis
Cystic Fibrosis Foundation
6931 Arlington Road
Bethesda, MD 20814
800/FIGHT-CF

Deaf-Blind
American Association of the Deaf-Blind
814 Thayer Avenue, Room 300
Silver Spring, MD 20910
301/587-1788

Helen Keller National Center for
  Deaf-Blind Youths and Adults
111 Middle Neck Road
Sands Point, NY 11505
516/944-8900

Diabetes
American Diabetes Association
PO Box 257575
1660 Duke Street
Alexandria, VA 22314
800/828-8293

Juvenile Diabetes Foundation International
432 Park Avenue, S
New York, NY 10016-8013
800/JDF-CURE

Epilepsy
Epilepsy Foundation of America
4351 Garden City Drive
Landover, MD 20785
800/EFA–1000

Head Injury and Coma
National Head Injury Foundation
1776 Massachusetts Avenue, NW,
 Suite 100
Washington, DC 20036
800/444–6443

Hearing Impairment
Alexander Graham Bell Association
 for the Deaf
3417 Volta Place, NW
Washington, DC 20007
202/337–5220

National Association for the Deaf
814 Thayer Avenue
Silver Spring, MD 20910
301/587–1788

Heart
American Heart Association,
 National Center
7272 Greenville Avenue
Dallas, TX 75231
800/242–8721

Hemophilia
National Hemophilia Foundation
212/219–8180

Kidney Disease
American Kidney Fund
6110 Executive Boulevard, #1010
Rockville, MD 20852
301/381–3052

National Kidney Foundation
30 E 33rd Street, Suite 1100
New York, NY 10016
800/622–9010

Leukemia
Leukemia Society of America
600 Third Avenue
New York, NY 10016
800/955–4LSA

National Leukemia Association
585 Steward Avenue, Suite 536
Garden City, NY 11530
516/222–1944

Liver Disease
American Liver Foundation
800/223–0179

Lung Disease
American Lung Association
1740 Broadway
New York, NY 10019–4374
800/LUNG-USA

Lupus Erythematosus
The American Lupus Society
3914 Del Amo Boulevard, Suite 922
Torrance, CA 90503
310/542–8891

The Lupus Foundation of America
800/558–0121
800/800–4532

Multiple sclerosis
Multiple Sclerosis Foundation
6350 N Andrews Avenue
Fort Lauderdale, FL 33309
305/776–6805

National Multiple Sclerosis Society
733 Third Avenue
New York, NY 10017
800/FIGHT-MS

Muscular Dystrophy
Muscular Dystrophy Association
3300 E Sunrise Drive
Tucson, AC 85718
602/529–2000

Organ Transplantation
Children's Transplant Association
PO Box 53699
Dallas, TX 75253
214/287-8484

Transplant Recipient International
  Organization (TRIO)
244 N Bellefield Avenue
Pittsburgh, PA 15213
412/687-2210

Ostomy
United Ostomy Association
36 Executive Park, Suite 120
Irvine, CA 92714
714/660-8624

Paralysis and Paraplegia
American Paralysis Association
500 Morris Avenue
Springfield, NJ 07081
800/225-0292

National Easter Seal Society
70 E Lake Street
Chicago, IL 60601
800/221-6827

National Spinal Cord Injury Association
600 W Cummings Park, Suite 2000
Woburn, MA 01801
800/962-9629

Paralyzed Veterans of America
801 18th Street, NW
Washington, DC 20006
202/USA-1300

Parkinson's Disease
National Parkinson's Foundation
1501 NW Ninth Avenue
Miami, FL 33136
800/327-4545

Parkinson's Educational Program
3900 Birch Street, Suite 105
Newport Beach, CA 92660
800/344-7872

Polio
International Polio Network
510 Oakland Avenue, Suite 206
St. Louis, MO 63110
314/361-0475

Polio Society
PO Box 106273
Washington, DC 20016
301/897-8180

Post-Polio League for Information and
  Outreach
703/273-8171

Sickle-Cell Anemia
Sickle Cell Disease Association of America
3545 Wilshire Boulevard, Suite 1106
Los Angeles, CA 90010
800/421-8453

Spina Bifida
Spina Bifida Association of America
800/621-3141

Stroke
American Heart Association
7272 Greenville Avenue
Dallas, TX 75231
800/242-8721, 214/373-6300

National Stroke Association
800 E Hampden Avenue, Suite 240
Englewood, CO 80110-2654
800/STROKES

Visual Impairment
American Council of the Blind
1155 15th Street NW, Suite 720
Washington, DC 20005
800/424–8666

American Foundation for the Blind
15 W 16th Street
New York, NY 10011
800/AF-BLIND

Other

National Organization for Rare Disorders
800/999–NORD

Alliance of Genetic Support Groups
   (genetic illnesses)
800/336–GENE

National Family Caregivers Association
9621 E. Bexhill Dr.
Kensington, MD 20895–3104
301/942–6430

National Institute on Aging Information
   Center
PO Box 8057
Gaithersburg, MD 20898–8057
800/222–2225, 301/587–2528

The National Library of Medicine's
DIRLINE lists over 1,000 organizations in
the health field.

Self-Help Clearinghouses

American Self-help Clearinghouse (for national U.S. listings and directories)
St. Clares-Riverside Medical Center
Denville, NJ 07834
201/625–7101 (TDD 201/625–9053)

State self-help clearinghouses (for help in finding or forming a self-help group)

California	800/222–LINK
Connecticut	203/789–7645
Illinois	708/328–0470
Iowa	800/952–4777
Kansas	800/445–0116
Massachusetts	413/545–2313
Michigan	800/777–5556
Minnesota	612/224–1133
Missouri	
Kansas City	816/472–HELP
St. Louis	314/773–1399
Nebraska	402/476–9668
New Jersey	800/FOR–MASH
New York	
Brooklyn	718/875–1420
Westchester	914/949–6301

New York City	212/586–5770
North Carolina	
Mecklenberg area	704/331–9500
Ohio	
Dayton area	513/225–3004
Toledo area	419/475–4449
Oregon	
Portland area	503/222–5555
Pennsylvania	
Philadelphia	215/482–4316
Pittsburgh area	412/261–5363
Scranton area	717/961–1234
South Carolina	
Midlands area	803/791–9227
Tennessee	
Knoxville area	615/584–6736
Memphis area	901/323–8485
Texas	512/454–3706
Washington, DC area	703/941–LINK

Some additional communities may have local clearinghouses offering information on self-help, social service and/or health topics, possibly maintained by the health department, Mental Health Association, or community mental health center.

Index